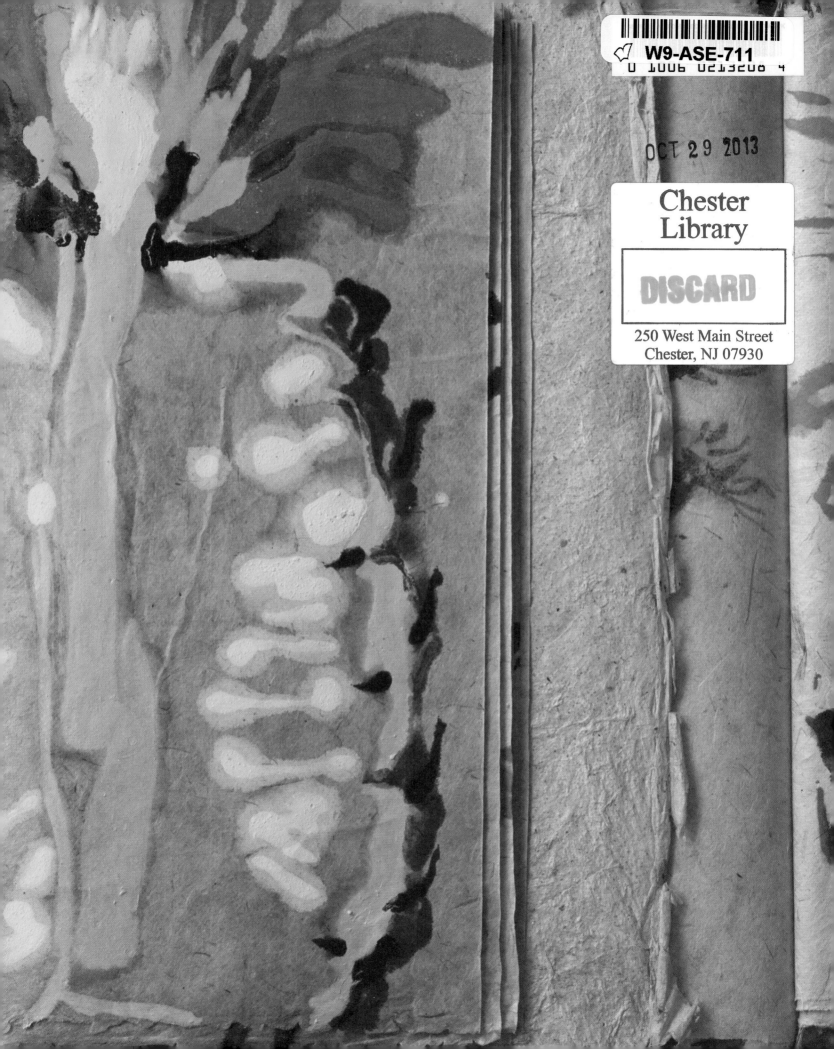

THE
GRAMERCY TAVERN
COOKBOOK

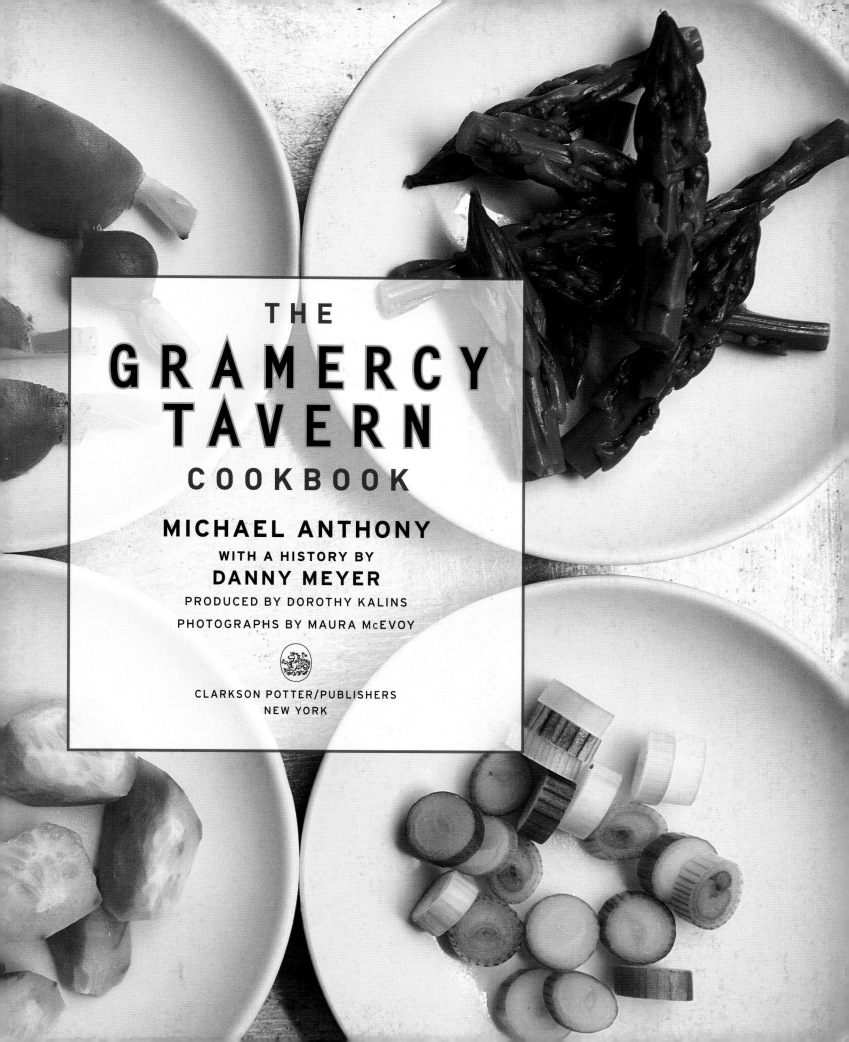

THE
GRAMERCY
TAVERN
COOKBOOK

MICHAEL ANTHONY

WITH A HISTORY BY
DANNY MEYER

PRODUCED BY DOROTHY KALINS

PHOTOGRAPHS BY MAURA McEVOY

CLARKSON POTTER/PUBLISHERS
NEW YORK

Copyright © 2013 by Gramercy Tavern Corp.
Photographs copyright © 2013 by Maura
McEvoy except as indicated

All rights reserved.
Published in the United States by Clarkson
Potter/Publishers, an imprint of the Crown
Publishing Group, a division of Random
House, Inc., New York.
www.crownpublishing.com
www.clarksonpotter.com

Library of Congress
Anthony, Michael, 1968–
  The Gramercy Tavern cookbook / Michael
Anthony with Dorothy Kalins.
      pages cm
1. Cooking, American. 2. Seasonal cooking.
3. Gramercy Tavern. I. Kalins, Dorothy.
II. Title.
  TX715.A6237 2013
  641.5973—dc23   2012047367

ISBN 978-0-307-88833-4
eISBN 978-0-385-34618-4

Printed in Hong Kong

Book design by Marysarah Quinn
Jacket design by Marysarah Quinn
Jacket photographs by Maura McEvoy
Recipe editor: Kathy Brennan

10 9 8 7 6 5 4 3 2 1

First Edition

PHOTO PERMISSIONS

Robert Kushner, Tavern Mural, *Cornucopia*,
1994, throughout. Endpapers: studies for
Cornucopia from the artist's notebook,
1993–94. *Pear Pavane*, 2011, page 197. By
permission of the artist.

Stephen Hannock, *Flooded River at Dawn
with Mauve Twins*, 2008, page 19. By
permission of the artist.

Andrew Millner, *Shaw's Magnolia*, 2006,
Lightjet print, pages 160–61, 234. By
permission of the artist.

David Heffernan, Tavern sign, 1994, page 18.
By permission of the artist.

Bentel & Bentel, restaurant floor plan, 1994,
page 192. By permission of the architects.

Restaurant Taillevent, Paris, 1994, page
12. Photograph: Alain Benainous/Gamma-
Rapho/Getty Images.

Union Square Cafe, 1993, page 13,
Photographs: Richard Bowditch.

Merrymaking in a Tavern, c.1670–74, page
14. Steen, Jan Havicksz, (oil on canvas),
(1625/26–79) / © Wallace Collection,
London, UK / The Bridgeman Art Library

Gramercy Tavern Staff Portrait, 1998, pages
16–17. Photograph: Bill Bettencourt.

Claudia Fleming, 2000, page 20.
Photograph: Catrina Genovese/Time & Life
Pictures/Getty Images.

New York magazine, July 18, 1994, page 21.
Cover photograph: Paul Manangan.

New York magazine article by Peter
Kaminsky, page 21. Photograph: Andrew
Bordwin.

Tom Colicchio, 1994, page 21. Photograph:
Andrew Bordwin.

Danny Meyer at Gramercy Tavern, page 22.
Photograph: Andrew Bordwin.

DEDICATION

This book is dedicated to the passionate and loyal
family and friends of Gramercy Tavern:
past, present, and future.

RECIPES

SPRING

SUMMER

FROM LEFT: Paul Wetzel, Alan Altizer, Howard Kalachnikoff, Jane Thompson, Kate Willer, Susan Chung, Angela Gauer, Md Komor Uddin, Hassan Ahmed, and Tracy Malechek.

AUTUMN

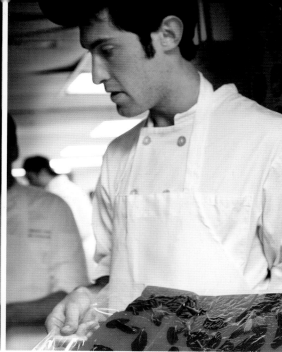

WINTER

FROM LEFT: John
Patterson, Ahasan Sokrul,
Roberta Bendavid, Ramon
Tavera, Juliette Pope, and
Micah Fredman.

THE MAKING OF
GRAMERCY TAVERN

by Danny Meyer

Gramercy Tavern seems so inevitable now, as if it has always been there. But after Union Square Cafe opened in 1985, I was never going to open a second restaurant. Period. I was viscerally afraid of expanding because of the mistakes I watched my father make as I grew up. He expanded his business in a major way twice. And he went bankrupt. Twice.

I had always felt like an imposter with Union Square Cafe. I knew it worked because we exceeded expectations, gave great value, made it personal, served good American food—much of it from the Greenmarket a half a block away. But I knew, too, that none of those ideas were originally mine. And there was nothing especially innovative about any of them. I was convinced that it was just luck. I could hardly believe it when Bryan Miller, restaurant critic at the *New York Times*, gave Union Square three stars in 1989, deeming it "a paragon among a new breed of restaurants that might be called international bistros."

Gramercy would never have come about had Tom Colicchio not approached me when Mondrian, his first restaurant, closed, saying, "I really want to do a restaurant with you." I respected him as a chef and admired his philanthropic values—we'd met through charity events for Share Our Strength's Taste of the Nation. It took someone whose outlook on food and the restaurant experience felt so comfortable and consistent with mine to make me go for it, to make me feel that it was a compelling enough opportunity. Gramercy Tavern was such a big dream, such a big vision, and everyone involved at the highest levels was at a point in their career where they had something important to prove. Tom had just closed Mondrian in Midtown. He had something to prove. The architects Bentel & Bentel had never designed a restaurant. Our first wine and service director, Steve Olson, had been praised in *Food & Wine* but had never worked in New York City. And I had to prove that I was not a one-hit wonder.

THE LOVE CHILD OF TAILLEVENT AND UNION SQUARE CAFE

But what would this new restaurant be? I started to think, "What if Union Square Cafe and Taillevent in Paris (the only three-star Michelin restaurant with a sense of humor I had ever been to in my life) could have a baby? What if you could take the ebullient local spirit of Union Square Cafe and make it prettier and a lot more refined? And what if you could take Taillevent, with its exquisite service and refined dining, and make it a lot more rustic?" I became obsessed with this notion of combining the two. Between Taillevent's owner, the late Jean-Claude Vrinat, who became my mentor, and Jean-Marie Ancher, now the director, their clockwork service always had a twinkle in its eye. That was a revelation, because for me, dining in a luxe restaurant had always meant enduring some level of self-reverential pretension. That made sense to Tom,

too, because his idea of Mondrian had been to make it sort of a junior version of Taillevent.

There are very few restaurants in the world where just knowing you have plans to go there that night is incredibly exciting. Taillevent is one of those places. The experience begins with heading toward the Place de l'Etoile and finding your way to the little side street called rue Lamennais. And then you see the tiny awning over the door (Gramercy's awning is rounder, but equally small). It's not a big-statement awning—it's just a gesture that says you're here, and you're welcome. You walk into a very generous, gracious foyer and are shown to a dining room that's broken into smaller episodes (exactly what we did at Gramercy Tavern). And you feel like you've arrived—like they've been expecting you, like they're excited you're here. You're one of the small handful of special people who actually got this golden ticket. At Taillevent, things happen when you're not looking. Before you even realize you need more

water, your glass is filled. And then really good food and wine begin to appear—and there's a lot of smiling. Before Taillevent, I had never been to such a fancy restaurant that was so down-to-earth, so serious and yet so winsome. Of course, the charm wouldn't matter if the food wasn't sensational. You can find equally fine food in a half dozen other places in Paris—but no one puts all the pieces together the way they do. I could go on about the seafood sausage, the foie gras torchon, the rack of lamb, and the wine list. I could definitely go on about the Cognac, but what I love most about that is they arrive at your table with a bottle and just put it down. It's a gesture that says, "Help yourself to as much as you like!" You used to see that generosity in family trattorias in Italy—generosity that means more than the quality of the Cognac, but the fact that it's exquisite Cognac is part of what makes Taillevent a peerless restaurant.

In contrast, Union Square Cafe was completely intuitive and nonintellectual from the start. What's great is that even decades later, I do not feel I've outgrown it. Union Square has all sorts of illogical design elements—a balcony that floats over the bar, a serpentine floor plan, and a minuscule kitchen—that are much more a function of what needed to be there than what ideally should have been there. After all these years, I know every nook and cranny of the place, and I realize how much I'm still in love with it: its imperfections, the idiosyncrasies of the physical layout, what you have to put up with to work there—that's what makes it special. Union Square Cafe remains a happy, bustling restaurant. It hums at lunch, at dinner, and all weekend, and when the place is humming, it's a party. Taillevent never feels like a party. It feels like a haven. We made sure the Tavern part of Gramercy Tavern brought along the party, and then the main dining room became like a haven.

FROM LEFT: At an extraordinary dinner honoring Taillevent at Gramercy Tavern in 1994, with my mentor, Jean-Claude Vrinat; the inviting dining room at Taillevent in Paris; Union Square Cafe, opened in 1985, has its own kind of warmth; with chef Michael Romano.

THE "TAVERN" IN MY MIND

The question of what the new restaurant would feel like morphed into the next question: "What would it be named?" In San Francisco in the early 1980s, it became chic to call a fine-dining restaurant a café or a bar and grill: Hayes Street Grill, Fourth Street Grill, and, earlier, the Washington Square Bar and Grill, and of course, Chez Panisse Café. These places successfully married an understated style of restaurant with an aspirational style of food and wine; they discovered how to strip away the pretentiousness of a highly refined restaurant experience and deliver a fresh kind of excellence. Unpretentiousness appeals to me because *home* is not pretentious. You don't get dressed up or put on airs to be *home*. I knew that the restaurants I most wanted to return to were always places where I didn't have to park my taste for good food and wine and caring service at the door. Nor did I have to be someone I was not in these restaurants. Which led me to the depth behind the word "tavern."

What a tavern means in almost every culture is the best—and sometimes only—local place to gather at the table. Taverns are international. There are tavernas in Greece; the restaurant where I learned to cook in Rome was La Taverna da Giovanni. In recent American history, the tavern had a boisterous blue-collar feel to it: you pulled up to a smoky bar and drank Pabst Blue Ribbon with the baseball game on TV. Some historic taverns right in Gramercy's New York neighborhood have that feeling. The Old Town Bar & Grill, just two blocks away on 18th Street, has been around since 1892. A little farther east on 18th is Pete's Tavern, which made it through Prohibition disguised as a flower shop and

has been open since 1864. We thought, "Why can't we introduce that kind of place today, in New York City?"

Taverns sprang up at a time when there were no telephones, never mind the myriad ways we communicate today. If you wanted to do business or politics or socialize with people, you went to a tavern. Traveling even farther back into American history, you reach the Early American era, which I am fascinated with, since my wife, Audrey, and I pretty much fell in love on bed-and-breakfast trips to her home turf, Bucks County, Pennsylvania. We drove throughout New England, and every one of those trips involved not just antiquing but also visits to charming old taverns that served food that was only okay. But we never encountered a contemporary place where the goal was to update the idea of a tavern as a place where you could just drop in at any time of day for excellent food and drink.

We'd also been spending a lot of time in Europe, and my favorite restaurants in the world then (different from those in the 1980s that led us to Union Square Cafe) were the two-star countryside Michelin restaurants in Italy and France. I was convinced we had to make all these disparate ideas come together in one restaurant: that refined restaurant in Paris with a twinkle in its eye, a trattoria in Rome, a rustic Early American watering hole, and our space in the heart of nineteenth-century Manhattan, literally down the block from the house where Teddy Roosevelt was born in 1858. To me, there was a visceral link between the taverns in Greece or Italy and taverns dating back to colonial America: they were always the best places to gather and eat in any town. And that's what Gramercy Tavern was meant to be.

Taverns were traditionally the best and often the only place for a community to gather, as in this seventeenth-century Dutch painting, *Merrymaking in a Tavern*, c. 1670-74, by Jan Havicksz Steen.

A NEIGHBORHOOD PLACE

Whoever wrote the rule that you can't have a restaurant that serves its neighborhood well day and night yet is so good that people will come there from *anywhere*? That was our thought as we began to look at spaces in 1993. The one requirement was that it be a short walk for me from Union Square Cafe and also a short walk from the glorious produce at the Greenmarket in Union Square, which would become the beating heart of the new restaurant. This, of course, is the essence of a tavern: it's the very definition of local. The first space we looked at was the just-shuttered Coach House on Waverly Place (which later became Babbo). Another location, the storefront of a building that was in bankruptcy, bordered on Union Square. We could have had the whole building, turning the two lower floors into the restaurant and converting the rest to rental space. I imagined living on the top two floors. Problem was, we'd have had to evict a bunch of tenants and that was not a business I was ever interested in being in. That building is now a Puma shoe store. We looked at the historic location of Max's Kansas City on Park Avenue South. But it just didn't lay out the way we wanted it to. It later became a Korean deli.

One day, a real estate broker told Tom about a space on 20th Street. The building was owned by a company called N. S. Meyer. The name alone, of course, piqued my interest. N. S. Meyer was a prominent American manufacturer and retailer of military medals, and there was a military uniform warehouse on the ground floor. But their business was declining and this seemed like a good time for them to make some money by leasing out the street floor. So we took over the wide-open space at 42 East 20th Street.

Taking a photograph of the entire GT staff each fall became a tradition and our holiday card. Each one hangs on the wall in the restaurant. This one is from 1998. Recognize anyone?

DOES THIS *FEEL* GOOD?

I am an entrepreneur and I'm proud of that. That means I'm excited to take business risks that involve trying to make a commercial enterprise out of something that gives me pleasure. I know myself well enough to know that if it's not something I enjoy, then I don't want to share it with others. I'm not just driven by judgment. The first thing that occurs to me is, "Does this *feel* good?" If it doesn't, I don't want to endorse it because I don't like what it says about me. My daughter Gretchen's art teacher once shared her philosophy with parents: "Whatever piece of art you create is a self-portrait. You're bringing your own point of view, you're telling

us something about yourself." Gramercy is a very clear expression of where I was then. And I've come to realize that whether Gramercy is a place or a song or a piece of art or a play, it is a reflection of where many of us were in our lives in the early 1990s. That was our expression of the restaurant then, and it remains so today.

I wanted to take on every aspect of conceptualizing the restaurant—designing it, choosing the architect, the colors, and the fabrics—just as I had at Union Square Cafe. But by that point, Gramercy was already a dividing cell. That was the first indication I had that this partnership would be different. I vividly remember Tom telling me one day in a meeting, "You've got to give me a voice here. If we're going to be partners, it's my restau-

rant, too." Up to that point, my view had been that Tom was just going to be the chef. Tom and I never ever had a dispute over taste. Whether it was food, art, or furniture, we shared an aesthetic. We also shared a belief (and part of this was a certain amount of business ignorance that we both brought to the party) that no amount of money was too much to spend in the spirit of "getting it right." But instead of deciding to buy more antiques or more expensive china, we spent it on making a difference in the spirit of the restaurant: throwing a staff Christmas party that became a long-standing tradition, taking a yearly staff photograph and turning it into a Christmas card, baking a treat our dinner guests could take home for breakfast. A defining idea was to close the restaurant for one night every year to host a dinner to raise funds for Share Our Strength, inviting guest chefs to cook in our home kitchen.

Over the years, every time we found the need to raise the prices at Gramercy, we would always add a little something extra to balance it. It was never just how much more can we *get*, it was how much more can we *give*? Truthfully, Tom and I were both undisciplined at cost control and I see now that our generosity—while effective—was sometimes an excuse for a lack of discipline. Eventually our relationship became a duet. I don't know who was the lyricist and who was the musician, but I suspect, personality-wise, that Tom was more like Lennon and I was more like McCartney!

FROM LEFT: As if it was meant to be, the building we eventually chose for Gramercy Tavern in 1993 already had the brass initials "N. S. Meyer" on the facade; David Heffernan, my brother-in-law, painted this tavern sign featuring our then two-year-old daughter, Hallie Meyer; Stephen Hannock's magical painting, *Flooded River at Dawn, with Mauve Twins*, 2008, greets every guest at the entrance.

AN AUTHENTIC SENSE OF PLACE

Authenticity meant drilling down deeply into the meaning of the word "tavern." It was our lead architect, Peter Bentel, a real intellectual with beyond-exquisite design sense, who helped keep us on a sane path. He said, "Whatever we do, this restaurant cannot appear like 'Ye Olde Tavern'" (see Peter in his own words on page 189). Initially, the entire restaurant was going to be what you now know as the Tavern, the casual no-reservations room in the front. It was only because we fell so in love with the entire space on 20th Street—and because there was so much of it—that we decided it was far too big for just a tavern. So Tom suggested, "Why don't I continue to cook the food I was doing at Mondrian in the back part of the restaurant?" We talked about the very upstairs/downstairs experience we'd enjoyed at Chez Panisse. The idea was to give people two different and distinct ways to dine under one roof: a tavern that was as intimate as an authentic tavern should feel and a destination-driven dining room with white tablecloths.

In fact, that's the great untold story of Gramercy Tavern—how the tavern and the restaurant came to enhance each other with an almost immeasurable alchemy. The Tavern sets a buoyant tone that benefits from the halo effect of the fine dining on the other side. You know that the food comes from the same kitchen, with the same selectivity of ingredients and the same quality of hospitality. But you also know that the price point is lower in the Tavern and the opportunity to be spontaneous is greater. Today, when you eat in the dining room, you have to walk through a party to get there—a down-to-earth, spur-of-the-moment gathering of people. Because you can't reserve in the Tavern,

everyone who's there has just dropped in! The fact that you absorb some of that spontaneous energy on the way to the dining room makes being there feel a lot less serious, without relaxing the standards of food or service. Each experience confers a richer depth to the other. In later years, when we opened Tabla and then The Modern, at the Museum of Modern Art, we deliberately borrowed from that duality. At The Modern, we dialed up the size of the bar and dialed down the space for the dining room, because we knew that moving into Midtown, we had to bring even more of a party atmosphere. That was a gift that Gramercy Tavern gave The Modern. The success of the Gramercy model later influenced our design for Maialino, as well as North End Grill.

Finding the furniture was half the fun. Before we had children, Audrey and I planned most of our week-end trips around antiquing, and we discovered many of the pieces now at Gramercy Tavern at antiques shows. We were learning, making great relationships with dealers. Along the way, we were fortunate to meet two remarkable men, Peter Ermacora and Evan Hughes, business and life partners who had an antiques business in the Berkshires. We fell in love with their taste, and as we were furnishing Gramercy Tavern, they signed on as our antiques rabbis. They gave us the courage to buy what we loved, such as the framed needlepoint sampler from Sotheby's (see page 316), which is to this day one of my favorites. It was made by Mary Ann Hobart and dated May 16, 1860. I still love its message: "Wisdom introduces the industrious to the temple of happiness and rejects the idle as unworthy."

FINDING THE RIGHT PEOPLE

I'll never forget how Robert Raeburn, owner of the N. S. Meyer building, allowed us to use his second floor to interview staff. The process took a couple of months, and I was there for every single interview for every single staff member of our opening team in a way that I certainly haven't been able to be since. I had a gut sense about the kind of people we were looking for, and I would say that's probably the thing I miss the most: there's no stronger impact you can have on how a restaurant grows than choosing the original team. We were fortunate to pick all kinds of terrific folks, many of whom we're still in touch with and have gone on to do great things.

Claudia Fleming, the pastry chef, was fundamental to the restaurant. I first met Claudia when she was a server at Union Square Cafe. A former dancer, she came to us from Jams, where she'd worked for Jonathan Waxman and Melvin Master. One day she asked me if she could intern in Michael Romano's kitchen, which she did, and she was drawn to the pastry station. Then she left and went to France, eventually working with the famed pastry chef Pierre Hermé at Fauchon. When we talked about pastry chefs for GT, Tom said, "What about Claudia Fleming?" I said, "*You* know Claudia?" And Tom said, "Of course I do." I thought it would be amazing to reunite with her. I had no idea how proficient she had become in such a short time. For Claudia, it was always flavor first, and her desserts came to have a dancer's elegance and grace that helped define Gramercy Tavern.

Does our success come from the team we selected in the early days? Kevin Mahan, Gramercy's managing partner, who has been a key part of the restaurant since he arrived in 1999 at age thirty, has recruited legions of excellent people and then helped them grow. In fact, it was Kevin who found our pastry chef, the talented Nancy Olson. Kevin knows that you are absolutely required to be really good at what you *do*, but it's just as important to be really good at who you *are*. And it can be exhausting. You must trust that the best way to take care of others is to first take care of yourself.

FROM LEFT: Pastry chef Claudia Fleming in 1994; Roberta Bendavid and Modesto Batista back in the day, and ever so loyal to this day.

Managing expectations for the debut of Gramercy Tavern most certainly would *not* have included this cover story in *New York* magazine, which appeared the day we opened, featuring my partner Tom Colicchio. **PAGE 22:** Showing a confidence I didn't yet feel at GT's opening.

MANAGING EXPECTATIONS

You might think that having a story about your brand-new restaurant in the city's hottest magazine would be a good thing. But we were staggered when the July 18, 1994, issue of *New York* magazine hit newsstands the day we opened. There, on the cover, was a photo of one of our matchboxes, with four stars and a question: "The Next Great Restaurant?" A parenthetical comment followed: "(It's the $3-million offspring of the Union Square Cafe. And it opens this week.)" The inside headline, "Why Ask for the Moon When He Already Has Three Stars?" blared across a double-page night shot of Gramercy Tavern.

Tom and I had agreed from the beginning that whatever you had to do to become a four-star restaurant was *not* in the spirit of a tavern. Reinventing the four-star restaurant was never our intention, but Tom's bravado quote in that article suggested otherwise: "'If we are serious about going up against Bouley,' says Colicchio, 'we are going to find these ingredients and charge for them.'" (In 1994, Bouley had four stars.) Peter Kaminsky is a fine writer and we had given him incredible access. He had spent months researching the story, which was originally intended for the *New Yorker*. It would have been a very different experience in that magazine. When the *New Yorker* eventually passed, however, and *New York* picked it up and put it on the cover suggesting a strategy we never had—well, even now it's difficult for me to go back and read it.

Because that piece became the way Gramercy Tavern was defined for the first year and a half of its life. The result was that people came in not to experience the restaurant for what it was, but to react to the presumption that we were touting ourselves as the next four-star restaurant. It set us up for disappointment all around.

MY FIRST SECOND RESTAURANT

For me, the biggest struggle of opening Gramercy was that it was "my first second restaurant." I had the awful feeling that I was doing damage to my firstborn, Union Square Cafe. When USC's chef Michael Romano saw the kitchen at Gramercy, he almost became ill. It wasn't that he didn't like it; it was that he had been cooking three-star food in a tiny kitchen and now this new sibling would have a palace! Michael and I had been working intensely for two years on the *Union Square Cafe Cookbook*, which came out in the fall of 1994, right after we opened Gramercy. I loved that book as much as I loved the restaurant. And it's not that Michael had any problem with Tom. It was that for nine years, I had spent sixteen hours a day in one restaurant. Now my loyalty had to be divided. We had not yet established operating systems or economics. Intellectually, I'd been anticipating that reality, but until you go through it, you just have no idea what that means.

On the day that Gramercy Tavern opened, I worked the front door for lunch at Union Square Cafe, because I wanted to show everybody that it still mattered. Thank God the two restaurants were only four blocks apart.

But despite their proximity, I couldn't get traction anywhere. I tried for the first month to do mornings and lunches at Union Square Cafe and afternoons and dinners at Gramercy. That worked because we weren't open for lunch yet at Gramercy. But what was tough was that all of a sudden, I had gone cold turkey from dinner at Union Square Cafe. So much of the culture of a restaurant team happens during the day when you're reviewing what you could have done better last night and planning how you'll do it better tonight.

I hadn't yet learned the hard lesson of empowering people. It was painful, because I couldn't seem to get a firm grip on either place. One restaurant thought I had abandoned it and the other restaurant was moving forward with its own engine (a baby will grow whether you are there to watch it or not). I was frustrated by my inability to shape some of the early decisions at GT, and I had to realize that if I wasn't there during the day, some of those decisions just had to get made without me.

But in that first month at Gramercy, I was increasingly biting my lip and not articulating things that were really troubling me. So in month two, I tried a new scheme: working Monday morning through Wednesday afternoon at Union Square and Wednesday evening through Friday night at Gramercy. (I refused to give up my weekends.) That failed, too. Even though I wasn't talking about it, my angst was clear to other people. I knew I was somewhat of a control freak—a style that had worked for me operating a single restaurant. I'd never been in a position where in order to succeed, I had to articulate what needed to get done, delegate it to the right people, and hold those people accountable.

ENLIGHTENED HOSPITALITY AS A WAY OF LIFE

Then I was lucky enough to have a bad thing happen. At Gramercy, a guest complained to the server about her salmon. The general manager told the server to leave the salmon on the woman's bill, since it was perfectly good—and since she had eaten half of it before complaining. When she left, someone presented her with a doggie bag containing the uneaten portion of her salmon. When the woman wrote to me to complain, I felt sick. I realized that these kinds of policy decisions were being made when I was at Union Square Cafe. This was also

a time when all the voices in me said: "Whatever you do, don't end up like your dad." But it suddenly became clear to me that my dad had not deputized the right people. He had not clearly established his priorities.

That low moment was a turning point, one that gave birth to my new philosophy. Right after Salmongate, I called a Saturday afternoon all-staff meeting in the Tavern to explain why that could never happen again. For the first time, I laid out the principles of what would become Enlightened Hospitality: nothing, I told them, would ever matter more than how we expressed hospitality to one another and then by extension to our guests, our community, our suppliers, and our investors. I was able to articulate these priorities at Gramercy Tavern because of this painful experience. In retrospect, it was an amazing gift. And it became the bedrock of everything that we've done since then. Not just at Gramercy, but at all of our restaurants.

THE BUSINESS OF THE BUSINESS

Gramercy Tavern was doing well. After just a few months, the restaurant was beginning to make money. (Ruth Reichl, the *New York Times* restaurant reviewer, gave it two stars three months after it opened, then three stars just a year and a half later.) The restaurant cost roughly $3 million to build in 1994 dollars and it took seven and a half years to pay all that back out of profits. That's a pretty long time. But we had patient, supportive investors who loved the restaurant and who had always trusted that it would end up in a good place. And that was even before we bought the space. We had signed a very long lease with Robert Raeburn and his family, and since the 1990s weren't bull-market years for medals or military uniforms, he thought it would be a wise time to close his business and sell the entire building to a condominium developer. Since we had so many years left on our lease, the developer said, "Why don't you guys just buy your space instead of having a bunch of apartment owners renting it to you?" So that's what we did. Today we are our own landlord and that's about as liberating as it gets. We don't have to worry about someone kicking us out or raising our rent, making it impossible to offer good food for good value. Or turning the space into a bank. Or a drugstore.

It probably took a year before we could feel truly proud, and it took a little longer before Gramercy Tavern felt as if it belonged in the same family as Union Square Cafe. Union Square was more feminine and Gramercy Tavern more masculine. But that was a lot about who was in the kitchen: many of the cooks at USC were women; at GT, the sous chefs were macho—there was more than one beer for everyone at the end of every service.

A DIFFICULT PARTING

Just four years into Gramercy, it became clear to me that Tom was getting itchy for a change. It was not that he and I were having a falling-out. He just wanted no part of Union Square Hospitality Group, where he'd have to play in the sandbox with my other partners. Really, he just wanted to do his own thing. But he *did* want me to do it with him. He would have been very happy to be a 50/50 partner. In fact, he invited me to do that with Craft, the restaurant he told me he wanted to open, but I did not want to turn my back on my partners. We had difficult conversations all through 1998, when USHG was opening Eleven Madison Park and Tabla. Not surprisingly, in the years after he opened Craft, in 2001, Gramercy Tavern went through a period that wasn't especially healthy. Tom kept sending signals that he wanted to do something else with me but not the USHG team. I had hugely mixed feelings, because

I didn't want to stop working with Tom and I was really concerned about derailing that relationship. I think we both knew that in Gramercy Tavern we had created a really wonderful and lasting restaurant.

Tom is much more shoot-from-the-hip than I am. He's much quicker to figure out how he feels about something and to act upon it. He had fewer misgivings than I had about expanding—I really believe that he had begun thinking about the next restaurant almost from the minute Gramercy opened. I was the one who kept saying, "Not yet, not yet, not yet." I had waited ten years before opening my second restaurant, and it just didn't seem right to me to open a third restaurant only a year after Gramercy opened. That difference was the seed for our ultimate separation as business partners, and from the perspective of what was best for the restaurant, it was a separation that probably took six or seven years longer than it should have. Even as he was starting his new company, Tom didn't want to leave Gramercy. My instincts were, "I'd hate to see you leave, but I don't think we can be both partners and rivals." And in fact that proved to be true. Because from the moment I told Tom I could not partner with him at Craft, an outflow of talent began from Gramercy to his new company. Craft's original chef, sous chef, pastry chef, service director, wine director, and general manager had all been Gramercy Tavern employees. That was not a good or healthy dynamic. Because we had competing interests, we were at a stalemate even as we moved forward in our respective businesses. There could be no new restaurants together, no Gramercy Tavern beyond New York, no Gramercy Tavern cookbook.

Gramercy went for too long a time without a full-time chef in the kitchen. Tom would show up for family meal in the afternoon, then leave for Craft, on 19th Street, for the rest of the night. And because he'd show up, I wouldn't. We both understood the reality (and danger) of the stasis, but neither one of us was willing to part ways with Gramercy Tavern. We each loved it too much, which is a credit to what we had built together.

I confess there were moments where I pondered whether I should just sell Gramercy Tavern to Tom. I imagined a scenario: why not agree on a fair price, flip a coin, and one of us would buy the restaurant from the other? But it never came to that. I remember being outside the restaurant one day with Audrey, looking up at those brass letters, N. S. Meyer, when she asked me, "How would you feel walking by this restaurant every day of your life if this were no longer yours?" The thought made me sick to my stomach. I knew she was right.

Tom ultimately became so consumed with his growing group of Craft restaurants and his television career that he finally felt safe enough to let go. But the restaurant's cracks had begun to show. In a 2007 review in the *New York Times* that awarded three stars to another of our restaurants, Eleven Madison Park, the critic Frank Bruni took a swipe at Gramercy Tavern: "Its luster had dimmed some even before the chef Tom Colicchio officially severed his ties."

ENTER MICHAEL ANTHONY

In 2006, some months before Tom and I parted ways, I received a letter from a gifted chef. Michael Anthony had recently left his position as executive chef at Blue Hill at Stone Barns, and he wanted to open his own restaurant. His letter included a business plan, and he asked if I would be willing to offer some input. We had met in Aspen in 2002, when Mike was a cowinner of one of *Food & Wine*'s Best New Chef awards. I'd enjoyed Mike's cooking at Stone Barns, and I liked him. And yet, uncharacteristically, I let that letter sit on a far corner of my desk for weeks. I knew I wasn't ready to open

Celebrating GT's fifteenth anniversary, Michael Anthony with staff members Katy Foley (left) and Theresa Mullen.

another restaurant, even with someone as talented as Mike. Yet there was a voice inside that asked, "What if?" I couldn't imagine at the time how, after all these years, Tom and I would separate (even though by then he was working on his *fifth* solo restaurant). But if we ever did, knowing Mike and his cooking, I thought he could be a perfect fit for Gramercy Tavern. When at last I decided that doing nothing was not an option, I spoke to Mike on the phone, told him I'd read his proposal, and gave him some feedback, with the understanding that I could not do a restaurant with him on the side. I said, "The last thing I would ever want to do is to stand in the way of the passion you feel for doing your own business. And

Celebrating at *Food & Wine* magazine's Aspen Classic in 2007. **FROM LEFT:** with Michael Anthony, his wife, Mindy Dubin, John Ragan, Nick Anderer, Wendy Anderer, and Kevin Mahan.

if that's where your heart is, that's what you should do. But . . . if you could ever imagine having a conversation about an opportunity within our company, I might have something to talk about."

We finally met in the kitchen of our catering company, now called Union Square Events. We had an opening for a chef there, and as a pretext for getting together I asked him, as an interim step, whether he might consider helping us out. He politely declined. Then I said, "I know you've been dreaming of owning your own restaurant, but could you imagine at this point in your career working for another restaurant company?" He replied, "You're about the only one I would consider doing it with." I smiled, then asked him, "If you could just wave a magic wand and head up one of our places, which one would you feel the most compatible with?" "That's easy," he said instantly. "Gramercy Tavern. And maybe Union Square Cafe." Once Michael answered that way, my mind couldn't stop. I knew it was time to act in the best interest of Gramercy Tavern.

I told Mike, "I'm not able to take this conversation any further right now, but I want you to know that I'm not going to waste your time. I've got some business to do on my side." I was discreet, but I think he knew I was very serious.

On August 23, 2006, the *New York Times* reported Tom Colicchio's departure from Gramercy Tavern. And on September 13, 2006, the restaurant announced its new executive chef, Michael Anthony.

It was difficult for Mike at the beginning, to come into a long-standing restaurant that was so big and so complicated, to be the outsider in such a deep-rooted culture, and to fill Tom's ample shoes. Gramercy Tavern is an intensely connected family, from the people who work there today back through to the folks who worked there years ago. It was a tough few months. But I had instructed him to lead an evolution, not a revolution. I felt he needed to take the time to understand the GT culture, to really know how the car drove before changing a thing. And Mike didn't come with his own team; he inherited Tom's sous chef, and kitchen staff, and servers. There were a couple of tough early reviews to endure, reviews for the menu Mike had inherited. But from the beginning, I always believed it would be fine, because I had full confidence in his skills and I trusted his capacity to lead. Mike's philosophies of sourcing and handling food were completely compatible with everything that Gramercy Tavern stands for, and I knew that Mike is a working chef who wants to be in his kitchen, but is also comfortable in the dining room

I think it took Mike two years to no longer feel like the restaurant's substitute teacher. But finally, in 2007, his own menu was reviewed by Frank Bruni in the *New York Times*. "[I]s there a restaurant in this city more beloved than Gramercy Tavern?" he wrote. ". . . What most diners want isn't nerve-jangling sensation. . . . It's a kind of unstrained graciousness and unlabored sophistication that Gramercy Tavern has pretty much defined." The restaurant retained its coveted three stars. We held an impromptu party that night and Tom Colicchio showed up to congratulate Mike and the team. He returned, too, in 2008, when Gramercy won the James Beard Award for Outstanding Restaurant in America.

But that was nothing compared to the explosive applause that rocked Lincoln Center in the spring of 2012, when Michael Anthony won the James Beard Award for Best Chef: New York City. Mike's level of taste and ability to cook good food are rare enough; add to that his refined sensibility and his willingness to teach other cooks, his kindness and his humility, and you have a combination that's almost unheard of in the world of professional chefs. His cooking techniques may be rooted in classical training in France and Japan, but they're driven by a reverence for ingredients that grow or graze on local soil. Mike's food at its best creates an experience that causes you to drop your conversation—and your fork—in amazement and delight. That's what led us to make Mike a partner in 2011.

There are a million ways Gramercy Tavern could have gone wrong, because we were putting together musical notes that didn't necessarily go together. And that was kind of the fun of it. We weren't certain how to make a chord out of those notes or even if that chord would endure. The music of Gramercy Tavern has now been listened to by so many people over the years that it has become *their* song. And the reason it may sound better than ever today is that it just gets richer and more soulful over time. It's like a play that different audiences have seen and reacted to. Different directors have driven it. Different actors have starred in it. A true tavern can only be defined by the way it is used by its community. You can't just build a place and decree that it become vital. That's why time matters. Now you know why this book took so long to write. We couldn't have done it any sooner than right now. Gramercy needed more time to develop more stories. More soul. More relationships. More memories. And, yes, more recipes!

INTRODUCTION

Gramercy Tavern has always been about creating a place where people can come together. I hope the recipes and stories in this book convey both the warm welcome of the restaurant and a sense of discovery about the food. My goal is not to have you try to slavishly reproduce dishes it takes a kitchen full of professionals to turn out every day. Let me say up front that this is not just a restaurant cookbook. What I encourage you to reproduce is the *spirit* of the cooking at GT, and to create your own versions of our recipes. My true mission here is to inspire you to cook healthy and inventive food in your own kitchen. Yes, the book will look great on your coffee table, but I want you to take it into the kitchen and use it well.

BRINGING GRAMERCY HOME

I cook differently at home than I do at the restaurant. Everything changes: the amount of time, space, equipment, number of helping hands, and, especially, the amount of cleanup I'm willing to do. What does that mean? A recipe cooked at Gramercy Tavern might require four or five pots and pans and several hours of preparation. At home, a meal has to happen in an hour, often less, using just a pan or two. My style of cooking is easily applied to both settings, even when it comes to making the food look beautiful. I don't cook food that is pretentious or overmanipulated. I practice what I call "the harmonious scatter"—meaning that I try to place the right ingredients together on a plate in a natural and beautiful way. No matter what the setting, I'm always searching for that special touch that will distinguish a dish, that will add another layer of flavor and intrigue. I accomplish this in a number of ways. Mostly I look for what's both freshest and immediately available: it could be something vibrant from the garden, or even just something crunchy from the cupboard. I'm not talking about

You can just imagine how the energy of these modest ingredients could enliven your cooking. **FROM LEFT:** carrots pulled from black dirt; handfuls of asparagus, leeks, bok choy, and spring onions; and vibrant fresh-picked thyme.

tossing around microgreens or special-ordering luxury ingredients. I'm talking about things like pickled vegetables, or freshly picked herbs, or toasted nuts, or thinly sliced raw vegetables, or a drop or two of aromatic vinegar added at the last moment.

I do not like to preach, but I do profoundly believe in cooking with unprocessed ingredients, produce that's the best each season offers, meat that's sustainably raised, and seafood that's thoughtfully sourced. Use this book as an invitation to discover how wonderful such ingredients can make a dish taste. When you choose to eat food from local sources, not only are you treating yourself to exceptional flavors, but you are learning about the story behind the food. The fact that you're cooking with great ingredients is more important than getting the recipes right. You can't screw them up. Relax when you're cooking, and it's going to taste great.

At the restaurant, presentation and imaginative plating keep you as the diner (and us in the kitchen) interested, entertained, surprised, and

There's magic in the monotony; we learn to value the repetition in our work, like slicing carrots with a mandoline, then julienning them *(above)*.

delighted. At home, you certainly don't need lots of flourishes, nor should you let them divert you from getting dinner on the table. The recipes in this book illustrate essential techniques, but as you're cooking, please don't worry if your dishes don't look exactly like our photographs. The ingredients themselves are beautiful enough on their own. Cooking at home should be loose, fun, and memorable.

In my family, we celebrate every holiday known to mankind and even make up some of our own, all with the goal of bringing our family together. During summers on Long Island, we've cooked entire pigs and used every single delicious part. In Ohio, we hunt for asparagus in the field next to my parents' home. And at home in New York City, we shop at the Union Square Greenmarket most Saturday mornings. Being a professional chef doesn't make me exempt from trying anything imaginable to get my kids to eat good food. I have even dressed up in my sushi chef's uniform to cook a Japanese night for my daughters, Gaby, Colette, and Adeline.

HOW I GOT TO GRAMERCY

I love cooking today for the same reasons I did when I began. I was lucky to realize early on how food can reveal a culture. I took every chance to travel the world and to learn how food and cooking can be a common denominator, how they open doors to discovering people. My particular story began with working in both stellar restaurants and home kitchens in Japan and in France, because I was fascinated with those cultures and those places. In fact, I cooked abroad for many years before I ever worked in a professional American kitchen. Each experience helped me figure out what was unique about that culture and has informed the way I cook today. My apprenticeship may have been roundabout, but the essence of Gramercy Tavern is that we cook the way we do because we're searching for what's unique about being right here, right now. We ask ourselves, "Who are we? And what makes the food we cook so special?"

I have spent years thinking about how I want my restaurant kitchen to feel. I left for Tokyo the day after I graduated from college and began my career working for my first chef, Shizuyo Shima, at her tiny twenty-seat restaurant, Bistro Shima. I didn't realize that I would be subjecting myself to the most humiliating—yet rich—experience of my life. In her minuscule space, Shima replicated the atmosphere of the brutal kitchens of famous

An impromptu moment with the sous chefs.
FROM LEFT: Saman Javid, Duncan Grant, Howard Kalachnikoff, Kyle Knall, and Geoff Lazlo.

restaurants in France where she'd worked. I tried to convince myself that her manner was tough love. This is the way restaurants have to function, I told myself. This is the way chefs have to behave. Shima taught me to embrace the restaurant business for its tough grittiness, not for its romantic side. She challenged me to understand that this kind of work is only for people who are deeply committed. For all the good and bad that came with her style of teaching, it did get me hooked.

After a year and a half, Shima told me she'd taught me everything she

Ours is a very busy kitchen, but I'm proud that we can maintain such a focused calm.

knew. She said it was time to move on, convincing me to get a vocational cooking degree at L'Ecole Technique Jean Ferrandi in Paris, where she had studied. Little did I know how valuable that advice would be. Three weeks after I arrived, Shima actually showed up in Paris to make sure I was doing it right: working diligently. She introduced me to her mentor, the famous old-school chef Jean Delaveyne. While at school, I worked three nights a week at his restaurant. I didn't understand then exactly why the mood was always so tense. I do now: it was another brutalized kitchen. The cooks were terrified of the chef. A lightbulb went off, and I put the pieces together; I understood why Shima had behaved that way. It was a kind of initiation rite she'd put me through.

I was moving toward my own idea of how a kitchen should be run, but there were still years of learning and soul searching ahead. I began to think, "Hey, it's not right (or productive) to treat people like this." I worked in many restaurants in Paris and in New York, including Jacques Cagna, Daniel, March, and Blue Hill at Stone Barns. It took working under these different chefs and observing their styles and temperaments to gradually develop and define a style of my own.

And it took working with Danny Meyer, and our partner at Gramercy Tavern, Kevin Mahan, to realize the sense of community that I had been looking for and dreaming about in a restaurant. Danny creates a learning environment. He's not just a brilliant guy, a great restaurateur who's grown a bunch of great restaurants. He is a visionary leader who continues to learn about himself and about the people who work with him. We share the value of cultivating Gramercy Tavern with our staff —and our guests—as a place where people are respected, where they have a home, where they have a purpose. It's a place where people are heard, where they're needed. I feel extremely proud to be where I am today. Gramercy Tavern is a community in every sense of the word. Now you're part of it, too.

At our annual Autumn Harvest Dinner, 2011. **FROM LEFT:** with Nick Anderer, Dan Dubin, Michael Senter, and Frank Hughes in the Tavern before the meal.

WELCOME

"Our relationship with a craft
brewer who's in a week-to-
week struggle to establish his
or her business is just like our
commitment to the small farmers
who pour their love and guts
into the soil."

— Kevin Mahan

BOURBON ON
THE ROCK

Kevin Mahan was determined to
serve the largest, purest cube of ice
he could find. So he searched out an
ice sculptor, and voilà!

ORANGE BLOSSOM

Our take on the traditional Champagne cocktail gets its fragrant floral note from elderflower essence and an orange twist; orange bitters temper the sweetness and add complexity. Drop 1 white sugar cube into a Champagne flute and soak it with 3 generous dashes of orange bitters. Add ½ ounce St-Germain elderflower liqueur and top with 5 ounces dry sparkling wine (pour slowly to keep the bubbles in). Twist a piece of orange peel over the glass, run it around the rim, and drop it into the glass.

MAKING SYRUPS

SIMPLE SYRUP

MAKES ABOUT 10 OUNCES

Simple syrup keeps forever, so make plenty and store it in the refrigerator. The proportions do not change, so you can scale it up easily. In a small saucepan, combine 1 cup sugar and 1 cup water and boil until the sugar dissolves. Cool and refrigerate.

HONEY SYRUP

MAKES ABOUT 4 OUNCES

This syrup is also wonderful as a sweetener for hot or cold tea. Combine ¼ cup honey and ¼ cup boiling water in a container. Stir until the honey dissolves, cover, and refrigerate. Honey syrup will keep in the refrigerator for about a month.

CRANBERRY SYRUP

MAKES ABOUT 7 OUNCES

The secret of our Cranberry Daiquiri, this syrup is delicious, too, in a vodka- or gin-based drink. In a small saucepan, combine 1 cup Simple Syrup, 2 wide strips orange zest, and 1 cinnamon stick and bring to a boil. Add 1¼ cups fresh cranberries and gently simmer. As soon as the first berry pops, remove 18 intact ones (enough for 6 drinks) and set aside, then continue simmering until most of the cranberries have popped. Let the mixture steep, off the heat, for 30 minutes. Strain into a container, pressing very gently on the solids with the back of a spoon—too much pressure, and you'll have jelly! Cool, then add the reserved berries, cover, and refrigerate. The syrup will keep in the refrigerator for up to a month.

MEZCALIENTE

A mezcal-based spicy, smoky margarita with a kick of jalapeño, crisped with fresh cucumbers. Infuse 8 ounces silver or blanco tequila with a halved jalapeño; taste after 20 minutes, then strain when you like the heat. Fill a cocktail shaker with ice and add 2 ounces of the jalapeño-infused tequila, $3/4$ ounce fresh lime juice, $1/2$ ounce mezcal, $1/2$ ounce Simple Syrup (opposite), and 3 halved slices of cucumber. Shake vigorously and pour.

RANSOM NOTE

A sophisticated drink built around gin and Germany's plum brandy barrel-aged Schraml mead (wine made from fermented honey). Fill a cocktail shaker with ice, add 2 ounces Ransom Old Tom gin, $3/4$ ounce Schraml mead, $3/4$ ounce Honey Syrup (page 44), and $1/4$ ounce fresh lemon juice. Shake and strain into a chilled martini glass.

> "Our Ransom Note cocktail features Ransom Old Tom gin, an Oregon microdistillery's reproduction of a nineteenth-century English malty, sweetened gin."
>
> —Juliette Pope

CRANBERRY DAIQUIRI

Spiced with cinnamon and orange zest and made with black rum instead of white, this is a holiday house specialty. Fill a cocktail shaker with ice. Add 2 ounces Gosling's black rum, 1 ounce fresh lime juice, and 1 ounce Cranberry Syrup (page 44). Shake, then strain into a chilled martini glass with 3 poached cranberries from the cranberry syrup.

SPRING

Roberta Bendavid *(far left)* reflects seasonal nuance on the ever-changing Tavern tablescape. She treats vegetables as flowers (a tangle of garlic scapes; bright sugar snap peas; even asparagus, leeks, and ramps); and flowers are never just bouquets. Lessons abound: vary the height, use timeworn containers of wrought iron, pewter, or sturdy New England saltware. Colors and themes should echo and repeat: a bunch of buttery ranunculus in a chubby pot appears again in a vase. Roberta says she's the only designer who "interviews" each contender before it's allowed on the table.

For Roberta

LIGHTLY CURRIED SWEET PEAS WITH SCAPES AND RAMPS

SERVES 4

Luxurious cooking has traditionally meant truffles, caviar, and foie gras. At Gramercy Tavern, however, we redefine luxury as the delicious progression of seasonal ingredients—like sweet peas. The decadent part of sweet pea season is racing the clock to eat as many spoonfuls as we can before the peas turn starchy and the weather becomes too hot to grow them. There is literally nothing like the pop of texture and crunch of a bowl of fresh peas. They're the star of this simple dish, which could include sautéed fiddlehead ferns, as shown. The peas are equally irresistible over rice or another soft grain like barley, farro, bulgur, or quinoa.

1 tablespoon olive oil

¼ cup diced garlic scapes or garlic

½ cup minced ramp or scallion whites (greens sliced and set aside)

½ teaspoon mild curry powder

½ cup buttermilk or whole milk

½ cup Vegetable Broth (page 118) or water

Salt

2 cups shelled fresh peas

½ tablespoon finely chopped herbs, such as tarragon, dill, or parsley

1 tablespoon unsalted butter

Fresh lemon juice

Pepper

In a medium saucepan, heat the oil over medium-low heat. Add the garlic and minced ramp whites and cook until softened, about 3 minutes. Add the curry powder and stir for about 30 seconds. Add the milk and broth, season with salt, and bring to a simmer. Add the peas and ramp greens and simmer until the peas are just tender, about a minute.

Stir in the herbs and butter, then season with lemon juice, salt, and pepper. Spoon the peas, broth, and herbs into a bowl.

A WORD ON SALT AND PEPPER

In this book, when I specify "salt" in a recipe, I mean kosher salt. This is what we use in our kitchen in our cooking, because it's easy to measure and sprinkle. When I specify "sea salt," I mean a finishing salt, like fleur de sel or another natural crystallized sea salt. This is a rare, hand-harvested product that should be used sparingly. I add sea salt after all the cooking is done, for its crystal crunch. Because it doesn't dissolve when you sprinkle it, a finishing salt adds another layer of interest to a dish.

I always have white peppercorns in my peppermill, and admit to liking white pepper, mostly for aesthetic reasons. In these recipes, I haven't stated a preference. Use whatever is easiest for you.

ROASTED ASPARAGUS SALAD WITH PICKLED SHALLOTS

SERVES 4

Making a great composed spring salad means focusing on just a few ingredients that really signal the season: here, asparagus, nettles, and shallots. Everything else is just a lovely accent, not crucial but delightful. In the restaurant, we have access to any number of fresh ingredients, like bamboo shoots, microgreens, borage, and other edible flowers, but when I'm making this salad at home, it's all about the asparagus. Roasting asparagus makes a difference, and I like to do it in a skillet with a drop of olive oil so the spears become slightly browned, a much more flavorful way of cooking them than boiling. To accentuate their asparagusness, I shave raw spears on top, which really shows off the vegetable.

For this recipe, I reach for some pretty special toppings straight from the Greenmarket. At home, use what's in your garden, like sprigs of herbs, or crunchy things from your pantry: a handful of sesame seeds or even just some coarse bread crumbs. The dressing is made from wild nettles, which are easily found at farmers' markets. In their raw state, they can irritate your skin; once washed and soaked, however, they're easy to work with. Nettles are one of the toughest plants around. That means that they have an amazing capacity to pull complex flavors from the earth, they pack the most intense green color, and they're supernutritious.

1/4 cup olive oil

1 cup minced onion

1/2 tablespoon minced shallot

1 teaspoon minced garlic

2 cups packed nettle leaves

1 cup cold Vegetable Broth (page 118) or water

24 asparagus spears, trimmed

Fresh lemon juice

Salt and pepper

12 inner hearts of romaine

16 petals Pickled Shallots (page 86)

Extra-virgin olive oil

Make the nettle puree. In a medium skillet, heat 2 tablespoons of the olive oil over medium-low heat. Add the onion, shallot, and garlic and cook until soft, about 10 minutes.

Meanwhile, blanch the nettles in a medium saucepan of boiling salted water for about 2 minutes, then drain and shock in ice water. Drain, squeeze out the excess water, and roughly chop the nettles.

In a blender, combine the nettles, onion mixture, and broth and process until smooth. Pass through a fine-mesh strainer into a medium bowl; cover and refrigerate.

In a large skillet, heat the remaining 2 tablespoons olive oil over medium-high heat. Add 20 of the asparagus spears and pan-roast, tossing occasionally, until just tender and lightly browned, about 6 minutes. Season with a squeeze of lemon juice and salt and pepper.

Shave the remaining 4 asparagus spears lengthwise with a vegetable peeler. Put the shavings in a medium bowl with the romaine hearts and pickled shallots and season with extra-virgin olive oil, lemon juice, salt, and pepper.

Stir 1/2 tablespoon extra-virgin olive oil into the nettle puree, add a squeeze or two of lemon juice, and season with salt and pepper. Spread the puree on the bottom of each plate (it should coat the plates like a sauce; thin with a little water if needed). Harmoniously scatter the roasted asparagus spears and the romaine, shaved raw asparagus, and pickled shallots over the puree.

SPRING ASPARAGUS WITH FLOUNDER

SERVES 4

I came up with this dish when the first asparagus finally showed up after waiting forever for spring to arrive. There's an unwritten restaurant rule that an ingredient shouldn't appear more than once on any menu. I've never believed that! When a seasonal ingredient like asparagus becomes available, we celebrate it in many ways, because it has a very short run. That's how this unconventional asparagus sauce came about. Here I serve it with delicate flounder fillets, but I also like it as a salad dressing or as a condiment with raw vegetables.

There are three easy steps to this chilled sauce (think of it as a tangy asparagus smoothie). You'll need a nice big bunch of asparagus. First marinate 1 cup of the stalks with green onions and vinegar. Then make a bright green base with another cup of the stalks, and finally blend the two with the herbs, yogurt, and avocado. The best tool for this job by far is the Vitamix blender. It turns out sauces and soups with an extraordinary silky-smooth texture—creamy without any cream or butter.

MARINATED ASPARAGUS

1 cup peeled and thinly sliced asparagus stalks (tips reserved)

2 tablespoons thinly sliced spring onions (white parts)

1 teaspoon minced garlic

3 paper-thin slices jalapeño pepper

2 tablespoons olive oil

1 tablespoon white balsamic vinegar

Salt and pepper

½ cup reserved asparagus tips

½ cup halved baby radishes

ASPARAGUS BASE

½ cup flat-leaf parsley leaves

¼ cup dill fronds

½ cup tarragon leaves

1 tablespoon olive oil

1 teaspoon minced garlic

2 tablespoons minced shallots

2 tablespoons minced onion

1 cup peeled and thinly sliced asparagus stalks

1½ cups Vegetable Broth (page 118) or water

1 cup packed baby spinach leaves

TO FINISH

½ ripe avocado

3 tablespoons Greek yogurt

Fresh lemon juice

Salt and pepper

½ cup diced small cucumbers

¼ tablespoon chopped dill

Extra-virgin olive oil

Four 6-ounce skinless flounder fillets

Olive oil for grilling or sautéing

First, marinate the asparagus. In a small saucepan, combine the asparagus, spring onions, garlic, jalapeño, olive oil, and vinegar. Season with salt and pepper. Let the asparagus marinate for an hour.

Meanwhile, in a small saucepan of boiling salted water, blanch the asparagus tips until crisp-tender, about 2 minutes. Drain, shock in ice water, and pat dry. Reserve the boiling and ice water for the next steps. Blanch the radishes for just a minute, then transfer to the ice water, drain, and pat dry. Set the blanched vegetables aside.

Make the asparagus base. Tie the parsley, dill fronds, and tarragon in a loose cheesecloth sachet and blanch for 30 seconds, then shock. Drain the sachet and gently squeeze out the water, then remove and discard the cheesecloth. In a small saucepan, heat the olive oil over medium-low heat. Add the garlic, shallots, and minced onion and cook until softened, about 3 minutes. Add the asparagus and stir briefly. Raise the heat to high, add the broth, and bring to a simmer. Add the spinach and stir just until wilted, about a minute. Immediately pour the asparagus base into a medium bowl, set it in an ice bath, and stir to cool.

Put the saucepan with the marinated asparagus over medium heat, bring to a simmer, and cook for 1 minute. Immediately pour the mixture into a medium bowl, set it in an ice bath, and stir to cool.

To finish the asparagus sauce, transfer the marinated asparagus and asparagus base to a blender, add the blanched herbs, avocado, and yogurt, and process until smooth. Pass through a fine-mesh strainer into a medium bowl. Season the asparagus sauce with lemon juice, salt, and pepper; refrigerate.

In a small bowl, combine the cucumbers, dill, and blanched asparagus tips and radishes. Season with extra-virgin olive oil, lemon juice, salt, and pepper.

If the flounder fillets are thick enough, grilling is a great option. If they're thin and delicate, sauté them in a skillet. Brush the fillets with olive oil and season with salt and pepper. Grill or sauté the fillets, turning once, until just cooked through, about 3 minutes per side.

Fill chilled shallow bowls with the asparagus sauce, lay the warm fillets in the sauce, and pile the asparagus tip mixture on top.

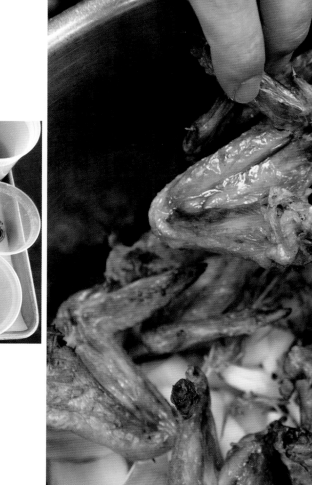

CHICKEN BROTH

MAKES ABOUT 3½ QUARTS

At home it's worth investing the time to make this light broth if you want to achieve something like the complex flavor we get in the restaurant. The process is close to what we go through to make a stock at GT, but I've shortened the cooking time and the number of ingredients to make it manageable; what's essential is to combine roasted chicken wings and bones with some fresh vegetables. The broth will add flavor to many recipes in this book.

2 tablespoons olive oil

1 large onion, roughly chopped

2 carrots, roughly chopped

2 celery stalks, roughly chopped

1 leek (white and pale green parts), roughly chopped

3 pounds chicken bones (backs, necks, carcasses), roasted (see method for roasting wings on page 61)

3 pounds chicken wings, roasted (see page 61)

5 flat-leaf parsley stems

2 sprigs thyme

1 bay leaf

½ tablespoon black peppercorns

½ tablespoon coriander seeds

In a large pot, heat the oil over medium heat. Add the onion, carrots, celery, and leek and cook, stirring occasionally, for about 10 minutes. Add the roasted chicken bones, wings, parsley, thyme, bay leaf, peppercorns, coriander, and 4 quarts water. Bring to a simmer and gently cook, skimming the foam once or twice, for about 2½ hours.

Pass the broth through a fine-mesh strainer into a container, then skim the fat. Or, if you're not using the broth right away, let it cool, then cover and refrigerate. The fat can easily be removed from the top of the chilled broth after it hardens. The broth will keep, covered, in the refrigerator for up to 5 days; it can be frozen for up to 3 months.

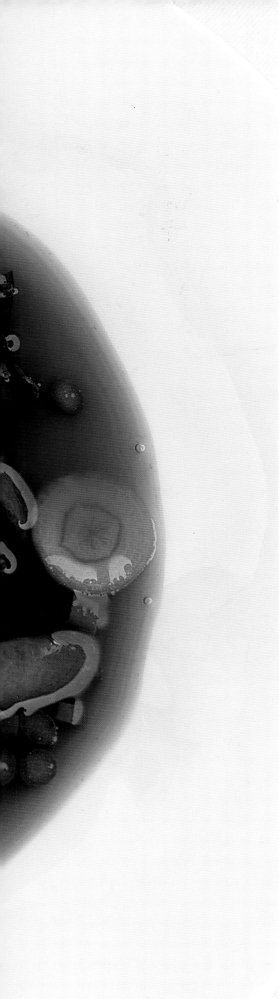

CHICKEN SOUP WITH SPRING VEGETABLES

SERVES 6

This soup is astounding to behold, with its abundance of vibrant vegetables in a rich broth. The intensity is reinforced by browning chicken wings and using a flavorful chicken broth, not water.

2 pounds chicken wings

3 tablespoons olive oil

1 onion, minced

1 carrot, minced

1 celery stalk, minced

3 garlic cloves, minced

One 1-inch piece of ginger, peeled and minced

2 tablespoons sherry vinegar

8 cups Chicken Broth (page 59)

1 cup shelled fresh peas, plus a few pea pods halved for garnish

1¼ cups sugar snap peas, trimmed and cut into pieces

1 cup thinly sliced baby carrots

1 cup thinly sliced baby turnips

1 cup diced asparagus

Salt and pepper

Fresh lemon juice

Shiro dashi (optional)

1 tablespoon finely chopped tarragon or flat-leaf parsley

Preheat the oven to 400°F.

Roast the wings. Put the chicken wings on a large baking sheet and toss with 1 tablespoon of the oil. Spread out the wings and roast, turning once about halfway through, until golden brown, about an hour.

When the wings are almost ready, in a large pot, heat the remaining 2 tablespoons oil over medium heat. Add the onion, carrot, celery, garlic, and ginger and cook, stirring often, until softened, about 6 minutes. Add the wings to the pot, then add the vinegar and cook until the vinegar has evaporated. Add the broth and bring to a boil, then reduce the heat and simmer gently for about an hour. Strain the broth and skim the fat.

Pour the broth into a medium pot and bring to a boil. Add the peas, snap peas, carrots, turnips, and asparagus, and simmer for 3 minutes. Season with salt, pepper, and a few drops of lemon juice. Add a tablespoon or two of shiro dashi, if you have it.

Fill bowls with the soup and vegetables and top with the tarragon.

of a successful yacht catering business, organizing parties and weddings for hundreds of people. It was all new to me, but I drew on my seemingly random summer job experiences: waitering, working in a grocery store meat department (where they let me rewrap leaky packages, unload 75-pound boxes of meat, and clean the band saws), bar backing, washing dishes, and parking cars. Not so much on the old finance degree.

In December 1995, I saw an ad for an assistant manager at a restaurant on Miami Beach. I met the chef/owner of A Fish Called Avalon in the Avalon Hotel. We sat on the balcony on Ocean Drive and talked for hours about our passion for food. My dad is a food and wine lover and my stepmother is a gourmet cook, interests I learned to appreciate while living with them in Venezuela as a kid. The restaurant hired me. The place was crazy fun and pretty much ran by itself.

A restaurant my dad frequented at the time was called Norman's, in Coral Gables, owned by the highly regarded chef Norman Van Aken. My dad said, "If you really love this business, you should try to work at Norman's." I interviewed and was offered a position as a food runner. On my first day, I was told to find a woman named Carol, a busgirl, who would train me. Carol was slicing bread as I introduced myself. She barely looked up at me and, in a half-grunt, said, "You will never make it here."

By then I was twenty-eight, and my finance degree seemed very far away. I'd had two nice stints in Spain and Australia. I certainly hadn't expected to wind up as a busboy. But it was my foot in the door to the serious side of the restaurant business. And at that level, I didn't know anything! I had never seen a tablecloth changed so flawlessly—never mind all of the other minute details executed to perfection by the busboy crew. I was a little disappointed to begin so far down, but I had to earn my stripes with that crew and prove I could keep up with the

KEVIN MAHAN

MANAGING PARTNER • SINCE 1999

Twenty years ago, parents didn't dream of their kids working in a restaurant. That job was something you'd fall back on, not what you'd aspire to. I grew up in Miami and lived in Venezuela for four years. I was a finance major at Boston University when my dad told me that we couldn't afford for me to go back my junior year, so I took a couple of classes at the University of Miami for a semester and then found a way to pay my way through the University of Florida. I studied finance and loved it, but I didn't stop to consider what or where finance jobs would be or whether I'd like them.

While in college, I worked as a "cater waiter" for the president of the university. After graduation in 1992, I was traveling all over Spain with a friend when I got a call offering me a job as the assistant to the first female president of the Florida Bar Association. I laughed and said, "I'm in Spain on vacation." But when I got back home to Miami, I signed on, and for two years I wrote articles for her and organized her schedule. When her term was over, I quit and spent three months in Australia. When I returned, I ended up as a manager other back waiters, busboys, and with Carol, one of the hardest-working people I have ever known. I took the tough treatment and worked as hard as possible. My saving grace was my fluency in Spanish; no one could haze me in Spanish without my understanding them!

At this point, my friends were on their way to becoming lawyers and doctors . . . and there I was serving them bread, butter, and water. It did hurt a bit. But at the end of the day, I realized I loved what I was doing. And starting at the bottom of the ladder was turning out to be an invaluable experience. After about a month, Carol looked at me and growled, "You're okay." That was a huge victory; a moment I'll never forget.

Did I want more responsibility? Sure. I went on to become a food runner and then server, which allowed me to develop relationships with the captains and managers, people much more serious about this business than anyone I'd ever met in Miami. I wanted to learn everything, not just about wine and service, but about food and cooking as well. I trailed in the kitchen whenever Norman would let me, which was not often—at first they did not take my enthusiasm very seriously. But when I asked for two weeks' vacation and spent it working full shifts in the kitchen, that changed. Many of Norman's veterans had worked at great restaurants in New York City. Two of them pulled me aside and said, "You need to go to New York." One even said I needed to be at a Danny Meyer restaurant. I had only been to New York once in my life. I had no idea who Danny Meyer was. But the seed was planted and heading north to work with the best became my new goal.

Here's where it gets incredible. In 1999, Norman was asked to be a guest chef for the Share Our Strength Autumn Harvest Dinner at Gramercy Tavern. There was a lot of chatter about that, because it's a huge honor to be invited to GT as a guest chef. Since SOS is a charity, chefs are asked to donate their food and labor. My dad suggested that I go to Norman and tell him I'd pay my own airfare and lodging and work the event for free. I somehow found the guts to ask for the opportunity, and for the permission to interview for a job at GT while there. Norman

FROM LEFT: with Michael Romano, Danny Meyer, Paul Bolles-Beaven, and Michael Anthony at Gramercy's fifteenth-anniversary celebration, 2009.

agreed and offered his help. So I worked with Norman at Gramercy and had a job interview with the GM, and within six weeks, I had moved to New York to start as a server.

I lived on a friend's couch for three months, through the beginning of December, when my friend said, "I don't know where you'll be for Christmas, but my family's coming here." I quickly moved into the smallest-imaginable apartment above Calcutta Restaurant on East 6th Street. My place was hot and smelled of curry. But it was worth it. I immersed myself in Gramercy, as a waiter and a cellar rat for wine-and-service director Paul Grieco. I delved deep into all aspects of his beverage program, taking on a lot quickly, like conducting a tasting of sherry and Roquefort cheese with the whole staff at family meal after only a few months. I loved the camaraderie, the adrenaline rush of service, and the pleasure-giving feeling you get from interacting with guests. This business is grueling, but watching people take a bite or sip of something that turns out to be the best thing they've ever tasted: that's fun.

After less than a year, I was promoted to floor manager. That was overwhelming—to this day, I still say that they must've been desperate! Two years later, I was made AGM (assistant general manager) and within a year, GM. Then in 2008, Danny made me the managing partner of Gramercy Tavern. Quite the crazy, unexpected, circuitous path from finance degree to restaurant career. For the record, I will admit to skipping some steps here at Gramercy—like being a back waiter or captain—but I swear I can change all the tablecloths!

ANTICIPATION

A dish is more than just the sum of its ingredients. It's about expressing emotion. The anticipation we feel about the arrival and departure of seasonal ingredients brings joy, a bit of sadness, and contemplation. For some people, cooking seasonally may seem like a cuisine of limits: self-deprivation. After all, we live in New York City, where we can get just about any ingredient we want just about any time we want it. But what's more powerful is the elation I feel the moment that ingredient first arrives in the market, the pure enjoyment of it in the height of its season, and then the melancholy that inevitably sets in as its season comes to an end. Anticipation represents the emotional side of eating; looking forward to cooking a special ingredient can turn a dull night in the middle of a week into an event. Expressing those emotions connects you to the world around you; it's a daily celebration that keeps us aware of the people who grow our food, focuses our attention on preserving nature, and gives us a way to pass on traditions from one generation to the next.

FRIED OYSTER AND SPINACH SALAD

SERVES 4

Oysters tell such a beautiful story of where they come from. All East Coast varieties derive from the same species, *Crassostrea virginica*, yet, amazingly, each variety—including the Island Creek and Fisher's Island oysters from the Long Island Sound that we serve at GT—is distinctly different and a perfect expression of its unique environment. Oysters are sustainable and act as healthy filters for the ocean water. Culturally they have been connected to New York's foodways from the very beginning (see Roasted Oysters, page 274). For these fried oysters, I like a quick vinegary marinade to season the carrots and daikon that enhances their crunch. Pickled daikon has a pungent aroma, but it tastes great! For even more flavor, add a bit of spicy kimchi.

1½ cups julienned carrots

1½ cups peeled and julienned daikon radish

¾ cup rice vinegar

2 tablespoons sugar

Salt

Grapeseed or peanut oil for frying

¼ cup all-purpose flour

1 egg

¾ cup panko or dried bread crumbs

2 handfuls of baby spinach

1 radish, sliced paper-thin

1 small shallot, thinly sliced

¼ cup torn mint leaves

Extra-virgin olive oil

Fresh lemon juice

Aleppo pepper

Pepper

16 shucked oysters, drained

"It's not every day that you see beautiful baby radishes like these from Eckerton Hill Farm, in Pennsylvania," Modesto Batista says, gleaming, at the Greenmarket.

In a medium bowl, combine the carrots, daikon, vinegar, ¾ cup water, the sugar, and 2 teaspoons salt and toss well. Cover and refrigerate for at least 1 hour, and up to 3 days.

When the pickles are ready, in a deep saucepan, heat 2 inches of grapeseed oil to about 375°F. Put the flour, egg, and panko in three separate small bowls. Whisk the egg with a little water to loosen it.

Thoroughly drain the pickled carrots and daikon and put a small handful in the center of each plate. In a medium bowl, combine the spinach, radish, shallot, and mint. Season with extra-virgin olive oil, lemon juice, Aleppo pepper, salt, and pepper just before serving.

Dredge each oyster in the flour, then the eggs, and finally the panko and put on a plate. Fry the oysters in the hot oil in batches, turning once, until golden brown, about a minute. Drain on paper towels and salt well. Arrange the oysters on top of the pickled daikon and carrot and top with the spinach salad.

ABOVE: Fried Oyster and Spinach Salad (page 65).
OPPOSITE: Elemental ingredients *(clockwise from top left):* three kinds of fresh spinach; julienned carrots and daikon; red onion rings and coins of daikon; just-shucked Island Creek oysters, panko bread crumbs, and eggs.

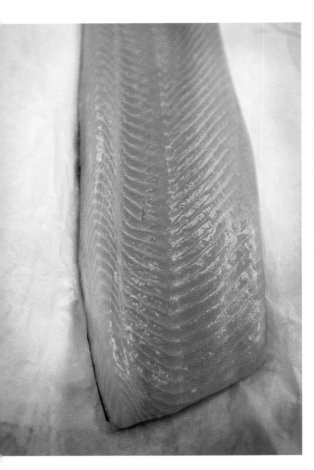

CITRUS-CURED CHAR

MAKES ABOUT 1¾ POUNDS

This fish undergoes a simple and magical transformation as it comes in contact with the aromatic salt, sugar, and spice cure. Unlike making gravlax, which can take days, you can cure char overnight. I like to cure a whole fillet for a dinner or party; it's amazingly practical and delicious. And I've found this cure to be a real lifesaver for dealing with pieces of tail and belly after you've cut fillets from a whole fish. While you're preparing to grill or sauté the fillets, you can bury the extra pieces in the spices and let them cure overnight for tomorrow's lunch. Then you've made two meals from one. This reminds me of the great French chef André Soltner, who is renowned for never missing the chance to make every last bit of any food delicious and even prized (for salmon, his trick was to make a mousse with just the scrapings from the bones).

1 cup kosher salt

½ cup sugar

½ tablespoon crushed coriander seeds

½ tablespoon crushed fennel seeds

½ tablespoon crushed star anise

Grated zest of 1 lemon

Grated zest of 1 lime

Grated zest of 1 orange

One 2-pound skinless Arctic char fillet, trimmed and any pin bones removed

In a small bowl, combine the salt, sugar, coriander, fennel seeds, star anise, and citrus zests. (Stop for a second and smell that aroma.) Spread half of the mixture in a strip down the center of a large piece of plastic wrap. Pat the fillet dry and set it on top of the mixture. Cover the fillet with the remaining mixture, then wrap tightly in two layers of plastic and transfer to a platter. Refrigerate, turning once, for at least 6 hours, or overnight.

Unwrap the fillet, rinse thoroughly, and pat dry. To serve, cut into thin slices at a slight angle. The cured char will keep, tightly wrapped, in the refrigerator for up to 5 days.

EGG CREPES WITH CRAB AND CARROTS

SERVES 6

Several years ago, I was invited to Japan to research traditional foods. Walking through the extraordinary Nishiki Market in the heart of Kyoto, past endless stalls of enticing artisanal foods (colorful pickles, crunchy croquettes, barbecued eel), I saw a man making *tamagoyaki*, a kind of dense omelet created by rolling fluffy layers of a thin egg batter in a square copper pan. When I returned to Gramercy Tavern, the sous chefs and I tried to translate those thin omelets to our American kitchen. Rather than imitate the Japanese technique, we homed in on one aspect of it—seasoning the egg mixture with shiro dashi and using a paper-thin layer of crêpe to veil sweet peekytoe crab and carrots.

5 large eggs

4 tablespoons (½ stick) unsalted butter, melted, plus 1 tablespoon

1 tablespoon shiro dashi

1 tablespoon all-purpose flour

Olive oil

1½ cups diced carrots

Pinch of sugar

Salt and pepper

Fresh lemon juice

1 pound jumbo lump crabmeat, picked over to remove any shells

1 tablespoon finely chopped chives

1 tablespoon finely chopped tarragon

½ tablespoon finely chopped shiso leaves (optional)

In a blender, combine the eggs, melted butter, shiro dashi, and flour and process until smooth. Pass the batter through a fine-mesh strainer into a bowl.

Heat a 7-inch nonstick skillet over medium-low heat. Brush the hot skillet with oil, then pour in ¼ cup batter and quickly swirl to coat the bottom evenly. Cook until the crêpe is just set but not browned, about 30 seconds. Carefully flip the crêpe and cook on the other side just until cooked through, about 15 seconds. Transfer to a plate and repeat the process with more oil and the remaining batter, stacking the crêpes as you go. (You will end up with 6 crêpes.) Trim with a sharp knife into about 5-inch squares. Set aside.

In a small saucepan, combine the carrots, the remaining 1 tablespoon butter, the sugar, and just enough water to cover; season with salt and pepper. Simmer until the water has evaporated and the carrots are tender. Add a small squeeze of lemon juice.

In another small saucepan, very gently heat the crabmeat; add the chives, tarragon, and shiso, if using, and season with a few drops of lemon juice, salt, and pepper.

Put a crêpe in the middle of each plate and spoon some of the crab mixture onto the corner closest to you. Spoon the carrots over the crab and fold the opposite corner over the top.

GRADUATING GREAT COOKS

When I arrived at Gramercy Tavern in 2006, I knew we needed to find people who could communicate within the kitchen at a level that was every bit as sophisticated as the interaction between the front of the house and our guests. I wanted people who could speak a common food language, express concerns, convey constructive criticism—and, most important, dream the same dreams about our food. I needed mature cooks who could both articulate and execute my vision of the kitchen. No one was more influential in helping me understand how to become a good manager than Paul Bolles-Beaven, a senior managing partner of USHG, with the title Chief People Officer. He gave me permission to care deeply for the people who work with us, he showed me how a leader can deal with unresolved tension, and he helped me value my own talent as a leader. All that helped build my confidence.

I'm a chef who runs a kitchen that's quiet and focused and thrives on communication. I wanted to hire a core group of people who complemented my vision and supported the way I ran the kitchen—and then could move on to run their own kitchens. Former GT chefs Nick Anderer, Chris Bradley, Joe Ogrodnek, Evyatar Lapidot, Kyle Knall, Geoff Lazlo, Alexandra Ray, and Gregory Marchand have all gone on to do just that. I'm extremely proud that the kitchen at Gramercy has become an elite graduate school for chefs. When I hire cooks, I look for people with the ability to grow. I never hire people just because they've had great experience. I want to find talented people who can work well together, add to our story, and then go on to do great things. I feel so lucky to be a part of that. I want to *graduate* great people.

I'd put my team of sous chefs up against *any* kitchen staff. **FROM LEFT:** with Duncan Grant, Kyle Knall, Saman Javid, Howard Kalachnikoff, and Geoff Lazlo.

SUGAR SNAP PEAS WITH LOBSTER

SERVES 4

Here is a different approach to a composed salad. This one has no leafy greens, and it swims in a bowl of sweet pea sauce. As soon as sugar snaps arrive in the Greenmarket, we start buying them by the bushel. We use lobster with coconut milk in this snap pea puree, along with pickled rhubarb and green tomatoes, to build a dish of such delicious contrasts that I eat it by the big spoonful. Sugar snap peas are so satisfying because after you've unzipped their pods to remove their fibrous strings, you can eat the whole thing. This dish is all about the peas, so feel free to try all sorts of variations with them, such as substituting seared scallops, or even just a scoop of fresh ricotta, for the lobster.

5 cups sugar snap peas, trimmed

1/2 cup cold Vegetable Broth (page 118) or water, plus more if needed

2 tablespoons unsweetened coconut milk

Extra-virgin olive oil

Fresh lime juice

Salt and pepper

Two 1 1/2-pound live lobsters

1/4 cup diced Pickled Rhubarb (page 87; optional)

1/4 cup diced Pickled Green Tomatoes (page 133; optional)

Fresh lemon juice

In a large pot of salted boiling water, blanch 1 cup of the sugar snaps until tender, about 3 minutes. Remove and shock in ice water. Then remove from the ice bath and reserve for pea sauce.

You want the sugar snaps for the salad to be crunchy, so blanch the remaining 4 cups peas just until crisp-tender, about 1 minute. Remove, shock in the ice water, and pat dry. Cut into pieces on the diagonal. Save the boiling water and ice bath for the lobsters; replenish the ice as needed.

Make the pea sauce. In a blender, combine the 1 cup tender sugar snaps, the broth, coconut milk, and 1/2 tablespoon extra-virgin olive oil and process until smooth and creamy. Pass the liquid through a fine-mesh strainer into a medium bowl. Thin with more broth if needed to create a light-bodied sauce. Season with a couple drops of lime juice, salt, and pepper, then refrigerate.

Remove the claws from the lobsters and put the claws and 3 bodies in the pot of boiling water. Cook the claws for 5 minutes and the tails for 4 minutes, then shock in the ice water. Drain and remove the meat from the shells. Cut the claws crosswise in half and cut the tails on the diagonal into 1/4-inch-thick slices.

In a large bowl, combine the lobster, sliced sugar snaps, pickled rhubarb, if using, and pickled green tomatoes, if using, and season with extra-virgin olive oil, lemon juice, salt, and pepper. Spoon the pea sauce into bowls and top with the lobster salad.

FOLLOWING PAGES: The downstairs prep room is the backbone of our kitchen; it's where all of our ingredients arrive directly from the Greenmarket. Our staff *(from left):* Iris Batista, Rose Weiss, Ramon Tavera, Luis Gomez, Modesto Batista, and Argentina Rosa.

WHAT MAKES A GREAT DISH

For me, three things make a great dish: First, it must be simple, undermanipulated but memorable. Second, the ingredients must be from *this* place and of *this* moment. Our message becomes more powerful with ingredients that come from around here. If I were dropped into the middle of Brazil, my dishes would have another taste and feeling altogether. The third quality is intrigue, a hook. It could be a surprising flavor combination; it could be the best incarnation of that ingredient, executed better than you've ever tasted (I'd nominate Hot-Smoked Trout, opposite). It could be discovering a new ingredient, like Japanese angelica sprouts. If you can do all that—convey a simple idea with a sense of place and a surprising twist—you've made a long-lasting food memory.

PICKLED CIPOLLINI ONIONS

MAKES ABOUT 1 PINT

Follow the Basic Pickling Recipe (page 86), substituting these ingredients. Remove the beet before transferring the onions to a container.

2½ cups thinly sliced cipollini onions, rings separated

¾ cup rice vinegar

¼ cup water

¼ cup sugar

1 tablespoon kosher salt

1 star anise

1 small beet, peeled and quartered

HOT-SMOKED TROUT WITH PICKLED CIPOLLINI ONIONS

SERVES 4

I first saw the technique of smoking in a small applewood chip–filled Weber grill set directly on a stovetop burner at March restaurant. There, Wayne Nish gave me the opportunity to become a sous chef in his tiny, jewel-like American kitchen. He also taught me to manage people with respect and to listen to my own voice. Wayne has always been an iconoclastic figure and this smoking technique is a good example of his intelligent, unorthodox approach. What is amazing about the method is that it allows us to smoke local trout one by one to order and serve the fish still warm, heightening its meltingly tender texture and lightly smoked flavor. Small stainless-steel stovetop smokers are now available, so you can actually smoke over wood chips indoors. Here I serve the smoked trout with an easy-to-make onion marmalade. At GT, this dish is a marker for us—it continues to inspire us to refine our ideas and keep them elegant and simple.

ONION MARMALADE

¼ cup red wine vinegar

¼ cup red wine

¼ cup port

½ onion, minced

1 teaspoon olive oil

Fresh lemon juice

Salt and pepper

Four 3-ounce skin-on trout fillets

Olive oil

Salt

¼ cup Onion Puree (page 215), warmed

20 rings Pickled Cipollini Onions (opposite)

Extra-virgin olive oil

Sea salt

1 tablespoon finely chopped chives

1 cup applewood chips

Make the marmalade. In a small saucepan, combine the vinegar, wine, port, onion, and ½ cup water. Add a few drops of cipollini onion pickling liquid for color. Bring to a simmer and cook until the onion is soft and the liquid has reduced to about ⅓ cup, about 10 minutes.

Remove from the heat, stir in the olive oil, and season with lemon juice, salt, and pepper. Set aside.

Prepare a stovetop smoker for smoking with the applewood chips; maintain a temperature of about 140°F.

Brush the trout fillets and the smoker grate with oil and season the trout with salt. When the wood chips are mostly gray, lay the fillets skin side up on the grate, cover, and smoke until just cooked through, about 5 minutes. You'll know the fish is ready when you can easily pull off the skin; discard the skin.

To serve, spread the onion puree and the marmalade on plates and top with the pickled onion rings. Lay the fillets on top, brush with a bit of extra-virgin olive oil, and sprinkle with sea salt and the chives.

HALIBUT AND RADISHES IN BEET DASHI

SERVES 4

This is a deceptively simple dish: one beautiful piece of olive oil–poached fish, slices of every kind of radish you can find, and an interesting twist on a Japanese broth. Dashi is the foundation of all Japanese soups and sauces. I wanted to take the respect I have for the technique of dashi and make it American by adding our seasonal touch: beets. In that way, a beet dashi truly belongs to us, instead of being fleetingly fusion. Just like our composed salads, this dish has its elemental ingredients and then the little flourishes we add for variety, like Swiss chard stems and Mexican gherkins.

---

4 cups plus 2 tablespoons olive oil, or more if needed

3 scallions (white and pale green parts), roughly chopped

One 1-inch piece of ginger, peeled and thinly sliced

2 star anise

¼ teaspoon fennel seeds

¼ teaspoon peppercorns

1 medium red beet, peeled and thinly sliced

1 cup thinly sliced red cabbage

Sugar

Salt

3 cups Dashi (page 82)

1 bay leaf

2 garlic cloves, smashed

4 sprigs thyme

1 tablespoon red wine vinegar

Pepper

Four 6-ounce halibut fillets

¼ pound slab bacon, diced

12 radishes of varied shapes and colors, quartered, plus 2 radishes, thinly sliced, for garnish

1 cup small Swiss chard leaves

Sea salt

In a medium saucepan, warm 2 tablespoons of the olive oil over medium heat. Add the scallions, ginger, 1 star anise, the fennel seeds, and peppercorns and cook, stirring often, for 2 minutes. Add the beet and cabbage and cook, stirring often, until softened, about 4 minutes. Add a pinch each of sugar and salt, stir in the dashi, and bring to a simmer. Gently simmer, covered, for an hour.

Remove the beet dashi from the heat and add the bay leaf, 1 garlic clove, 2 thyme sprigs, and the remaining star anise. Cover and let steep for 15 minutes.

Pass the beet dashi through a cheesecloth-lined strainer into a small saucepan. Stir in the vinegar and season with sugar, salt, and pepper. Keep hot over low heat.

Add the 4 cups olive oil, or enough to cover the fish by 1 inch, to a deep skillet just large enough to hold the fish. Gently infuse the olive oil with flavors of the remaining garlic clove and 2 thyme sprigs by heating them in the olive oil over medium heat until it reaches 140°F. Season the fish with salt and pepper and gently place in the oil. Poach until just cooked through, 12 to 15 minutes, maintaining the temperature of the oil.

Meanwhile, in a large skillet, cook the bacon until crisp. Pour off the fat.

While the bacon cooks, blanch the quartered radishes in a small saucepan of boiling salted water until just tender, about 3 minutes. Drain and add to the pan with the bacon. Fold in the Swiss chard and cook over medium heat until it just wilts. Season with salt if needed.

With a spatula, transfer the poached fish to a paper towel–lined plate and pat dry. Sprinkle with sea salt and then put each fillet in a shallow bowl. Spoon the radish mixture next to the fillets, pour in the beet dashi, and top with the sliced radishes.

DASHI

MAKES 3 CUPS

In a Japanese kitchen, every single day a pot of water is set on the stove and brought to a simmer. Then just two essential ingredients are added to make dashi: kombu, which is dried and aged seaweed, and katsuobushi, dried bonito flakes—the basic flavor combination fundamental to all Japanese cooking. Although there are so few ingredients, every kitchen has its own way of making dashi. A discreetly flavored broth, dashi is the basis for so many dishes, but it is not a soup in itself, so don't be surprised if you're underwhelmed at first taste. At Gramercy Tavern, our American cooking is inspired by the Japanese reverence for essential ingredients like kombu and katsuobushi. We appreciate how the source of every ingredient defines the way it tastes.

One 4-inch-square piece of dried kombu

1 cup loosely packed katsuobushi (dried bonito flakes)

A few drops of shiro dashi (optional)

In a small saucepan, bring the kombu and 4 cups water to a simmer and cook for 20 minutes. Remove from the heat and discard the kombu, then add the bonito flakes, stir, and let steep for 15 minutes.

Pass the broth through a fine-mesh strainer into a bowl. To intensify the flavor, add several drops of shiro dashi, if you like. Use dashi the day you make it.

LEARNING FROM A JAPANESE HOME KITCHEN

My time spent living in Japan was not exactly glamorous. I found a one-room apartment in a small town outside Tokyo. Way outside—an hour-and-a-half commute each way to the restaurant where I worked. Because I was so far from friends or family, I made friends, in a very funny way, with a middle-aged neighbor who dragged me along to the hilarious setting of her "culture club." I traded English lessons for Japanese lessons, cooking lessons, and excursions with their straw-hat hiking club. Cooking with this bunch of ladies, I learned to make Japanese home dishes, including all kinds of pickles, the essential dashi, miso-based soups, salted and grilled whole fish, light-as-air vegetable tempura, simmered root vegetables (carrots, potatoes, daikon), sukiyaki-style braised meats, and crispy breaded pork cutlets. Japanese people eat an amazing variety of carefully prepared foods every day, but that kind of home cooking hardly ever finds its way to Japanese restaurants in the United States. Both the wide variety of their everyday diet and the delicate, skillful touch those housewives give each ingredient have influenced the way I create dishes.

A few of the ingredients from those ladies' home kitchens have found their way into my cooking. In a restaurant kitchen in New York City, we can get whatever we want whenever we want it from anywhere in the world. At Gramercy Tavern, we choose to think about food in the context of the Northeast; the spirit of our food is focused on where we cook and live. But it's not a religion. We have favorite ingredients from all over the world that make our dishes special. I do not expect you to go out and hunt down every specialty ingredient in order to reproduce recipes in this book. If you stick to the basic ingredients of each recipe, you'll be closer to the idea of a Gramercy dish than if you substituted something else. This is really important to me: I don't want you not to make a dish because you can't find a specific condiment or herb or spice. That said, there are some distinct Japanese flavors and ingredients that I really love.

Shiro dashi is a smoky, salty, wheat-brewed bottled condiment that I use to season fish, sauces, and soups.

White miso is fermented Japanese soybean paste that I love for its earthiness in dressings.

Kombu is dried aged Japanese seaweed, used to make the elemental Japanese broth, dashi.

Bonito flakes, readily available in bags, are shaved dried fish, also used for dashi.

Panko is a crunchy Japanese bread crumb. I use it to make Fried Oysters (page 65) and Baked Clams (page 271), and in other dishes.

PRESERVING THE SEASON

Simple pickling *(following pages)* allows us to extend our use of fresh ingredients. **CLOCKWISE FROM TOP LEFT:** Swiss chard stems, smoked jalapeños, fennel, chipotle peppers, golden beets, red beets, hon-shimeji mushrooms, cauliflower, carrots, and ramps.

BASIC PICKLING RECIPE:
PICKLED SHALLOTS

MAKES ABOUT 1 PINT

Here's our basic method for quick refrigerator pickles. This pickled shallot recipe illustrates how easy it is. Sure, each ingredient benefits from its own personalized seasonings (carrots take well to ginger and fennel seeds, turnips to saffron and coriander, Swiss chard stems to beet, for a little color), but learning this ratio is a good place to start: 3 parts rice vinegar, 1 part water, 1 part sugar, and a pinch of salt. The technique is always the same: boil the brine and pour it over the ingredient to be pickled. When this process becomes familiar to you, it's easy to combine many different spices and herbs to develop different flavors. Check the Index for more pickle recipes and ideas throughout the book.

Most pickles are ready in 6 hours or less. Packed into a jar and kept in the refrigerator, they will stay bright and crunchy for up to a month.

2 cups shallot petals (halve trimmed shallots lengthwise and pull apart the layers)

3/4 cup rice vinegar

1/4 cup water

1/4 cup sugar

1 tablespoon kosher salt

Put the shallots in a medium bowl.

In a small saucepan, combine the vinegar, water, the sugar, and salt. Bring to a boil over high heat, stirring until the sugar and salt are dissolved. Pour the pickling liquid over the shallots and cover with a plate to keep them submerged. Let cool to room temperature.

Cover the bowl with plastic wrap and refrigerate for at least 6 hours, or overnight. Transfer the pickles and liquid to a container, cover, and refrigerate.

PICKLED RHUBARB

MAKES ABOUT 1 PINT

Follow the Basic Pickling Recipe (opposite), substituting these ingredients.

2 cups sliced rhubarb (2-inch pieces)

¾ cup rice vinegar

¼ cup water

¼ cup sugar

1 tablespoon kosher salt

½ tablespoon peeled and minced ginger

PICKLE EXPLORATION

I've been fascinated with pickles since I lived and cooked in Japan. There, pickles are an exciting and crucial element of so many meals. At Gramercy, they work their way into the composition of numerous dishes, too. Pickling is a traditional and natural method of preservation that captures the season and lengthens the life of ingredients that are available for only a short time. But the way we use pickles at Gramercy Tavern is hardly old-fashioned: we use them to add important and unexpected hits of acidity to our dishes while enhancing their brightness.

Living in the Northeast, we don't get red, ripe tomatoes until well after the Fourth of July, but green tomatoes arrive earlier and have a much longer season—they just need some help. We pickle green tomatoes (see page 133) not simply to preserve them, but also to show off another way to appreciate them. Yet pickling does allow us to deal with ingredients as they come into season. Ramps have a tiny window of availability; we'll buy as many as Modesto can bring back from the market and pickle them as fast as we can clean them. Cucumbers, baby turnips, cherries, and ají dulce peppers all fall into this category. Buy them, pickle them, keep them. I'm talking about quick refrigerator pickles. No special equipment necessary.

Pickling allows us to be thrifty, to use parts of plants that are often discarded. Take Swiss chard stems. How many of those have you thrown away? But pickled (see page 188), they add wonderful color, crunch, and acidity to a dish. In fact, Swiss chard stems occupy the place in our kitchen that preserved truffles take in a classic French restaurant kitchen—where it's an honor to stay late to preserve the truffles. We feel the same way about pickling ginger, mushrooms, rhubarb, jalapeños, watermelon rind, onions, shallots, sunchokes, daikon, carrots, and cauliflower. We're interested, too, in fermentation, and we make kimchi-style cabbage, red cabbage sauerkraut, and even *nukazuke*, rice-bran fermented vegetables.

Pickling is such a significant part of our kitchen—and our imaginations—that we have an entire station dedicated to studying and producing pickles: pickle exploration. Cooks rotate through that station as part of becoming a chef. One of our former cooks, Michaela Hayes, inspired the pickle station; she was so enamored with the pickling and fermenting in our kitchen that she went on to create her own company, Crock and Jar.

A word about pickles in our recipes: At the restaurant we have a larder full of the wonderful pickles we make all year long. So when I specify a pickle or two in a recipe, it's great if you have them on hand. But if you don't have them or the time to make them, don't skip the recipe. Substitute a different one or buy some great pickles from your farmers' market or from an artisanal producer.

CHICKEN LIVER MOUSSE

MAKES ABOUT 2 CUPS

On my first day of cooking school in Paris, we learned how to eviscerate a chicken, extricating the liver and gizzards. I called my mother and told her that the essence of cooking is learning to be a five-year-old again—playing with your food. What I really meant was the joy of discovery. She reminded me that good cooking is also about thrift—using every delicious morsel. Chicken liver mousse satisfies those two essential elements: discovery and economy.

MOUSSE

2 tablespoons olive oil

1½ cups chicken livers, trimmed and patted dry

Salt and pepper

1 cup thinly sliced shallots

1 tablespoon minced garlic

1 sprig thyme

1 bay leaf

Large pinch of ground cloves

Large pinch of ground nutmeg

Small pinch of ground cinnamon

½ cup Cognac

2 tablespoons white wine

6 tablespoons (¾ stick) unsalted butter, melted

¼ cup heavy cream

Red wine vinegar

1 tablespoon minced chives

Coarsely cracked black pepper

Grilled bread or crackers

Make the mousse. In a large skillet, heat 1 tablespoon of the oil over medium-high heat. Season the livers with salt and pepper, then add to the skillet and cook, turning once, until browned but still a bit pink inside, about 3 minutes. Transfer to a plate.

Add the remaining 1 tablespoon oil to the skillet, reduce the heat to medium, and add the shallots, garlic, thyme, and bay leaf. Cook, stirring often, until the shallots are softened, about 4 minutes. Add ¼ teaspoon pepper, the cloves, nutmeg, and cinnamon and stir for a few seconds. Pour in the Cognac and white wine, scrape the bottom of the skillet, and simmer to reduce the liquid by half.

Discard the thyme and bay leaf and transfer the mixture to a blender. Add the reserved livers and any juices, the butter, and cream and process until smooth. Pass the mousse through a fine-mesh strainer, then assertively season with salt and vinegar.

Transfer the mousse to a 2-cup serving dish (or two 1-cup dishes), loosely cover with plastic wrap, and refrigerate until cold. The mousse will keep, covered with plastic wrap pressed over the surface, in the refrigerator for up to 5 days.

Sprinkle the mousse with the chives and cracked black pepper and serve with grilled bread.

ABOUT SOUS VIDE

As soulful and natural as Gramercy Tavern feels, the kitchen team strives to stay ahead of the curve when it comes to understanding and using modern technology. Bruno Goussault is one of the world's leaders in teaching sous vide cooking, and I met him in the early '90s, when I was at cooking school in Paris. His research lab began there as a facility for the government; he then turned it into a culinary research center, working with the chef Joël Robuchon. I attended his seminars at school, and over the years, I've had many exchanges with Bruno, both in his lab and at the restaurants where I've worked in New York. From early on, I understood the value of integrating sous vide (which literally means "under vacuum") cooking into my kitchens.

The technique of cooking foods sous vide allows us to treat exceptional ingredients with great care and to highlight their inherent flavors. We do this by sealing food in an airtight bag and cooking it in a water bath for a long time at precise low temperatures. This process ensures tenderness, preserves moisture, and keeps all the flavor intact. The sous vide process has endless uses in the kitchen, but here's an easy way to understand it: Traditionally, a pork roast is seared over high heat and roasted in the dry heat of a hot oven, then, ideally, rested for an equal amount of time before it is served. The sous vide process lets us cook that roast at a very low temperature, so the meat stays supple, moist, and flavorful. When conventionally roasted, the pork is blasted with high heat, which ultimately causes the proteins in the meat to tense up, toughen, and lose moisture (which equals flavor). The window of opportunity for getting that roast cooked just right is very small. Cooking meat sous vide drastically improves our chances of getting it perfect every time.

It may seem counterintuitive, but at GT, sometimes technology allows us to cook with more care and to enhance the rustic nature of our cooking. A good example is our Four Story Hill Farm milk-fed poularde. Since I consider this bird one of the best available in the country, it's important to preserve its flavor nuances. We use sous vide to do most of the cooking—and then finish it over the open wood-burning fire. This produces the most delicious char on the outside, reminiscent of a campfire or the food at a state fair, but the meat remains more moist than you could ever imagine. At Gramercy Tavern, sous vide is not a novelty—it is just one of the many techniques we use in our modern kitchen.

CHICKEN WITH SUGAR SNAP PEAS, PICKLED RAMPS, AND ALMOND MILK

SERVES 4

At the restaurant, we treat our guests to the complex flavor and dense texture of chickens raised by Sylvia and Steve Pryzant at Four Story Hill Farm in Pennsylvania. Their expertise and careful handling makes this chicken dish one of the most interesting things on our menu. I hope that you will search out someone near you who raises birds on a small scale, because that extraordinary flavor will make all the difference. We top it with our own nutty almond milk, which is far lighter than a cream-based sauce, and a scattering of microgreens.

1 cup nonfat milk

½ cup blanched slivered almonds, toasted

1 thin slice peeled ginger, plus ½ teaspoon peeled and minced ginger

1 tablespoon almond oil (optional)

4 cups sugar snap peas, trimmed

Salt and pepper

Four 6-ounce skin-on boneless chicken breast halves

¼ cup olive oil

½ cup roughly chopped raw almonds

½ cup sliced scallions (white parts)

½ teaspoon minced garlic

2 tablespoons thinly sliced Pickled Ramps (opposite)

2 tablespoons chopped tarragon

2 tablespoons unsalted butter

Fresh lime juice

Preheat the oven to 350°F.

Make the almond sauce. In a small saucepan, heat the milk over low heat, without allowing it to boil. Add the slivered almonds, ginger slice, and almond oil, if using, and let steep, stirring occasionally, for about 45 minutes, keeping the milk at just below a simmer.

Meanwhile, in a large pot of boiling salted water, blanch the sugar snaps for 30 seconds. Drain and shock in ice water. Drain again, pat dry, and slice on the diagonal into ¼-inch pieces.

Pass the almond milk through a fine-mesh strainer and return to the saucepan. Season with salt and pepper and keep warm.

Season the chicken with salt and pepper. In a large ovenproof skillet, heat 2 tablespoons of the oil over medium-high heat. Add the chicken skin side down and cook until the skin is golden brown, about 5 minutes. Flip the chicken,

immediately put the skillet in the oven, and bake until just cooked through, about 10 minutes. Transfer the chicken to a cutting board and let rest for about 5 minutes.

Meanwhile, finish the sugar snaps. In a large skillet, heat the remaining 2 tablespoons oil over medium heat. Add the chopped almonds and cook, stirring occasionally, for about a minute. Add the scallions, minced ginger, and garlic and cook, stirring occasionally, for about a minute. Add the blanched sugar snaps, pickled ramps, tarragon, and butter, then season with a healthy squeeze of lime juice and salt and pepper and heat for 2 minutes.

Mound some sugar snaps in the center of each plate. Slice the chicken breasts and set on top. Finish each with a few spoonfuls of almond milk (if you have a hand blender, here's a chance to froth the almond milk).

PICKLED RAMPS

MAKES ABOUT 1 QUART

Ramps are wild leeks and are one of the most celebrated foraged foods in the Northeast. For many of us they're the first sign of spring. Since they've become so popular, we buy only small batches and cook the whole plant: sautéing or grilling the greens to eat immediately and pickling the white bulbs to use throughout the year.

Follow the Basic Pickling Recipe (page 86), substituting these ingredients. Note that since ramp season is so fleeting, this recipe makes a quart, not a pint like the others.

5 cups ramp bulbs with white stems

1½ cups rice vinegar

½ cup water

½ cup sugar

1½ tablespoons kosher salt

¼ teaspoon coriander seeds

¼ teaspoon fennel seeds

¼ teaspoon mustard seeds

¼ teaspoon black peppercorns

DUO OF BRAISED AND ROASTED BEEF

SERVES 4

We buy trustworthy beef from people we know. We've set up the restaurant so we can purchase entire sides of beef from small farms. I've taught our full-time butcher the skills to break them down into cuts for multiple dishes. Try to find a butcher near you knowledgeable enough to answer your questions and deliver the cut you want. There are many ways today to find good beef: the Internet, farmers' markets, and specialty stores. Spend your money on smaller quantities of better-quality meat. In this recipe, we pair just a few slices of great sirloin with cubes of unctuous braised flatiron steak and lots of vegetables. This dish is decadent as a duo (and a necessity at GT, since we want to use every bit of the whole animal), but you can certainly make it happen with one or the other of these beef preparations: just the sirloin or just the braised beef.

One 1-pound sirloin steak, about 1½ inches thick

4 cups liquid from Braised Beef (page 97; if there's not enough liquid to make 4 cups, add Beef Broth, page 96, or water)

¾ pound Braised Beef (page 97)

Salt and pepper

2 fennel bulbs, trimmed and cut into 8 wedges each, fronds reserved for garnish

1 teaspoon cumin seeds

1 star anise

1½ cups orange juice

1 tablespoon olive oil

4 tablespoons (½ stick) unsalted butter

1 garlic clove, smashed

2 sprigs thyme

1 sprig rosemary

2 cups sugar snap peas, trimmed

½ cup black olives, halved and pitted

About 30 minutes before cooking it, remove the sirloin from the refrigerator.

In a wide saucepan, bring the braised beef liquid to a brisk simmer and reduce it until it's thick enough to coat a piece of the meat, about 1 cup. Add the braised beef to the sauce, add salt and pepper, cover, and keep warm over very low heat.

Meanwhile, arrange the fennel wedges in one layer in a wide saucepan and season with salt and pepper. Add the cumin, star anise, orange juice, and about 1½ cups water, enough to barely cover the fennel. Bring the liquid to a boil, then reduce the heat and simmer, covered, until the fennel is tender, about 20 minutes; add water if the pan gets dry. Transfer the fennel to a plate. Boil down the liquid until it is reduced to a glaze.

While the liquid reduces, season the sirloin with salt and pepper. In a small skillet, heat the oil over high heat until hot but not smoking. Add the sirloin and brown on both sides, about 3 minutes per side. Add 2 tablespoons of the butter, the garlic, thyme, and rosemary, reduce the heat to medium, and cook, basting the meat, just until medium-rare, about 2 minutes more. Transfer the steak to a cutting board and let rest for about 5 minutes.

Meanwhile, blanch the sugar snaps in a large pot of boiling salted water for 20 seconds. Drain and transfer to the saucepan with the orange glaze. Add the fennel and olives and stir in the remaining 2 tablespoons butter; keep warm over low heat.

Cut the steak against the grain into generous slices. Serve it with the braised beef chunks and fennel mixture, spooning some of the sauce over the top, and garnish with a few fennel fronds.

BEEF BROTH

MAKES ABOUT 3 QUARTS

It takes a surprising amount of beef to generate truly tasty broth. As noted in other recipes, you can always substitute water in recipes that call for beef broth, but this rich broth can be made ahead and frozen, then used to enrich so many dishes. I like to use some oxtail (which is, again, about making good use of every part of the cow), because it adds more flavor and a bit of gelatin to the broth.

Olive oil

4 pounds boneless beef chuck, cut into 2-inch pieces

1 pound oxtails (optional), cut into 2-inch pieces

2 onions, roughly chopped

2 carrots, roughly chopped

1 celery stalk, roughly chopped

1 leek (white and pale green parts), roughly chopped

¼ cup tomato paste

6 flat-leaf parsley stems

3 sprigs thyme

1 bay leaf

In a large pot, heat 2 tablespoons olive oil over medium-high heat. Add the beef and oxtails, if using, in batches (using more oil as needed) and brown well on all sides, about 10 minutes per batch. Transfer the beef to a platter. Reduce the heat to medium, add a little more oil if needed, and then add the onions, carrots, celery, and leek. Cook the vegetables, stirring occasionally, for about 12 minutes; a little browning is good.

Add the tomato paste and cook, stirring, for about a minute. Add the browned beef and juices, the parsley, thyme, bay leaf, and 4 quarts water. Bring to a boil, then reduce the heat and gently simmer, skimming any foam once or twice, for about 2½ hours.

Pass the broth through a fine-mesh strainer into a container, then skim the fat. Or, if you're not using the broth right away, let it cool, then cover and refrigerate. The fat can easily be removed from the top of the chilled broth after it hardens. The broth will keep, covered, in the refrigerator for up to 5 days; it can be frozen for up to 3 months.

BRAISED BEEF

SERVES 4; MAKES ABOUT 1½ POUNDS

If the basic task of a cook is to make something delicious from very little, then this dish is the perfect example. In braising, you're creating succulent meat and a versatile and valuable sauce that will make *anything* taste good. So while you do have to invest some time, you're taking part in a little bit of cooking magic, where deep flavor is slowly coaxed from a few basic ingredients. In the restaurant, we braise beef in beef broth to intensify the flavor of the sauce, but at home, I use water for a lighter, more aromatic finish. As a practical note, braised beef can and should be made in advance, to make your life easier the day you're serving it. To keep it moist, refrigerate the meat in the strained liquid (or freeze it), and complete the recipe later. Braised beef appears in this book in Open Ravioli (page 213), as well as the Duo of Beef (page 95), but you can serve it over pasta or whole grains, too.

One 2-pound piece flatiron steak or 2 pounds boneless beef chuck, cut into chunks

Salt and pepper

Olive oil

2 onions, chopped

1 carrot, chopped

1 celery stalk, chopped

1 garlic clove, minced

1 tablespoon tomato paste

1 cup red wine

5 cups Beef Broth (opposite) or water

Preheat the oven to 325°F.

Season the beef with salt and pepper. Heat 1 tablespoon of oil in a heavy ovenproof pot, one that is just large enough to hold the beef snugly and has a tight-fitting lid, over medium-high heat. Add the beef in batches and brown well on all sides, about 10 minutes per batch. Transfer to a platter.

Reduce the heat to medium, add the onions, carrot, celery, and garlic, and cook, stirring occasionally, until softened, about 10 minutes. Add the tomato paste and cook, stirring, for a minute. Add the red wine and stir, scraping the bottom of the pot to loosen the browned bits, then simmer to reduce the wine until it is almost gone.

Return the beef to the pot, along with any accumulated juices, and add the broth. Bring the liquid to a boil, cover the pot, and transfer to the oven. Cook until the beef is very tender, about 2 hours. Transfer the beef to a plate.

Pass the liquid through a fine-mesh strainer into a large saucepan, pushing down on the solids to extract every bit of delicious juice. Simmer the sauce to the consistency you like. Season with salt and pepper. Add the cooked beef and coat with the sauce.

RHUBARB STREUSEL TART
(PAGE 102)

PEACH PIE WITH PECAN CRUMBLE
(PAGE 168)

FRESH STRAWBERRY PIE
(PAGE 106)

NANCY OLSON

PASTRY CHEF • FROM 2006 TO 2013

I am lucky. I grew up in Napoleon, North Dakota, population 1,000. My mom and grandma were great bakers, so I already had a sense of what I liked to eat. My first New York City job was in a high-end restaurant with a lot of frou-frou things on the menu that didn't appeal to my frugal Midwestern practicality. I wanted to give guests something from my heart. If I made apple pie, I didn't want it to be some deconstructed version. It was never about my ego as a chef to do something crazy. I've always been happiest making things that take you back home, that make you feel loved, as if you were sitting at the kitchen counter watching your mom bake. Even if you never were that kid, you can still relate. At Gramercy, my style is to take homey, comforting flavors—desserts you recognize!— and make them as excellent as I can. I always tell my team that if we have the courage to put apple pie on the menu, it should be one of the best apple pies that anyone's ever eaten. I like to be very detail-oriented about the things we make, so that when people eat it, they think, "Wow! That's a seriously good apple pie." It makes them remember us.

To have graduated from the Culinary Institute of America in March 2001 and then become the pastry chef of Gramercy Tavern by August 2006—that's kind of crazy. After my freshman year of college, I was a nanny for a summer. The family wanted to have a Fourth of July party at their lake cabin and pulled out an issue of *Bon Appétit* (July 1991), with a big spread on a Texas-style barbecue. I'd never seen a food magazine before. It opened things up for me. I hung on to that magazine and cooked out of it. Leafing through the pages, I found listings of cooking schools, which stuck in the back of my mind. I began watching food shows on television: Emeril's *How to Boil Water*, Sara Moulton, *Two Hot Tamales*. *Frugal Gourmet* was probably my favorite.

I had great training at the Fargo Country Club in North Dakota. It was a ten-hour-a-week job that turned into a line cook position, that turned into five years in that kitchen. Many people say that Gramercy Tavern is the best place they've ever worked, and I can say I'm so fortunate I have two of those places. I landed in a kitchen where they taught me everything I wanted to learn; they were nurturing, but they also left me to figure it out on my own.

In Fargo, I started cooking out of Maida Heatter's books on Monday nights, when it was very slow at the country club. The line cooks would hang out and play cards and I'd pull out a Maida book. I love her writing style. I made some awful messes! But I did get into pastry and I pushed the club's pastry program. The chef I worked for has been there for some forty years (he is still there). He'd gone to CIA when it was still on the Yale campus. I adore him and thought everything he did was so great; I decided I would go to CIA, too—in the pastry track. But I was a small-town girl and I was afraid of New York, worried that I'd have less experience and knowledge than my classmates. When I arrived, I realized that I was twenty-seven and the rest of my classmates were seventeen-year-olds just out of high school. So I needn't have worried. The experience was so valuable and taught me confidence.

After my first New York City job, I worked at a number of other restaurants: Django, Union Pacific, BLT Fish, Peacock Alley. I was pastry chef at Dona when I got a call about the Gramercy job. I later discovered that Kevin Mahan had sent Scott Reinhardt and Paul Walsh in on a secret mission to taste my desserts. Kevin had called Laurent Tourondel and had already conducted a background check on me. I started at Gramercy about a week before the news: Mike Anthony was taking over as executive chef. We had never worked together and we had to map out a vision for GT together.

Mike is very nurturing to everyone. He has taught me how to settle down. My unwavering pursuit of excellence has sometimes turned me into a very demanding, crabby person, but Mike's style has rubbed off on me over the years. We've developed a sense of trust, whether we express it to each other or not. One of the key things that Danny asks of his team is to have self-awareness. I think Mike and I both have that. We are both constantly looking for what we can learn about ourselves and from each other. I may be stubborn, but my desserts are always evolving. My style is homey and literal, and Mike is a visionary. He really is. He'll slowly slip in a suggestion or two, and I'll balk at first. New ideas are hard for me. That's one of the things that Mike and I work on. He gives me little ideas, then lets them take root. "Nancy Olson," he'll say, "I think this dessert should be a bit smaller." Then he'll leave and I'll think about it for a long time, and then one day, I tell myself, "This dessert should be smaller."

Building a team is not easy. Claudia Fleming, GT's original pastry chef, is one of my heroes. The organization she set up at Gramercy before I arrived was a great starting point. I've gotten better at building a team over the years. It was difficult at first to step out of the role of cook and into the role of leader. It was a challenge to let go of the idea that I could do anything better than any of my cooks, or that I could do all the work by myself. At Gramercy Tavern, we turn out four hundred desserts a day. We are a team of twelve, and it takes every single one of us giving every single thing we have to make that happen. Since I began, I've learned to let go and to trust people. That's helped my team. People work so much better when they know you trust them and

they can take pride in what they do. In my kitchen now, there are people who are way better cooks than I am. I hire trustworthy people and then train them really well.

I've learned better interviewing skills. I tell everyone that if we're going to spend twelve hours a day together, we should like each other. Our ultimate goal is to make desserts that make people happy, but we can't do that if we can't make each other happy. Everyone new starts in the same position and moves through each station, so that he or she is trained by everyone else who has been there. It's a circular thing, and it makes the cooks better teachers, too. I do not have to be in the kitchen for every single step of the way. I get to see my cooks grow along with their confidence. Our pastry team is nurturing. In restaurants, pastry winds up nurturing everyone. If someone is having a bad day, it's usually something a chocolate chip cookie can fix.

RHUBARB STREUSEL TART WITH STRAWBERRY ICE CREAM

MAKES ONE 9-INCH TART

Nancy loves working with rhubarb because it reminds her of her childhood, the rhubarb plants in her Grandma Zerr's garden, and her rhubarb jam. This tart is made of several distinct components—the shell, the pastry cream, the rhubarb jam, and the streusel topping. Each one can be made in advance and then the tart can be assembled right before serving. (The jam is so delicious on its own, you can make it as soon as the first stalks of rhubarb hit the market.) Nancy serves the tart with Strawberry Ice Cream made with first-of-the-season berries.

Pastry Dough (opposite)

All-purpose flour for rolling

PASTRY CREAM

1½ cups whole milk

⅓ cup sugar

1 tablespoon cornstarch

1 large egg

3 large egg yolks

1 tablespoon unsalted butter, at room temperature

STREUSEL TOPPING

1 cup all-purpose flour

⅓ cup sugar

4 tablespoons (½ stick) unsalted butter, cubed and chilled

¼ teaspoon ground cinnamon

Pinch of salt

1⅓ cups Rhubarb Jam (page 105)

Strawberry Ice Cream (page 105)

Preheat the oven to 375°F, with a rack in the middle position.

On a lightly floured surface, roll out the dough, then fit it into a 9-inch tart pan with a removable bottom. Trim excess dough and crimp the edges. Line with parchment paper and fill with pie weights.

Bake the shell for 20 minutes. Remove the paper and weights and continue to bake until evenly golden brown and cooked all the way through, 10 to 15 minutes more. Let cool. Lower temperature to 350°F.

Meanwhile, make the pastry cream. In a small saucepan, bring 1 cup of the milk to a boil over medium heat. In a medium bowl, whisk together the sugar and cornstarch, then whisk in the remaining ½ cup milk. Whisk in the egg and yolks.

When the milk comes to a boil, slowly whisk it into the egg mixture in a steady stream to temper it, then pour the contents of the bowl back into the saucepan. Cook the mixture over medium heat, whisking constantly and getting into the edges to keep it from sticking or burning, until it thickens and the first bubbles form. Immediately remove from the heat and whisk in the butter. Cover the surface with plastic wrap and refrigerate until cool, for about an hour, or overnight.

Make the streusel topping. In the bowl of a stand mixer fitted with the paddle attachment, combine the flour, sugar, butter, cinnamon, and salt and mix on medium-low speed until small crumbs form. Spread the topping in a baking pan and bake, scraping up the mixture and spreading it out again a couple of times, until golden, about 15 minutes. Let cool. Leave the oven on.

Spread the cooled pastry cream in the tart shell (if it's difficult to spread, let it warm up a bit). Bake until the top is set, about 15 minutes. Let cool.

Spread the rhubarb jam over the cooled tart and then cover with the streusel topping, breaking up any large pieces with your fingers. Serve the tart at room temperature or chilled. The tart is best the day it is made.

PASTRY DOUGH

MAKES ENOUGH FOR ONE 9-INCH
TART OR SINGLE-CRUST PIE

This is a reliable recipe for a classic
pastry dough. We also use it for the
Lemon Meringue Pie (page 321).

1¼ cups all-purpose flour

¼ cup sugar

8 tablespoons (1 stick) unsalted
butter, cubed and very cold

1 large egg yolk

In the bowl of a stand mixer fitted
with the paddle attachment,
combine the flour and sugar. Add
the butter and mix on medium-low
speed until the mixture looks like
sand. Add the yolk and mix just until
a dough forms. Some dry patches
and crumbs are okay; they will
moisten as the dough rests.

Form the dough into a ball,
flatten, and wrap well in plastic
wrap. Refrigerate for at least
2 hours, or overnight. The dough can
be frozen for up to a month; thaw it
overnight in the refrigerator.

STRAWBERRY ICE CREAM

MAKES ABOUT 1½ QUARTS

Every summer, Nancy tries to make an even-better version of strawberry ice cream. She likes her fruit ice creams to taste like frozen fruit with a little cream, as opposed to the reverse. She uses cornstarch instead of eggs to thicken the ice cream base, because egg yolks can mask the fruit's flavor. This basic recipe can be used to make almost any fruit ice cream. Nancy makes the most wonderful ice creams by simply pureeing fresh fruit like strawberries, as here, Concord grapes, or raspberries and adding the puree to the base. With fruits such as rhubarb, blueberries, peaches, and plums, cooking helps intensify their flavor and release their natural pectins.

1¼ cups heavy cream

¾ cup whole milk

1 cup plus 2 tablespoons sugar

¼ cup cornstarch

3 cups pureed strawberries (about 2 pounds whole berries), chilled

In a medium saucepan, combine the cream, ¼ cup of the milk, and 1 cup of the sugar and bring to a boil over medium heat, stirring until the sugar dissolves. Meanwhile, in

a medium bowl, whisk together the remaining 2 tablespoons sugar and the cornstarch, then whisk in the remaining ½ cup milk.

When the cream mixture comes to a boil, remove it from the heat and slowly whisk about a cup of the hot liquid into the cornstarch mixture in a steady stream. Pour the contents of the bowl back into the saucepan and bring to a boil, whisking constantly. Be sure to get into the edges of the pan to keep the mixture from sticking or burning. Boil for a full minute, whisking constantly, then pass through a fine-mesh strainer into a large bowl. Let cool.

Cover the ice cream base and refrigerate until thoroughly chilled, or preferably overnight, for the creamiest results.

Add the strawberry puree to the chilled ice cream base and whisk until smooth. Pour into an ice cream maker and freeze according to the manufacturer's directions. Transfer the ice cream to a freezer container, cover, and freeze until firm enough to scoop.

RHUBARB JAM

MAKES ABOUT 2 CUPS

Spread this delicious jam on toasted, buttered brioche. It's also wonderful over Sweet Cream Ice Cream (page 173).

3 cups finely diced rhubarb

1½ cups sugar

In a medium saucepan, combine 1½ cups of the rhubarb and the sugar, bring to a boil over medium heat, stirring constantly, and boil, stirring until the consistency of jam, about 5 minutes. Stir in ¾ cup of the remaining rhubarb and boil, stirring constantly, until just tender, about 2 minutes. Repeat with the remaining ¾ cup rhubarb. Transfer the jam to a medium bowl and let cool. The jam will keep, covered, in the refrigerator for at least a week.

FRESH STRAWBERRY PIE

MAKES ONE 9-INCH PIE OR SIX 4½-INCH INDIVIDUAL PIES

When Nancy was growing up in North Dakota, her family had a large strawberry patch in the backyard that was so bountiful they always had more berries than they knew what to do with. One of the desserts she learned to make was a pie very similar to this one, with gorgeous lightly glazed strawberries in a crumbly graham cracker crust. Using the most flavorful berries makes all the difference in this simple no-bake dessert.

¾ cup plus 1 tablespoon sugar

¼ cup cornstarch

⅛ teaspoon salt

3 cups hulled and quartered strawberries, plus 4½ cups (cut very large berries into eighths and leave very small ones whole; about 3 pounds whole berries total)

1⅛ cups finely ground graham crackers (about 9 crackers)

8 tablespoons (1 stick) unsalted butter, melted

½ cup heavy cream, lightly whipped

In a medium saucepan, whisk together ¾ cup of the sugar, the cornstarch, and salt, then whisk in ⅓ cup cold water. Add 3 cups of the strawberries and roughly mash the fruit with the end of the whisk. (Depending on the firmness of the berries, it may be easier to use an old-fashioned potato masher or a large fork.) Bring the mixture to a boil over medium heat, whisking constantly and further mashing the strawberries until they are broken down (some lumps of berries are okay). Boil for a full minute, whisking constantly. Transfer the strawberry mixture to a large bowl and let cool to room temperature.

Meanwhile, make the crust. In a large bowl, stir together the graham crackers, the remaining 1 tablespoon sugar, and the melted butter until the crumbs are evenly moistened. Very lightly press the crumbs into your mold(s), starting with the sides and then covering the bottom.

When the strawberry mixture is at room temperature, gently stir in the remaining 4½ cups strawberries, then spoon the filling into the graham cracker crust(s). Refrigerate for at least 2 hours, or up to 2 days. Serve with the whipped cream.

FRESH MINT ICE CREAM WITH HOT FUDGE

SERVES 8

If you make this ice cream with just-picked mint, like peppermint, you'll be rewarded with intensely minty ice cream. Serve topped with Hot Fudge. The yield for the ice cream is about 1½ quarts.

Follow the recipe for Sweet Cream Ice Cream (page 173), adding 1 cup tightly packed mint leaves, torn, to the saucepan with the milk, cream, and sugar. As soon as the mixture comes to a boil, remove from the heat and let infuse for 10 minutes. Strain out the mint leaves, pushing down on the leaves with a spoon to extract as much liquid and flavor as possible; proceed with the rest of the recipe. Serve topped with Hot Fudge.

HOT FUDGE

MAKES ABOUT 1¾ CUPS

I love the very experience of making people around me smile with something as simple as hot fudge or Caramel Sauce (page 267).

2 ounces unsweetened chocolate, finely chopped

2 tablespoons unsalted butter

1 tablespoon light corn syrup

³⁄₄ cup heavy cream

1 cup lightly packed dark brown sugar

½ teaspoon vanilla extract

⅛ teaspoon salt

In a small heavy-bottomed saucepan, melt the chocolate with the butter and corn syrup over low heat. Add the cream and brown sugar, increase the heat to medium, and bring the mixture to a full boil, stirring gently but constantly with a spatula to keep the mixture from burning.

Remove from the heat and stir in the vanilla and salt. If you're not using the sauce immediately, transfer to a container and let cool completely, then cover and refrigerate for up to a week. You can reheat the hot fudge over low heat. If the consistency is too thin, boil it for a few minutes; if it's too thick, stir in a little hot water.

CHOCOLATE PUDDING

SERVES 6 TO 8

Desserts at Gramercy evoke nostalgia and deliver a complex experience. You can make this creamy chocolate pudding more intriguing by serving it with the slightly bitter salted caramel sauce, deeply caramelized croutons, and a pinch of sea salt.

4 cups whole milk

1 cup sugar

¼ cup cornstarch

3 tablespoons unsweetened cocoa powder

¼ teaspoon salt

4 large egg yolks

6 ounces bittersweet chocolate, finely chopped

1 tablespoon unsalted butter

2 teaspoons vanilla extract

Salted Caramel Sauce (page 112)

¾ cup heavy cream, lightly whipped

Brioche Croutons (page 112)

Sea salt

In a medium saucepan, bring 3½ cups of the milk and ¾ cup of the sugar to a boil over medium heat, stirring until the sugar dissolves. Meanwhile, in a medium bowl, whisk together the remaining ¼ cup sugar, the cornstarch, cocoa, and salt.

Whisk in the remaining ½ cup milk, then whisk in the yolks.

When the milk mixture comes to a boil, remove it from the heat and slowly pour about a cup of the hot liquid into the egg mixture, whisking constantly to temper it. Pour the contents of the bowl back into the saucepan and bring to a boil over medium heat, whisking constantly; be sure to get into the edges of the pan to keep the mixture from sticking or burning. Boil for a full minute, whisking constantly, then pass the mixture through a fine-mesh strainer into a large bowl.

Whisk in the chocolate, butter, and vanilla until smooth. Transfer the pudding to a large bowl, cover the surface with plastic wrap placed in direct contact with the pudding, and refrigerate until cold. Serve the pudding topped with the salted caramel sauce, the whipped cream, brioche croutons, and a pinch of sea salt.

SALTED CARAMEL SAUCE

MAKE ABOUT 2½ CUPS

Caramel sauce is simply cooked sugar with cream and butter. Since the sugar is cooked at a high temperature, it does require a bit of caution, but otherwise, this recipe is easy and watching the transformation from raw sugar to caramel is so rewarding. To clean the saucepan, just soak it in hot soapy water until the hardened bits of sugar dissolve.

2 cups heavy cream

1 cup sugar

6 tablespoons (¾ stick) unsalted butter

1 teaspoon kosher salt

In a small saucepan, bring the cream to a boil over medium heat.

Meanwhile, in a medium saucepan, combine the sugar and ¼ cup water (being careful not to get sugar on the sides of the saucepan, where it can crystallize), and bring to a boil over medium-high heat, stirring until the sugar is dissolved. Boil the syrup, without stirring, until it becomes an amber color (about 340°F on a candy thermometer), about 8 minutes.

When the caramel is ready, immediately remove it from the heat. Very slowly and carefully pour the hot cream down the side of the saucepan into the caramel, making sure your hand and arm are not over the saucepan. Stir to combine, getting into the edges of the saucepan to keep the mixture from burning or sticking. Then stir in the butter and salt. (Resist the urge to taste the caramel immediately, because it is seriously hot.) If the sauce is lumpy, stir it over medium heat until the lumps dissolve. If you're not using the sauce immediately, transfer to a container and let cool, then cover. Salted caramel sauce will keep, covered in the refrigerator, for 2 weeks; reheat before serving.

BRIOCHE CROUTONS

MAKES ABOUT 2 CUPS

If you sit on the bench in the waiting area of the restaurant in the late afternoon, you can smell the aroma of the brioche wafting up from the downstairs kitchen. I'm certainly not going to suggest you make brioche from scratch just for these croutons, but you will appreciate the difference if you do. Use challah as a substitute or brioche from a good bakery. Caramelizing the croutons takes time, so be patient and stir them until they color properly.

2 tablespoons unsalted butter

¼ pound Brioche (page 260), or other bread, crusts removed and cut into 1-inch cubes (about 2 cups)

¼ cup confectioners' sugar

In a large skillet, melt the butter over medium-low heat. Add the bread, stir to coat, and sprinkle with the sugar. Stir gently and constantly with a spatula until the sugar melts and the croutons are caramelized on all sides. Transfer to a baking sheet and let cool completely. The croutons are best the day they are made.

OPPOSITE: Anita Villacreses has been part of Gramercy Tavern for fifteen years. As lunch maître d', Anita's is often the first smiling face you see. "I am a better host here than I am at home," she confesses. "I sense people's time constraints and I try to take care of them. Gramercy is my pride and joy," she says. "It's the passion. If you're here for just a job, it won't work."

SUMMER

CHILLED ZUCCHINI SOUP

SERVES 4 TO 6

A hint of garlic and basil is a wonderful way to heighten the flavor of the ubiquitous zucchini that overflows summer gardens. Here that zucchini base becomes a vehicle for a whole basketful of summer ingredients. A soup is most interesting when every bite contains a variety of textures and flavors, like bits of turnip, tomatoes, and cucumbers, seasoned with lemon juice, good olive oil, salt, and pepper.

SOUP

2 tablespoons olive oil

1 onion, thinly sliced

5 shallots, thinly sliced

1 leek (white part), halved lengthwise and thinly sliced

3 garlic cloves, thinly sliced

5 sprigs lemon thyme

6 cups Vegetable Broth (page 118) or water

2 pounds zucchini, halved lengthwise, seeded, and sliced (about 6 cups)

Salt

3 cups packed baby spinach

A large handful of flat-leaf parsley leaves

10 basil leaves

GARNISH

6 baby turnips, peeled and quartered

12 Sun Gold or other small cherry tomatoes, halved

1/3 cup seeded and finely diced cucumber

Fresh lemon juice

Salt and pepper

Extra-virgin olive oil

Make the soup. In a large pot, heat the olive oil over medium heat. Add the onion, shallots, leek, and garlic and cook, stirring occasionally, until the onion is softened, about 6 minutes. Add the lemon thyme and cook, stirring, for a minute, then add the broth and bring to a simmer.

Raise the heat to high, add the zucchini, season with salt, and bring to a boil. Cook until the zucchini is tender, about 3 minutes. Add the spinach, parsley, and basil. As soon as the greens are wilted, no more than a minute, pour the mixture into a large bowl, set it in an ice bath, and stir to cool it quickly and preserve the vegetables' green color.

Discard the lemon thyme. Transfer the solids to a blender in batches, and process until very smooth and creamy, adding enough of the liquid to the blender to achieve a thin consistency. Pass through a fine-mesh strainer into a container. Season with salt, cover, and refrigerate. Reserve any remaining broth. (The soup will likely thicken as it chills, so thin with a bit of the reserved liquid or water.)

Just before serving, prepare the garnish. Blanch the turnips in boiling salted water until tender, about 5 minutes. Drain, shock in ice water, then drain again. In a small bowl, season the turnips, tomatoes, and cucumber with lemon juice, salt, and pepper. Laddle the soup into bowls, and top with the garnish and a drizzle of extra-virgin olive oil.

PRECEDING PAGES: Hayden Guialdo *(left)*, Roberta Bendavid's assistant, creates towering floral arrangements inside the front door, and seasonally changes the branches in the metal tub that sits on the bar. For summer, he fills it with 135 sunflowers.

VEGETABLE BROTH

MAKES ABOUT 10 CUPS

We rely on this light vegetable broth rather than a heavier meat or chicken stock for many of our recipes in this book. The taste of vegetable broth is subtle; it's not a soup on its own. But I believe it adds layers of discreet flavor. You can make it in advance and freeze it, but to really experience the magic, make it in small batches and use it right away. Which reminds me: forget about that image of a huge stockpot boiling away on the stove for hours; this broth comes together quickly and simply. This is a basic recipe. You might try flavoring the sweet broth with branches of herbs like lovage, dill, bay, or basil.

2 tablespoons olive oil

3 onions, roughly chopped

2 carrots, roughly chopped

2 celery stalks, roughly chopped

1 leek (white and pale green parts), roughly chopped

5 garlic cloves, smashed

3 sprigs thyme

1 teaspoon black peppercorns

1 teaspoon coriander seeds

In a large pot, heat the oil over medium heat. Add the onions, carrots, celery, leek, and garlic and cook, stirring occasionally, until softened, about 10 minutes. Add the thyme, peppercorns, coriander, and 3 quarts water. Bring to a boil, reduce the heat, and gently simmer for about an hour.

Pass the broth through a fine-mesh strainer into a container, pressing on the solids to extract as much liquid as possible. The broth will keep, covered, in the refrigerator for up to 5 days; it can be frozen for up to 3 months.

FINISHING A DISH

Any dish, from a soup to a main course, becomes much more intriguing when topped with unexpected bites of crunchy texture and flavor. The last touches to a dish are so important to my food, and they should be thoughtful. They play a role that goes beyond just looking pretty. Here's where your imagination can wander. Instead of worrying about executing these recipes down to that last little detail in the photographs, I'd rather you feel free to use whatever fresh ingredients you have at your fingertips to add a personal touch. Did you find a great bunch of basil in the market this morning? Use that to finish the Heirloom Tomato Tarts (page 151). Is parsley coming up in your garden? Snip it and sprinkle it on the Spring Asparagus with Flounder (page 56). Have some Pickled Ramps (page 93)? They'll taste great with the Lightly Curried Sweet Peas (page 52). Is there an extra carrot in your fridge? Shave it over the Carrot and Calamari Salad (page 221). Mince the green parts of scallions for the Grilled Zucchini and Corn Salsa (page 147). Even simple sliced cucumbers can add the interest and texture I'm talking about to a sautéed fish fillet.

Michael Anthony
Gramercy Tavern

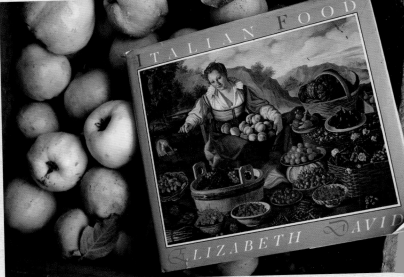

ROBERTA BENDAVID

FLORAL DESIGNER • SINCE 1994

The flowers at Gramercy Tavern are never about just one piece; it's always a vignette, a narrative, a layering. I began in the fashion business, in menswear, and I was good at layering: textures, colors, and fabrics in photo shoots, advertisements, and especially the clothes—which were so unbelievable you just had to touch them to appreciate the way they all worked together. It was incredibly sensual. I love doing that, styling, putting clothes together. I worked for Bill Kaiserman at Rafael Fashions—he was the American Armani in the '70s. We met when I was at Esquire magazine and I produced all his fashion shows and ad campaigns. He won every award. Our shows were incredible and somehow there were always extraordinary flowers.

But by 1987, I'd had it with fashion. I'd been a vegetarian forever, and at the Union Square Greenmarket, I met the people from Blooming Hill Farm in Blooming Grove, New York. They were the first organic farmers to bring in mesclun. They quickly realized my passion for flowers, and in the autumn and winter, when the organic greens and vegetables were at their end, their means of making a living was foraging, bringing down branches and making fantastic arrangements at the market. There was nothing like it. They made me an offer of $100 a week and all the arugula I could eat if I would come work for them. So I did! I finished my commitments, moved up to a little house on their farm in Orange County, and began foraging. I was in charge of the flowers. They'd been selling flowers on a limited basis and when I moved up, we expanded that business. We made bouquets of dried sunflowers with pine boughs and pods and brought them to the Greenmarket. It was a wonderful way to use every growing thing. People would line up to buy our flowers. It was an incredible business. It was a dream. Unbelievable. It was exactly what I needed. I didn't even own a pair of jeans before that.

I lived upstate for three years. Then I decided I had the design part down, but I needed to know everything about how to handle flowers, how to cut a flower, how to condition a hydrangea. So I went to work at a florist in New York City, where a British woman took me under her wing. They hired me as an apprentice and they paid me. I had to punch a time card—something I'd never done in my life. There were old-time florists there who would say, "She's got the hand!" as I made the bouquets. You have to have a feel for it. I did and I really wanted to learn.

At about that time, my brother was opening a restaurant up in North Bennington, Vermont. I went up to help him cook and to do the flowers. One day, back in New York, I happened to stop by Rizzoli, where I picked up a cookbook called *Italian Food* by Elizabeth David. It blew me away. It was filled with voluptuous Renaissance paintings of food. On the cover was a painting by the Italian Vincenzo Campi, dating from 1580, called *The Fruit Seller.* The woman was displaying dozens of kinds of glorious fruits and vegetables in baskets and buckets and bowls and platters and plates. It was then that I understood how fruits and vegetables could *be* the flowers. When I saw that book, I knew I hadn't made a mistake by leaving fashion. It was divine intervention, and it gave me the courage to approach Danny Meyer.

The previous five years, he had seen my work, because I did the decorations for Share Our Strength events. There was no budget, and when there's no money and all these great people volunteering, it can be an unbelievably creative endeavor; that was one of the most fruitful times of my life. I'd heard Danny was opening

a restaurant on 20th Street. When we first spoke, the restaurant was supposed to be a seventeenth-century tavern, open for lunch and dinner, a neighborly place to meet, to come play checkers. My vision, when we first walked through the space, was that it was surrounded by meadows! I saw it as a tavern that sat on lush fields where I would gather flowers and branches and put whatever I had gathered on the Tavern table. I've stayed so true to that vision that I have never been able to put anything in the restaurant that I couldn't envision growing right outside the door. So I used delphiniums when the restaurant opened because July was delphinium season. When January came around, I was stuck. That's when I went back to the bounty of the fruits and vegetables of the Elizabeth David book. Now, because of the superlative way Michael Anthony uses vegetables in the kitchen, I always incorporate vegetables into the floral design.

CHILLED CORN SOUP

SERVES 4 TO 6

This soup, which can also be served hot, is wonderful made with water, but if you have a little extra time, it's far better with corn broth. Not only does the broth enhance the flavor, but it gets the most out of the fresh corn, so nothing goes to waste. Simply put the stripped cobs in a large pot with some chopped onions, carrots, celery, and garlic, cover with water, and bring to a boil, then reduce the heat, let it simmer for about 30 minutes, and strain. If you have some left over, you can use corn broth for many other things: making polenta, braising vegetables, or whenever you need a vegetable broth.

SOUP

2 tablespoons olive oil

3 shallots, thinly sliced

2 garlic cloves, thinly sliced

1 leek (white and pale green parts), halved lengthwise and thinly sliced

8 cups corn kernels (from about 16 ears)

Salt and pepper

1 teaspoon honey

6 cups water or corn broth

Fresh lime juice

GARNISH

1 teaspoon olive oil

1/2 cup corn kernels (from about 1 ear)

1/2 cup finely diced zucchini

Salt and pepper

12 cherry tomatoes, halved

1 radish, very thinly sliced

Extra-virgin olive oil

2 shiso leaves, julienned (optional)

Make the soup. In a large pot, heat the olive oil over medium-low heat. Add the shallots, garlic, and leek and cook, stirring often, until the leek is softened, about 6 minutes. Add the corn kernels, season with salt and pepper, and stir for 2 minutes. Add the honey and water or corn broth, bring to a simmer, and cook until the corn kernels are just tender, about 3 minutes.

Transfer the solids to a blender in batches and process until very smooth and creamy, adding enough of the liquid to the blender to achieve a thin consistency. Pass the soup through a fine-mesh strainer into a container. Season with salt, pepper, and lime juice, then cover and refrigerate. Reserve any remaining liquid. (The soup will likely thicken as it chills, so thin with a bit of the reserved liquid or water.)

Just before serving, prepare the garnish. In a small skillet, heat the olive oil over medium heat. Add the corn and zucchini and cook until just crisp-tender, about 3 minutes. Season with salt and pepper.

In a small bowl, season the tomatoes and radish with extra-virgin olive oil, salt, and pepper.

Ladle the soup into bowls and top with the corn mixture and the tomatoes and radishes. Sprinkle with shiso leaves, if you like.

FLOUNDER with MARINATED CUCUMBERS and YOGURT SAUCE

SERVES 4

All of the elements of this dish—the crunchy cucumber salad and creamy yogurt sauce—are meant to be chilled except for the flounder served straight from the pan. I prefer to make the salad with Persian cucumbers because I like their small size and lack of seeds; and their skins aren't bitter, so you don't have to peel them. If you can find Mexican gherkins (they look like tiny watermelons, left), they make a nice addition.

3 small cucumbers

2 tablespoons plus 1 teaspoon white balsamic vinegar

2 tablespoons plus 1 teaspoon fresh lime juice

2 tablespoons fresh lemon juice

1 teaspoon finely chopped dill

Salt and pepper

½ cup Greek yogurt

¼ teaspoon honey

2 teaspoons finely chopped cilantro

1 teaspoon finely chopped mint

1 teaspoon finely chopped tarragon

Four 6-ounce skinless flounder fillets

1 tablespoon olive oil

Extra-virgin olive oil

1 tablespoon finely chopped chives

Using a mandoline or a sharp knife, cut 2 of the cucumbers lengthwise into very thin, supple slices; discard the first and last slices, which will be mostly skin. In a large bowl, combine the sliced cucumbers with 2 tablespoons of the vinegar, 2 tablespoons of the lime juice, the lemon juice, and dill and season with salt and pepper. Toss gently to coat the cucumbers; marinate for about 30 minutes.

Meanwhile, peel the remaining cucumber, halve lengthwise, seed, and slice. Set aside.

In a small bowl, combine the yogurt, 2 tablespoons water, the remaining 1 teaspoon vinegar and 1 teaspoon lime juice, the honey, 1 teaspoon of the cilantro, the mint, and tarragon. Stir until you have a smooth, spreadable sauce, thinning it with a bit more water if necessary. Season with salt and pepper, cover, and refrigerate.

Season the flounder with salt and pepper. In a large nonstick skillet, heat the olive oil over medium heat. Lay the fillets in the pan and cook until lightly browned on the bottom, about 3 minutes. Flip the fillets and cook until just cooked through, about a minute more.

While the fish is cooking, season the sliced cucumber with extra-virgin olive oil, salt, and pepper.

Spread a large spoonful of the yogurt sauce in the middle of each plate. Drain the marinated cucumbers, pat dry, and mound on the sauce. Top with the flounder fillets, spoon the sliced cucumbers over the fish, and scatter the chives and the remaining 1 teaspoon cilantro on top.

BABY ARTICHOKES WITH SUMMER BEANS AND SUN GOLD TOMATOES

SERVES 4

Some dishes are about flavors that are layered on the plate; others, like this one, are about melding the flavors in the pan as they cook. Here the tomato water that is released at the last moment when you gently heat the Sun Golds is where the magic lies. It makes the neighboring ingredients taste like something brand new, but it's really drop-dead simple. I like to scatter the finished dish with baby bok choy and tiny mustard greens just before serving.

½ lemon

12 baby artichokes

2 tablespoons olive oil

1 shallot, minced

1 garlic clove, minced

Large pinch of coriander seeds, smashed

Small pinch of fennel seeds, smashed

½ cup white wine

¼ cup white wine vinegar

¼ cup orange juice

2 cups Vegetable Broth (page 118) or bean liquid plus water

Salt and pepper

1 cup peeled fava beans or lima beans

1¼ cups White Beans (page 129)

12 Sun Gold or other small cherry tomatoes, halved

1 tablespoon extra-virgin olive oil

Grated zest of ½ orange

1 teaspoon fresh lemon juice

1 tablespoon finely chopped flat-leaf parsley

1 teaspoon finely chopped tarragon

2 tablespoons unsalted butter

Squeeze the juice from the lemon into a large bowl of cold water. Trim the top of each artichoke and snap off a few outer leaves until you reach the tender pale green ones underneath. Peel the stems and trim the ends, then halve the artichokes lengthwise and submerge in the lemon water.

When all the artichokes are trimmed, drain them and pat dry. In a large pan, heat the olive oil over medium-high heat. Add the artichokes cut side down and brown, about 2 minutes. Add the shallot and garlic and cook, stirring occasionally, for a minute, then add the coriander and fennel seeds.

Pour in the wine and vinegar and bring to a simmer. When the liquid is reduced by half, add the orange juice and reduce again by half. Add enough broth to just cover the artichokes, season with salt and pepper, and simmer until the artichokes are just tender, about 15 minutes.

Meanwhile, blanch the fava beans in boiling salted water until tender, about 1 minute. Drain, shock in ice water, and drain again.

Add the fava beans, white beans, and tomatoes to the artichoke mixture and heat through.

Remove from the heat, add the extra-virgin olive oil, orange zest, lemon juice, parsley, and tarragon, and stir to combine. Swirl in the butter and ladle into bowls.

LEFT: Tony Gibbons began as a host at Gramercy in 2008; now he's a maître d'. Some of the time. Garden State Urban Farms claims the rest of his life. A New Jersey-based business begun by his enterprising mother, Lorraine Gibbons, GSUF is devoted to community-based gardening projects that yield employment opportunities as well as the freshest, crispest greens *(far left)*, which I'm proud to buy for the restaurant all year long.

CARE AND FEEDING

Gramercy Tavern is a quilt. We celebrate diversity of character and colorful personalities. We search for and attract people with those qualities. As a result, we are a dynamic team of individuals, each with a particular strength. When I'm hiring or promoting waiters and managers, I prize individuality and an instinct for hospitality. As Danny puts it, "We hire hard and train easy," meaning that from the very first interview, we pay attention to the way a person listens, looks, and feels.

All of our dining room managers have grown with us; they've seen the restaurant from many vantage points. Almost every one of them began here as a server, a host, a bartender, or a cook. I'm always proud of the long tenure of our front-of-the-house employees—our seven managers have a collective seventy to eighty years of experience at Gramercy Tavern alone—and the unusually long tenure extends to the back of the house, too, where turnover is remarkably low for restaurants in our category. We've heard people say we don't hire superstar waiters. It's true; we hire people who can provide great hospitality but who are not always experienced servers. That's because I believe I can teach a server technical skills, but I can't teach him or her how to make a table that's meeting their in-laws for the first time feel really comfortable and relaxed. I can't make him listen to someone who says, "Oh my God, my mom used to make celery soup all the time but I haven't had it in years" and then bring her over a little cup to taste. That type of service blows people away. People can be technically accomplished but not great listeners or great givers.

What's different about Gramercy is that the managers genuinely want to see their colleagues grow. In addition to our emphasis on performance, we work to create a family-like atmosphere. We're devoted to personalized, quirky ways of connecting with each other, like reading *The Grinch* at Christmas or giving people birthday cakes (as on Assistant General Manager Scott Reinhardt's birthday, below). And then there is National Poetry Month, when every afternoon work stops so someone can read a poem. Our traditions are genuine and they run deep. They are a gift to ourselves and to each other, meant to celebrate the uniqueness and color each person adds to this quilt. At most restaurants, your job is your job. I don't want it to be like that. I want our staff to honor and respect what's best for each other. I'm excited by the idea of trying to get people to fall in love with what we do. I look for people who come in and are a little lost, like I was, and then watch them get it and learn and become a part of our family.

—Kevin Mahan

WHITE BEANS

MAKES ABOUT 2 CUPS

The great thing about cooking beans is that the liquid they're cooked in becomes a delicious broth. It gives backbone to the recipe at hand and can be used in many other recipes as well. So make sure there's enough liquid in the pot to store the beans in once they're cooked. They'll also taste better!

I use fresh shell beans, like these cranberry beans (right), whenever I can. But dried beans are a wonderful ingredient to have in your pantry: they're easy to keep on hand, and you can prep them whenever you like, first soaking them overnight. I like to add lots of carrots, onions, and garlic to the beans to infuse them with rich flavor. Because they are so good and versatile, consider making a bigger batch by doubling or tripling this recipe. Remember, if you're using fresh beans, you don't have to soak them and the cooking time is shorter.

Once the beans are cooked, you're just a step away from any number of delicious meals, such as bean soup for lunch, or in my case, bean salsa for dinner for my daughters, Gaby, Colette, and Addie. Or use them in recipes like Ruby Red Shrimp with White Beans and Kale Salsa Verde (page 279), as well as in the baby artichokes (see page 126).

1 carrot, halved

½ small onion

1 garlic clove, smashed

1 bay leaf

1 sprig thyme

1 cup dried beans, soaked overnight in water, drained, and rinsed

Salt and pepper

In a small pot, combine the carrot, onion, garlic, bay leaf, thyme, and 2 cups water; bring to a simmer, and cook for 20 minutes.

Add the beans, then add enough water to cover them by 2 to 3 inches and simmer for 30 minutes. Season with salt and pepper and continue to simmer until the beans are just tender, about 20 minutes longer. Remove from the heat and let the beans cool in their liquid.

Drain the beans, reserving the liquid, and discard the vegetables and herbs. You can keep the cooked beans, submerged in the liquid, in the refrigerator for up to 3 days.

CARROT AND POLE BEAN SALAD WITH CARROT VINAIGRETTE

SERVES 4 GENEROUSLY

I try to make dishes that are both memorable and intriguing. Sometimes even an unfamiliar ingredient can be memorable; other times, a simple ingredient is given a new twist. When we call a carrot by its specific name, Kyoto carrot, for instance, that name is a flag that says, "There's a story here." It's me begging a guest to ask, "What *is* this purple carrot? Where did you get it?" I have a cool story about the Kyoto carrot. In Japan, while visiting vegetable farmers with Japanese chefs, I tasted a Kyoto carrot just pulled from the soil.

I asked myself, "Can we grow these amazing carrots back home?" That involved getting the seeds from Japan, finding a farmer who would plant them in New York, and then hoping and hoping. That first summer crop was a failure—it was far too warm. But the fall crop was magic! And immediately anyone who discovered Kyoto carrots at the Greenmarket was excited by them, without knowing that Gramercy Tavern had brought the seeds to New York or that Zaid Kurdieh is an amazing farmer who made them grow in his soil at Norwich Meadows Farm in central New York in an exemplary way. Thus, a simple carrot can generate a story of discovery.

The fields at Norwich Meadows also produce long, flat pole beans that taste so green and earthy you can eat them just blanched in salted water, with a drizzle of olive oil. To make this radiant salad, we marry these two incredible ingredients—Kyoto carrots and pole beans—in an intense carrot vinaigrette.

CARROT VINAIGRETTE

2 cups carrot juice

1 large egg yolk

2 teaspoons white miso paste

2 teaspoons whole-grain mustard

2 tablespoons apple cider vinegar or white wine vinegar

²/₃ cup grapeseed oil

Fresh lemon juice

Salt and pepper

1¹/₂ pounds green and yellow pole beans, cut on the diagonal into 1-inch pieces

Salt

4 carrots, sliced paper-thin on the diagonal

12 cherry tomatoes, halved

¹/₄ cup diced Pickled Green Tomatoes (page 133; optional)

20 gooseberries (optional)

1 shallot, minced

1 tablespoon finely chopped chives

Make the carrot vinaigrette. In a small saucepan, bring the carrot juice to a simmer and reduce by two-thirds, stirring occasionally. Remove from the heat and let cool.

In a blender, combine the reduced carrot juice, the egg yolk, miso paste, mustard, and vinegar and process until smooth. With the machine running, slowly add the oil in a thin stream. Season with lemon juice, salt, and pepper.

In a large pot of boiling salted water, blanch the beans until crisp-tender, about 4 minutes. Drain, shock in ice water, and drain again.

In a large bowl, combine the beans, carrots, cherry tomatoes, pickled green tomatoes, if using, gooseberries, if using, shallot, chives, and ¹/₂ cup of the carrot vinaigrette and toss well. Serve with more of the vinaigrette.

GRAMERCY TAVERN

SEPTEMBER 19, 2011
Summer Tasting Menu

Summer Squash and Crab Rolls

Compressed Watermelon Salad
Roasted Beets, Blue Cheese and Hazelnuts

Fairytale Eggplant with Olives, Tomato and Lardo

Warm Maine Lobster
Caramelized Corn, Eckerton Tomatoes, Lobster Sauce

Kyoto Carrots and Creamy Cayuga Barley
Shiso, Apples and Carrot Juice

Roasted Pekin Style Duck Breast and Open Ravioli of Confit
Pole Beans, Swiss Chard Leaves and Stems, Foraged Maine Herbs

Nectarine Tarte Tatin
Bourbon Crème Anglaise and Butter Pecan Ice Cream

Petit Fours

MICHAEL ANTHONY, EXECUTIVE CHEF/PARTNER

HOW I NAME A DISH

You can tell from reading the names of the dishes on the menus at Gramercy Tavern, and in this book, that simplicity is my style. I like the name to be said in one breath: Open Ravioli of Beef and Carrots; Hot-Smoked Trout with Pickled Cipollini Onions; Carrot and Calamari Salad. The names are designed to be easily remembered and unpretentious. In this way, the name of a dish opens a dialogue between the diner and the cook, because I really want our guests to feel a sense of discovery that can get lost if we overexplain. Why miss all the fun, the element of surprise?

By not cluttering up the name of a dish with the precise provenance of each ingredient, we open the door to rich conversation about our respect for the farmers and growers as the diner becomes intrigued with the food he or she is tasting. We're giving our guests the opportunity to fall in love with the physical sensations of dining: the look, the aroma, the flavor of what's on their plates.

OPPOSITE: When guests are served a special tasting dinner, the next day we e-mail a menu like this one, illustrated by Mindy Dubin. That way they can remember their great time and share it with friends.

PICKLED GREEN TOMATOES

MAKES ABOUT 1 QUART

Follow the Basic Pickling Recipe (page 86), substituting these ingredients.

1½ pounds green tomatoes, thinly sliced

1½ cups rice vinegar

½ cup water

½ cup sugar

1½ tablespoons kosher salt

¼ teaspoon coriander seeds

¼ teaspoon fennel seeds

¼ teaspoon mustard seeds

1 garlic clove, smashed

1 sprig thyme

1 sprig tarragon

WATERMELON AND BEET SALAD

SERVES 4

This refreshing chilled summertime salad is made special with Forono beets, a surprisingly sweet variety with a long carrot-like shape (the shape its cousin, the standard beet, used to have). The salad's vibrant red colors grab your attention on a plate, but of course it is just as good tossed and served in a bowl. I like to eat it very cold.

RASPBERRY VINAIGRETTE

1/2 pint raspberries

1 tablespoon extra-virgin olive oil

1 teaspoon red wine vinegar

1 teaspoon raspberry vinegar

Salt

4 small red beets (about 1/2 pound, without greens), cooked, peeled, and quartered

1 small yellow beet, peeled and sliced paper-thin

4 cups watermelon chunks

1 plum, halved, pitted, and diced

1/4 cup diced Pickled Watermelon Rind (optional)

1/4 cup hazelnuts, toasted, skinned, salted, and halved

2 ounces blue cheese, crumbled

2 teaspoons raspberry vinegar

2 teaspoons hazelnut oil

Salt and pepper

Fennel fronds, chopped, for garnish

Make the raspberry vinaigrette. In a blender, combine the raspberries, olive oil, red wine vinegar, and raspberry vinegar and process until smooth. Pass through a fine-mesh strainer into a small bowl and season with salt.

Put the red and yellow beets, watermelon, plum, pickled watermelon rind, if using, hazelnuts, and blue cheese in a large bowl. Sprinkle with the raspberry vinegar and hazelnut oil, season with salt and pepper, and gently toss.

Spoon the salad onto plates, drizzle some of the raspberry vinaigrette around the edges, and top with the fennel fronds.

PICKLED WATERMELON RIND

MAKES ABOUT 1 QUART

A small watermelon yields more than enough rind for these pickles. Slice the rind into crescents, cut away the flesh, and remove all traces of the green peel. I like to use large rectangular pieces about an inch thick. What's important is that the pieces be about the same size and shape so they'll pickle evenly. The beet adds a lovely color.

Follow the Basic Pickling Recipe (page 86), substituting these ingredients. Remove the beet before transferring the watermelon rind to a container.

4 1/2 cups rectangular pieces peeled watermelon rind

1 1/2 cups rice vinegar

1/2 cup water

1/2 cup sugar

1 1/2 tablespoons kosher salt

1/4 teaspoon coriander seeds

1/4 teaspoon fennel seeds

1/4 teaspoon mustard seeds

1/4 teaspoon black peppercorns

1/2 small beet, peeled and halved

MODESTO GOES TO MARKET
MODESTO BATISTA

CHIEF STEWARD •
SINCE 1994

I have been at Gramercy since the week after it opened in 1994. I was working at La Côte Basque and I got the call for help from a sous chef I'd worked with. It's hard to tell you what I do except to say I am in charge of making sure everything is all right.

I come in at 6:30 a.m. and I take my big, deep rolling cart and walk to the Greenmarket in Union Square every day it's open. I know everyone there and they know me! I buy whatever the chefs need, but sometimes a vegetable or fruit or herb will look so good I just buy a bunch and I know the cooks will figure out what to do with it.

I'm always looking ahead to what will be ripest. And I'm always watching for what needs to be done, in the kitchen, or for Roberta and her flowers, or I'll fix a wobbly table base.

I came to the United States in 1984 from the Dominican Republic. My wife, Iris, works in the prep kitchen downstairs. My older son, Junior, is a manager at Shake Shack, my younger son, Angel, is a student at MIT. I love the restaurant and I love Mike. We make a good team.

Four times a week, Modesto rolls his cart just a few blocks away to our favorite stands at the Union Square Greenmarket: Paffenroth Gardens; Bodhitree Tree Farm; Lani's Farm; Berried Treasures; Norwich Meadows Farms; Eckerton Hill Farm; and Phillips Farm. (See Where We Shop, page 338.)

GRAMERCY

TAVERN

☎ GR7-0777

"When you look in from the street, you get a frisson: Oooh, there's a glow inside. You want to be there. I love the idea of a couple on a first date pulling up in a cab and wondering, 'Did we pick the right restaurant? *Yes we did!!!*'"

—Peter Bentel, Architect, Bentel & Bentel

PICKLED FAIRY TALE EGGPLANT

MAKES ABOUT 1 QUART

Follow the Basic Pickling Recipe (page 86), substituting these ingredients; submerge the eggplants in the hot liquid for 2 minutes instead of pouring the liquid over them in a bowl. This slight adjustment will help soften the eggplants.

6 Fairy Tale eggplants, peeled and kept in lemon water

1 1/2 cups white wine vinegar

1/2 cup water

1/2 cup sugar

1 1/2 tablespoons kosher salt

WARM SALAD OF FAIRY TALE EGGPLANTS

SERVES 4

Typically eggplant is pickled to remove bitterness and to preserve it. My Italian grandmother used to take the big garden variety, salt and squeeze it, and then submerge it in vinegar seasoned with onions and red chile peppers. The Fairy Tale eggplant, however, which is small (about 2 inches long) and a beautiful pale lavender, is celebrated for more than its cuteness: it has no bitterness and only imperceptible seeds. So pickling it isn't necessary to counteract bitterness—but it does add another layer of flavor in this salad, where warm plays against cold, tender against crunchy, and sweet against acid. It's an excellent example of how I like to build flavors just by layering them.

EGGPLANT PUREE

1 large eggplant (about 1 pound)

2 tablespoons olive oil

Salt and pepper

$\frac{1}{2}$ teaspoon sherry vinegar

2 tablespoons extra-virgin olive oil

4 Fairy Tale eggplants

Salt and pepper

2 tablespoons olive oil

6 thin slices of small heirloom tomato, halved

8 Sun Gold or other small cherry tomatoes, halved

$\frac{1}{4}$ fennel bulb, trimmed and sliced paper-thin, fronds chopped for garnish

Pinch of Aleppo pepper

Extra-virgin olive oil

Fresh lemon juice

1 tablespoon sherry vinegar

1 tablespoon honey

1 tablespoon white miso paste

1 tablespoon shiro dashi

1 tablespoon unsalted butter

4 Pickled Fairy Tale Eggplants (page 139), quartered

Preheat the oven to 400°F.

Make the eggplant puree. Halve the eggplant lengthwise and pierce the halves several times with a fork. Rub with the olive oil and season with salt and pepper. Put the eggplant cut side up on a rimmed baking sheet and roast until browned and completely soft in the center, about 40 minutes.

When the eggplant is cool enough to handle, scrape the flesh into a blender. Add the vinegar and extra-virgin olive oil and process until smooth. Season the eggplant puree with salt and pepper,

transfer to a small saucepan, and keep warm.

Halve the Fairy Tale eggplants lengthwise. Score the cut sides and season with salt and pepper. In a medium skillet, heat the olive oil over medium heat. Add the eggplants cut side down and cook, turning once, until just tender, about 3 minutes per side.

Meanwhile, in a medium bowl, gently toss the tomatoes and fennel with the Aleppo pepper. Season with extra-virgin olive oil, lemon juice, salt, and pepper.

Remove the pan from the heat and stir in the vinegar, honey, miso, shiro dashi, and butter. This should form a nice glaze; if it is too thick, stir in a little water. Coat the eggplants with the glaze.

Spoon the eggplant puree onto plates. Layer the glazed eggplants, pickled eggplants, and tomato mixture on top and garnish with the fennel fronds.

HEIRLOOM TOMATO SALAD WITH PICKLED CHERRIES

SERVES 4

This is *the* salad to serve when tomatoes are at their ripest. I like to use a colorful variety of heirlooms and pair them with a dense, sweet ricotta cheese like Salvatore ricotta from Brooklyn. We serve the salad on individual plates, but it looks wonderful displayed on a platter. Dollop the ricotta on top so it looks rustic and delicious.

4 heirloom tomatoes, cut into thin wedges

12 Sun Gold or other small cherry tomatoes, halved

1 shallot, minced

1 tablespoon sherry vinegar

8 Pickled Cherries, halved, plus 1 tablespoon of the pickling liquid

1 tablespoon extra-virgin olive oil

Salt and pepper

2 radishes, sliced paper-thin

Fresh lemon juice

12 large butter lettuce leaves, torn

1/4 cup roasted, salted sunflower seeds

1/4 cup ricotta cheese

In a large bowl, combine the tomatoes, shallot, vinegar, pickling liquid, and olive oil. Season with salt and pepper, toss gently, and let marinate for about 10 minutes.

In a small bowl, season the radishes with lemon juice, salt, and pepper. Add the radishes, lettuce, sunflower seeds, and pickled cherries to the tomatoes. Gently toss and serve immediately, topping each serving with a spoonful of ricotta.

PICKLED CHERRIES

MAKES ABOUT 1 QUART

As soon as Bing cherries come into season, we pickle them by the case. We use them to brighten salads and cocktails, and I like their pop in pork, duck, and venison dishes. We use a slightly different recipe than for our Basic Pickles (page 86), but this is just as easy to make.

4 cups Bing cherries

1 clove

1/2 vanilla bean, split lengthwise

1/2 cinnamon stick

One 1/2-inch piece of ginger

2 cups sugar

1 cup champagne vinegar

Put the cherries in a medium bowl. Set aside.

Tie the clove, vanilla bean, cinnamon, and ginger in a piece of cheesecloth to make a sachet and toss into a medium saucepan. Add the sugar, vinegar, and 1 cup water, bring to a simmer, stirring, and cook for 10 minutes.

Pour the pickling liquid over the cherries. Put a plate over the cherries to keep them submerged and let cool to room temperature.

Discard the sachet, then cover the bowl with plastic wrap and refrigerate for 6 hours.

Transfer the pickles and liquid to a container, cover, and refrigerate. The pickled cherries will keep, covered and submerged in their liquid, for about a month in the refrigerator. Remove the pits before using.

THE TAVERN GRILL

The Tavern wood-fired grill is not just our version of an American backyard grill. It is also a primitive way to cook—over an open fire. Our goal is to capture authentic, rustic smoky flavors using a combination of full flame and indirect low heat. We cook *in* it, putting sweet potatoes directly in the embers; we cook *on* it, laying thin strips of zucchini, fish fillets, or kielbasa sausages on the hot grill or soft-smashed beets on the cast-iron griddle; and we cook *over* it, baking clams and roasting oysters in the ovens set above the smoky fire. The controlled char we get on the edges of our lasagna or the outside of leeks contrasts beautifully with the creaminess within. We use white oak, which gives off a delicious, distinctive aroma that wafts into the neighborhood. Even before you hit 20th Street, the perfumed air tells you you're near Gramercy Tavern.

GRILLED ZUCCHINI AND CORN SALSA

SERVES 4

While I love corn on the cob, there is nothing like the pleasure of a mouthful of fresh corn in each bite of this salsa. Enhanced by a zucchini puree and smoky slabs of grilled zucchini, it is all about highlighting homegrown flavors rather than about being a fancy restaurant dish. Ají dulce peppers make this salsa sing.

2 tablespoons olive oil

1/3 cup minced onion

1 tablespoon seeded and minced jalapeño peppers

1/3 cup diced ají dulce or red bell pepper

2 cups corn kernels (from about 4 ears)

1 small tomato, halved, seeded, and diced

Fresh lime juice

Salt and pepper

1/2 cup Zucchini Puree (page 148)

Vegetable Broth (page 118) or water, as needed

12 thick slices small zucchini (about 4 inches long)

A chunk of Parmigiano cheese for grating and shaving

1/3 cup red currants (optional)

A handful of small basil leaves

Preheat a charcoal or gas grill to medium-high heat.

Meanwhile, in a large skillet, heat 1 tablespoon of the olive oil over medium-low heat. Add the onion, jalapeños, and ají dulce pepper and cook, stirring often, until softened, about 5 minutes. Increase the heat to medium-high, add the corn, and cook until crisp-tender, about 2 minutes. Stir in the tomato and season with lime juice, salt, and pepper. Keep warm.

In a small saucepan, gently heat the zucchini puree, then thin with the broth. Season with salt and pepper and keep warm.

In a large bowl, toss the zucchini slices with the remaining tablespoon of olive oil and season with salt and pepper. Grill, turning once, until just tender, about 4 minutes per side.

Arrange the grilled zucchini on plates and spoon the corn salsa on top. Drizzle the zucchini puree around the zucchini. Grate some Parmigiano and scatter cheese shavings on top, along with the red currants, if you like, and basil.

ZUCCHINI PUREE

MAKES ABOUT 1$\frac{1}{3}$ CUPS

This is a flavorful and versatile way to use zucchini. Besides the Corn Salsa, I'll stir the puree into Chilled Zucchini Soup (page 116), serve it under Striped Bass with Summer Squash and Pepper Sauce (page 156), and like it alongside Pork Tenderloin and Shell Beans (page 164).

$\frac{1}{2}$ cup tightly packed flat-leaf parsley leaves

$\frac{1}{2}$ cup loosely packed basil leaves

Leaves from 2 sprigs tarragon

6 large mint leaves

1 tablespoon olive oil

$\frac{1}{2}$ cup sliced scallions (white and pale green parts)

1 garlic clove, thinly sliced

1 pound zucchini, halved lengthwise, seeded, and thinly sliced (about 3 cups)

Salt and pepper

1 cup plus 3 tablespoons Vegetable Broth (page 118) or water

3 tablespoons extra-virgin olive oil

Fresh lemon juice

In a large saucepan of boiling salted water blanch the parsley, basil, tarragon, and mint for about 15 seconds. Drain, shock in ice water, and pat dry. (Save the ice bath for the next step.)

In a large skillet, heat the olive oil over medium-low heat. Add the scallions and garlic and cook, stirring often, until softened, about 4 minutes. Increase the heat to medium-high, add the zucchini, season with salt and pepper, and cook, stirring often, for about 2 minutes. Add the 1 cup broth, bring to a simmer, and cook for 2 minutes. Transfer the zucchini mixture to a bowl and set the bowl in the ice bath to cool the mixture, replenishing the ice if needed.

Squeeze the excess water from the blanched herbs. Transfer to a blender, add the zucchini mixture, the remaining 3 tablespoons broth, and the extra-virgin olive oil, and process until smooth. Season with lemon juice, salt, and pepper, then pass through a fine-mesh strainer into a container. The puree will keep, covered, in the refrigerator, for up to 3 days.

A POWERFUL WELCOME

It was eerily reminiscent of the movie The Day the Earth Stood Still; *no power, no phones, waves of people moving through the street, disoriented, needing to get home to loved ones or to find a place of refuge. This was August 2003, just after 4:10 p.m. on a sweltering Thursday. After they realized the scope of the power outage, many of our staff took off in their separate directions; others lingered in the comfort of their place of work, a place of camaraderie, security, and comfort: this was the Tavern, after all. On that Thursday, regulars and friends of the restaurant began to stop by, some to see if there was anything they could do to help, others hoping to find reprieve in a glass of wine. Unfortunately, with no power, we were forced to turn them away. All but Shirley Munyon, that is. Mrs. Munyon, one of the restaurant's faithful longtime guests, was stranded alone at home with no way to contact her husband, Winthrop, who was trapped in his forty-fifth-floor office in Midtown. As dusk began to creep in, with no sign of power being restored, Mrs. Munyon ventured outside with the faint hope of finding solace at her usual table in the front window of the Tavern. A former Gramercy captain encountered her attempting to cross 20th Street at Park Avenue and escorted her to our door.*

Without missing a beat, the staff that was left slipped seamlessly into action, as though this were the standard Munyon Sunday lunch. Terry seated Mrs. Munyon at her regular table, while Ben lit candles and Terry poured her usual sparkling water with ice on the side. Before I knew it, her place was set with silverware, her preferred bread delivered, and a plate of roast chicken that had been destined for our family meal that afternoon was set before her. Only one ingredient was more glaringly absent than a menu or proper lighting or fellow diners—her husband of sixty-two years.

Concerned, and still unable to contact Winthrop, Mrs. Munyon ate her chicken, sipped a glass of wine, and waited. Having known her for years, the staff enjoyed the chance to take care of her. They quickly assembled a plate of cheese, which she nibbled while studying the passing figures on the shadowy sidewalk, eating so very slowly now, hoping that Mr. Munyon would arrive in time for dinner.

Somehow, eventually, Mr. Munyon escaped his office and materialized to join his wife in the candlelit Tavern. She greeted him with a hug that appeared a bit stronger and longer than usual. They resumed their normal places at the front window, and Mrs. Munyon described the dinner menu to her husband: "They have some really nice chicken," she said sweetly. The staff made Mr. Munyon comfortable, brought him a place setting, some of that roast chicken, and a wine list. As I watched Terry at Mr. Munyon's side, in shorts and T-shirt, opened wine list and flashlight in hand, I knew that our corner of the world was clearly in order.

If the Munyons noticed the growing heat in the un-air-conditioned room, the staff's casual attire and festive mood, or any other aspect of this highly unusual Gramercy meal, they didn't let on. In fact, clad in a three-piece suit, with his relieved wife on his right and a fine white Burgundy in his glass, Mr. Munyon seemed as content as if they were enjoying this candlelight repast at their own dining room table. How Mr. Munyon found Mrs. Munyon in the Tavern during the blackout, I still have not discovered. But what I do know is that all of us here on that strange New York evening shared a unique experience, during which the Tavern's customary warm hospitality took on an entirely new glow.

—Kevin Mahan

HEIRLOOM TOMATO TARTS

MAKES SIX 3-INCH TARTS

These tarts are all about celebrating the flavor of tomatoes, both cooked and raw and in their prime. Even the best tomato on its own is not a symphony of flavor; it needs a little help. I like to add ingredients that scream summer, such as husk cherries and gooseberries or even blackberries. All those sweet-and-tart fruits that ripen at the same time amplify the flavor of the tomatoes.

½ recipe Flaky Pie Dough (page 170), made with ⅓ cup lightly packed finely grated Parmigiano cheese and ¼ teaspoon coarsely cracked black pepper added to the flour

All purpose flour, for rolling

1 tablespoon olive oil

1 shallot, minced

1 garlic clove, minced

1 tablespoon sherry vinegar

1 teaspoon balsamic vinegar

8 plum tomatoes, peeled, halved, seeded, and diced

1 sprig thyme

Salt and pepper

3 small heirloom tomatoes, preferably different colors, cut into thin wedges

5 Sun Gold or other small cherry tomatoes, halved

Extra-virgin olive oil

2 tablespoons finely diced Pickled Watermelon Rind (page 135; optional)

A small handful of small basil leaves

12 gooseberries (optional)

4 husk cherries (optional), halved

Preheat the oven to 350°F, with a rack in the middle position. Put six 3-inch tart molds on a baking sheet.

On a floured surface, roll out the dough to about ⅛ inch thick. Cut six circles from the dough. Carefully fit the dough into the molds. Trim the excess dough from the edges. Line each ring with parchment paper and fill with pie weights. Bake until the shells are deep golden brown all over, about 30 minutes. (Note that this time can vary a bit, so start checking a little sooner and don't worry if it takes a little longer.) Remove the paper and weights and allow the tart shells to cool before removing from the molds. (The shells can be baked up to a day ahead, cooled, and stored, covered, at room temperature.)

Make the tomato compote. In a medium saucepan, heat the olive oil over medium-low heat. Add the shallot and garlic and cook until soft, about 4 minutes. Add 1 teaspoon of the sherry vinegar and the balsamic vinegar, scrape the bottom of the pan, and add the plum tomatoes and thyme. Partially cover and gently simmer, stirring occasionally, until all the liquid has evaporated, about an hour. (It's ready when you draw a line through the tomatoes with a wooden spoon and no liquid runs into the line.) Remove the thyme sprig, season the tomato compote with salt and pepper, and let cool to room temperature.

Put the heirloom and Sun Gold tomatoes in a medium bowl and season with extra-virgin olive oil, the remaining 2 teaspoons sherry vinegar, salt, and pepper.

Spread about 2 tablespoons tomato compote in each tart shell. Fill the shells with the raw tomatoes, being careful to drain off the liquid. Top with the pickled watermelon rind, basil, and gooseberries and husk cherries, if you like. Serve immediately (the shells start to get soggy quickly).

JULIETTE POPE

BEVERAGE DIRECTOR • SINCE 1997

I get to taste an incredible range of wines every day. My job is all about sharing my discoveries and passions with the people I work with. Sure, choosing wines that complement Mike's cooking and that fit into the budget is a large part of it, but my pleasure, really my whole existence here, revolves around teaching our staff. Danny set up this restaurant in a uniquely American way, without one sommelier in charge of passing all wine information on to our guests. At GT, our whole team of managers and servers is the sommelier; we all convey an amazing amount of enthusiasm and information to our guests. It is my job to educate the team.

The daily forum for that education is family meal, which happens at 4:30 p.m. before dinner service. We open different wines every day and taste them side by side. We often do blind tastings and ask the staff to give us their impressions of the wines. We talk about where

they fit in the whole list and what would be delicious to eat with them. In addition, I teach wines-by-the-glass classes to new employees, hold full-staff wine training classes monthly, and teach a company-wide wine course.

The funny thing is that when I taste for our list, I can't help but think of which captain is going to love this one or which bartender is going to hate that one. I love knowing the staff this way. My challenge is to get them personally connected with the wine. I don't want them to parrot what I say; I want them to be excited themselves. Because wine is very personal.

I came to this position in a typical GT way, which is to say I did almost every other job before becoming beverage director. I was a banker in a suit in Atlanta when I fell in love with home cooking. Fast-forward to cooking school at Peter Kump's in 1994. My first paid job was as a line cook at Zoë in Soho, where I met my husband, Ralf Kuettel. Next was a line cook job at Union Square Cafe. In December 1997, I landed in garde manger at Gramercy Tavern. I worked my way through every station, ending at the top, nighttime meat roast. Chef Tom Colicchio asked me to eventually replace sous chef Marco Canora, whom he had tapped to open his restaurant Craft. In the meantime, I wanted to do a six-month stint in pastry with Claudia Fleming. That was a huge leap. But I loved it and learned so much from Claudia.

Yet all along, my chef-husband and I were thinking about opening a restaurant. We knew that one of us needed to see the "other side," and it was definitely not going to be him. Luckily for me, GT has always been a place where you can reinvent yourself. I ultimately passed on the sous chef position and decided to start from scratch as a waiter. Typically there is an unfortunate disconnect between the cooks and the diners (though that has changed tremendously at Gramercy Tavern under Mike). Seeing the dishes I used to cook actually hit the table was eye-opening for me.

Within a week of my becoming a waiter, wine-and-service director Paul Grieco lured me into being one of his wine-cellar rats (he clearly knew a sucker when he saw one). I was drawn in deeper and deeper through our daily staff tastings. Paul has a strong, even magnetic, personality. His excitement about wine was infectious. Being a line cook had appealed to one side of me, the side that loves getting down and dirty and loves the adrenaline rush. But I am a geek at heart, and wine appealed to my inner geek.

I continued as a waiter and then captain, working in the cellar all the while. In May 2002, I became a manager, still with a strong interest in beverage. Then Paul left to open Hearth, and Karen King came over from Union Square Cafe to run our program. I was her assistant for a year and a half. When Karen left, GM Kevin Mahan gave me the chance to take over the program and I ran with it, though not without some personal turmoil. Taking the new job meant opting out of the restaurant venture with Ralf. He went on to open Trestle on Tenth in 2006. He is still its chef, wine guy, you name it. I am a partner but not directly involved.

I jumped even deeper into my own wine education— reading a ton, attending off-site industry tastings, digging deeper into the Gramercy cellar, soaking up everything—while also figuring out how to educate the staff. New worlds were opening for me, full of intriguing stories told by intriguing people, visiting winemakers who put their wines in front of me to taste and talk about.

Lucky for me, Gramercy Tavern is a destination restaurant, which means we're also a destination for winemakers with something to sell. We have access to the most amazing wines in the world. So many of the people involved in making these wines are interesting, passionate, and down-to-earth. For me, it's about not just what's in the bottle, but also how it came to be there, in terms of nature and the human beings involved.

I choose wines for our list that are made with care and passion—it's the artisanal side of winemaking that truly interests me. I like wines with stories to tell, especially those from growers working off the beaten path. Some favorites come to mind, such as the wines of the Jura in eastern France, possibly unlovable at first pass but hard to resist as you get to know them; Rieslings, saddled with all kinds of image problems but too glorious to overlook (an addiction inherited from Paul, my mentor); and the wines from our backyard, Long Island and upstate New York, slow to earn wide respect but deserving of our attention. Our list of underdogs could go on and on.

My palate undoubtedly leans toward Old World wines, which is a plus, since Mike's dishes complement these wines: lighter in body, higher in acid, clean and fresh on the palate, but still complex in flavor, and rich with history. New World wines have taken me longer to love. Oregon was easy, California a little tougher. But California wines have become more intriguing to me, especially bottles from the little guys—small-scale winemakers with a real point of view. Take Arnot-Roberts, whose barely red Trousseau is true in style to the grape's Jura roots, though grown in California. Or Kalin, whose unique thirteen-year-old Semillon we pour by the glass. The interesting options are growing every year. I can't wait to share them with you.

Juliette holds regular wine tastings for the staff at dinner family meal (*below left*). For a New York restaurant, Gramercy has a very generous space to store wine properly (*below right*).

STRIPED BASS WITH SUMMER SQUASH AND PEPPER SAUCE

SERVES 4

In the heat of the summer, zucchini and summer squash grows faster than you can cook it. My mom and dad in Ohio complain that they can't keep up with their garden. Because we use the squash raw, that just-picked quality really matters. So get to a farmers' market—or knock on your neighbor's door. Somebody's got to be growing summer squash around here!

2 tablespoons olive oil

¼ cup minced onion

2 garlic cloves, 1 minced, 1 smashed

1½ pounds summer squash, halved lengthwise, seeded, and diced (about 4 cups), plus 16 paper-thin ribbons yellow squash

Fresh lemon juice

Salt and pepper

Four 6-ounce skinless striped bass fillets

2 tablespoons unsalted butter

2 sprigs thyme

⅓ cup Vegetable Broth (page 118) or water

Extra-virgin olive oil

Aleppo pepper

6 large basil leaves, thinly sliced

¾ cup Zucchini Puree (page 148), warmed

¼ cup Pepper Sauce (page 158), at room temperature

In a large skillet, heat 1 tablespoon of the olive oil over medium-low heat. Add the onion and minced garlic and cook until softened, about 4 minutes. Increase the heat to medium-high, add the diced squash, and cook, stirring often, until just tender, about 4 minutes. Season with lemon juice, salt, and pepper and keep warm.

In another large skillet, heat the remaining tablespoon of olive oil over medium-high heat. Season the striped bass with salt and pepper (see page 216). Lay the fillets skinned side down in the pan and cook until lightly golden on the bottom, about 5 minutes. Flip the fillets and cook for 2 minutes more. Add the butter, smashed garlic, thyme, broth, and a splash of lemon juice. Baste the fillets with the pan juices and continue to cook, basting regularly, until just cooked through, 2 to 3 minutes more.

Meanwhile, in a medium bowl, season the squash ribbons with extra-virgin olive oil, lemon juice, Aleppo pepper, salt, and pepper. Add the basil at the last minute. Spoon the zucchini puree onto plates and top with the diced squash and fish. Spread a thin layer of the pepper sauce on each fillet and top with the squash slices.

PEPPER SAUCE

MAKES ABOUT 1¼ CUPS

This sauce tastes as wonderful on grilled meat and vegetables as on the Striped Bass (page 156). I even like it on crackers! The recipe comes from the Spanish family of our executive sous chef Howard Kalachnikoff.

1 red bell pepper, cored, halved, and seeded

1 large tomato, halved and seeded

½ red onion, sliced

3 tablespoons extra-virgin olive oil

Salt and pepper

½ dried ancho chile

½ cup grapeseed oil

2 garlic cloves

½ cup dried bread cubes

¼ cup skinless whole or slivered almonds

½ teaspoon sweet paprika

½ teaspoon pimentón

2 teaspoons red wine vinegar

2 teaspoons sherry vinegar

Preheat the oven to 400°F.

In a small baking pan, toss the bell pepper, tomato, and onion with 1 tablespoon of the olive oil; season with salt and pepper. Spread out in one layer, the pepper and tomato cut side down, and roast until softened and slightly charred, about 45 minutes. Remove from the oven, cover the pan with foil, and let stand for about 10 minutes.

Meanwhile, soak the ancho chile in 1 cup hot water for 10 minutes to soften.

In a small saucepan, heat the grapeseed oil over medium heat. Add the garlic and cook, stirring often, until golden, about 2 minutes. Remove the garlic and set aside, then add the bread cubes to the pan and fry, stirring, until golden and crisp, about 2 minutes. Remove the bread cubes, add the almonds to the pan, and cook, stirring, until lightly toasted, about 2 minutes. Remove from the pan.

Peel the pepper and tomato and put them in a blender with the onion. Drain the ancho chile, reserving the soaking liquid, seed it, and add to the blender, along with the garlic, bread cubes, almonds, sweet paprika, pimentón, red wine and sherry vinegars, and the remaining 2 tablespoons olive oil. Pulse until smooth. The consistency should be spreadable; thin with some of the chile soaking liquid if needed. Season with salt. The pepper sauce will keep for a few days, covered, in the refrigerator; bring to room temperature before serving.

OUR FAMILY MEAL

We use family meal as a way to communicate togetherness. Twice a day the entire restaurant staff stops to share a meal before service. Responsibility for cooking is distributed among the kitchen stations. The staff sits down for lunch at 11 a.m. in the Tavern. For dinner at 4:30 we gather under the vaulted ceilings of the side dining room (*following pages*), around Andrew Millner's drawing, *Shaw's Magnolia*. Simply by relaxing together, we work better together.

MARINATED ARCTIC CHAR AND CUCUMBER BROTH

SERVES 4

Our sous chef Saman Javid (below) plates this dish with skill and poetry. If you make it without all the flowers and flourishes, it will taste just as good. The pleasure lies in the even balance of fish and cucumbers. I like char because it has the same mouthfeel as salmon but far fewer sustainability issues. Persian cucumbers have tiny seeds, complex flavor, and no bitterness.

MARINADE

¼ cup extra-virgin olive oil, plus more for seasoning

2 tablespoons shiro dashi

2 tablespoons fresh lemon juice, plus more for seasoning

1 tablespoon white balsamic vinegar

½ garlic clove, thinly sliced

Salt and pepper

4 baby turnips, peeled and quartered

5 radishes, 4 quartered, 1 sliced paper-thin

1 cup diced cucumbers, plus 2 tablespoons minced cucumber and a 1-inch piece of cucumber, sliced paper-thin

1 large shallot, minced

One ¾-pound skinless Arctic char fillet, cut into dice slightly larger than the cucumbers

A few dill fronds

Make the marinade. In a medium bowl, whisk together the olive oil, 3 tablespoons water, the shiro dashi, lemon juice, vinegar, garlic, and a pinch each of salt and pepper.

In a small saucepan of boiling salted water, blanch the turnips for 1 minute, then add the quartered radishes and blanch for just 1 minute. Both the turnips and radishes should still be crisp. Drain and shock in ice water. Drain again and add to the marinade, along with the diced and minced cucumbers and the shallot. Toss and then marinate for 4 minutes.

Lightly season the char with salt. Add to the vegetables, gently toss, and marinate for a minute more. Meanwhile, in a small bowl, season the sliced radishes and cucumbers with olive oil, lemon juice, salt, and pepper. Divide the char, vegetables, and marinade among shallow bowls. Scatter the raw radishes and cucumbers over them and top with the dill. Serve immediately.

PORK TENDERLOIN AND SHELL BEANS

SERVES 4

Pork tenderloin is wonderful in summertime because it cooks quickly and doesn't take me away from the beach and the kids. It's a light, lean cut that still delivers delicious flavor. The moistness in this recipe comes from the zucchini and soft beans. At the restaurant, we prepare tenderloin cut from whole Berkshire pigs on the Tavern grill in summer.

6 tablespoons olive oil

⅓ cup fresh lemon juice

1 heaping teaspoon mild curry powder

4 garlic cloves, 3 smashed, 1 minced

One 1-inch piece of ginger, smashed

1 sprig rosemary

1 large pork tenderloin (about 1¼ pounds)

Salt and pepper

1 onion, minced

1 cup finely diced zucchini

1 cup finely diced yellow squash

1½ cups cooked pinto beans (see page 129)

1½ cups peeled fava or lima beans

About 3 cups Vegetable Broth (page 118) or bean liquid plus water

1 tablespoon Garlic Puree (page 231; optional)

2 tablespoons unsalted butter

2 tablespoons finely chopped flat-leaf parsley

Extra-virgin olive oil

Sea salt

In a medium bowl, combine ¼ cup of the olive oil, the lemon juice, curry powder, smashed garlic cloves, ginger, and rosemary. Add the tenderloin, turn to coat with the marinade, and marinate at room temperature for an hour, turning occasionally.

Preheat a charcoal or gas grill to medium heat.

Remove the pork from the marinade and season with salt and pepper. Grill, turning occasionally, for about 10 minutes—good pork is best cooked medium-rare. Transfer the pork to a cutting board and let rest for 10 minutes.

Meanwhile, in a medium saucepan, heat the remaining 2 tablespoons olive oil over medium-low heat. Add the onion and minced garlic and cook, stirring occasionally, until the onion is softened, about 6 minutes. Add the zucchini, yellow squash, pinto and fava beans, and enough broth just to cover, and then season with salt and pepper. Bring to a simmer, stirring occasionally. The mixture should be loose but not soupy. Add the garlic puree, if using, butter, and parsley. Season with salt and pepper.

Cut the pork into very thin slices. Spoon the bean mixture onto plates and drizzle with extra-virgin olive oil. Top with the sliced pork and sprinkle with sea salt.

GOOD PORK MAKES COMMON SENSE

Raising, buying, cooking, and eating higher-quality meat is crucial for every part of the food chain. As an enthusiastic and engaged eater, parent, and chef, I am pleased that many Americans are now demanding to know more about where their food comes from. Part of this involves learning the actual names of the foods we eat. Berkshire pork, for example, is just one of many breeds of pig that deserves our attention. It's very good eating, but don't get caught up on labels or in the race to find the next hot breed of pig. What I'm more interested in is participating in developing the most authentic and flavorful ingredients we can find, raised by people we know. It takes an excellent small farmer to raise good pork. The visionary writer Wendell Berry tells us that animals are a necessity on such farms because they complete the natural cycle of farming. We know for sure that without a diversity of healthy animals, there would be no healthy vegetables.

Like winemakers, some pork producers believe that single varietals—i.e., a pure breed—are the best expression of a place. Other producers feel that biodiversity and blending are key to long-term health and distinctive flavor. As a chef, I have preferences, but I do not need to take sides—I'm interested in all of it, restlessly in search of excellence. I just want to encourage you to participate in the amazing evolution of the quality of the food we eat. You can vote with your pork! It's simple—buy pork only from a small producer you know and trust.

Cooks come to Gramercy to learn. They walk in with a natural curiosity and a strong dedication to the craft of cooking. **CLOCKWISE FROM ABOVE:** Margot Protzel, Geoff Lazlo, Duncan Grant, and Louis Bayla.

PEACH PIE WITH PECAN CRUMBLE AND SWEET CREAM ICE CREAM

MAKES ONE 9-INCH PIE

This is the ultimate crumble-top peach pie, and it's a bestseller for the few weeks a year it's on the menu. In order to ensure a properly cooked bottom crust, the shell is first blind-baked and then the filled pie is baked on the oven's lowest rack. I love it with Sweet Cream Ice Cream, but it's perfect on its own.

½ recipe Flaky Pie Dough (page 170)

All-purpose flour for rolling

PECAN CRUMBLE

½ cup all-purpose flour

¼ cup packed dark brown sugar

Scant ½ teaspoon salt

5 tablespoons unsalted butter, cubed and chilled

½ cup pecan pieces

¼ cup cornstarch

⅓ cup sugar

¼ teaspoon salt

2½ pounds ripe peaches (about 7 medium), halved, pitted, and cut into thin slices

Grated zest of 1 lemon

2 tablespoons fresh lemon juice

Sweet Cream Ice Cream (page 173; optional)

Preheat the oven to 375°F, with racks in the bottom and center positions.

On a floured surface, roll out the dough. Fit it into a 9-inch pie dish, trim any excess dough, and crimp the edges. Line the pie shell with parchment paper and fill with pie weights. Bake on the center oven rack for 30 minutes. Remove the paper and weights and bake until the crust is evenly browned and cooked all the way through, about 10 minutes more. Let cool.

Make the pecan crumble. In a food processor, pulse the flour, brown sugar, and salt until combined. Add the butter and pulse just until a crumbly mixture forms. Transfer to a medium bowl and gently mix in the pecans.

Make the filling. In a large bowl, stir together the cornstarch, sugar, and salt. Add half of the peaches, the zest, and lemon juice. Thoroughly combine, then lightly mash the fruit with the end of a sturdy whisk just until their juices moisten the dry ingredients. Add the remaining peaches and stir until well combined.

Pour the filling into the crust and top evenly with the pecan crumble. Put the pie on a baking sheet (the juices will bubble up) on the bottom oven rack and bake until the topping is dark brown and the juices are bubbling furiously, 60 to 70 minutes. Serve the pie with the ice cream, if you like.

FLAKY PIE DOUGH

MAKES ENOUGH FOR ONE 9-INCH DOUBLE-CRUST PIE
OR TWELVE 3-INCH TARTS

Nancy Olson makes the flakiest pie crust you've ever tasted! She is a master of the fine points of baking. For instance, she's found that freezing the flour overnight is a secret to a more delicate crust. And, sure, you can make the dough in a food processor, but Nancy thinks it turns out flakier by hand.

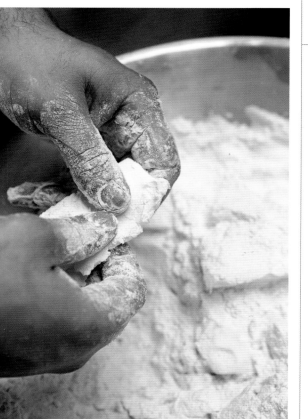

3 cups all-purpose flour, plus more for rolling

1 teaspoon salt

10 tablespoons (1¼ sticks) unsalted butter, cut into small cubes and chilled

½ cup plus 2 tablespoons vegetable shortening, chilled

Up to 1 cup ice water

In a large bowl, stir together the flour and salt. Add the butter and toss to coat with the flour, then flatten the bits of butter between your fingertips. Add the vegetable shortening, toss to coat with the flour mixture, and then flatten into pieces a little bigger than the butter. (Using just the tips of your fingers helps produce a flaky crust.) Sprinkle ¾ cup of the ice water over the flour mixture and gently toss to incorporate. Use a rubber spatula to push the dry flour into the liquid, but do not stir the mixture. This gentle process of "hydrating" the flour without stirring makes all the difference. If the mixture is too dry and won't come together when you gently squeeze a handful, sprinkle with another tablespoon of water and toss again. Continue the process until the dough just holds together, adding as little water and handling the dough as little as possible. Some dry patches and crumbs are okay—they will moisten as the dough rests.

Divide the dough into 2 balls, flatten into disks, and wrap well in plastic. Refrigerate for at least 2 hours, or overnight. The dough can be frozen for up to a month; thaw overnight in the refrigerator.

SWEET CREAM ICE CREAM

MAKES ABOUT 1½ QUARTS

As with all the ice creams (and sherbets) in this book, the ice cream base should be chilled overnight for the smoothest result. Cold ingredients take less time to freeze, reducing the risk of overchurning. This is a great ice cream on its own, but we also use it as the base for many flavor variations, including Fresh Mint Ice Cream (page 109).

1 quart whole milk

2 cups heavy cream

1½ cups sugar

¼ cup cornstarch

1½ teaspoons vanilla extract

In a medium saucepan, combine 3½ cups of the milk, the cream, and 1¼ cups of the sugar and bring to a boil over medium heat, stirring until the sugar dissolves. Meanwhile, in a small bowl, whisk together the remaining ¼ cup sugar and the cornstarch, then whisk in the remaining ½ cup milk.

When the milk mixture comes to a boil, remove it from the heat and carefully ladle about a cup of the hot liquid into the cornstarch mixture in a steady stream, whisking constantly. Pour the contents of the bowl back into the saucepan and bring to a boil, whisking constantly; be sure to get into the edges of the pan to keep the mixture from sticking or burning. Boil for a full minute, whisking constantly, then remove from the heat and stir in the vanilla. Pass through a fine-mesh strainer into a large bowl. Let cool. Cover the ice cream base and refrigerate until thoroughly chilled, or preferably overnight for the creamiest results.

Pour the base into an ice cream maker and freeze according to the manufacturer's directions. Transfer the ice cream to a freezer container, cover, and freeze until firm enough to scoop.

LEMON VERBENA GRANITE WITH BLUEBERRY SORBET

SERVES 8

This dessert may look plain, but the flavors absolutely pop. The granité is wonderful on its own or over a handful of raspberries. If lemon verbena is hard to find, substitute fresh lemon balm or lemon thyme.

Many granité recipes require you to scrape the mixture regularly as it freezes, but this one just needs to be scraped once, when it's fully frozen. If the mixture has frozen too solid, just set it on the counter for about 5 minutes before you scrape it.

A very large handful of lemon verbena leaves

⅔ cup sugar

3 tablespoons fresh lemon juice

4 nectarines, halved, pitted, and cut into wedges (optional)

4 scoops Blueberry Sorbet (opposite)

Gently tear the lemon verbena leaves to help release their scent. In a medium saucepan, combine the verbena, 4 cups water, the sugar, and lemon juice and bring just to a boil over high heat, stirring until the sugar dissolves. Remove from the heat and let the herbs infuse for 30 minutes.

Pass the mixture through a fine-mesh strainer into a 9-by-13-inch nonreactive baking pan; discard the herbs. Let cool and then freeze until firm, about 5 hours, or overnight.

Remove the pan from the freezer and scrape the mixture with the tines of a fork, crushing any lumps. If not using immediately, cover the pan with plastic wrap and refreeze, then scrape again before serving. (The granité keeps, tightly covered, in the freezer for a few days.) To serve, divide the nectarines, if using, among bowls. Top with a scoop of blueberry sorbet, followed by a generous mound of granité.

BLUEBERRY SORBET

MAKES ABOUT 1½ QUARTS

3½ cups blueberries

1½ cups sugar

½ cup fresh lemon juice

In a medium saucepan, combine the blueberries, 3¼ cups water, the sugar, and lemon juice and bring to a boil over high heat, stirring until the sugar is dissolved. Remove from the heat as soon as the mixture comes to a boil, transfer to a large bowl, and let cool. Cover the sorbet base and refrigerate until completely chilled, or overnight.

Process the sorbet base in batches in a blender until smooth. Pass through a fine-mesh strainer, pour into an ice cream maker, and freeze according to the manufacturer's directions. Transfer the sorbet to a freezer container, cover, and freeze until firm enough to scoop.

BLACKBERRY LIME SHERBET

MAKES ABOUT 1 QUART

Sherbet is simply sorbet made with milk, but this recipe takes sherbet to a whole new level when the acidity of lime and the fruitiness of blackberries meet mellow milk and cream.

2¼ cups whole milk

¾ cup plus 2 tablespoons sugar

¾ cup heavy cream

⅓ cup light corn syrup

Grated zest of 2 limes

2 tablespoons cornstarch

1 cup blackberries

½ cup fresh lime juice

In a medium saucepan, combine 2 cups of the milk, ¾ cup of the sugar, the cream, corn syrup, and lime zest and bring to a boil over medium heat, stirring until the sugar dissolves. Meanwhile, in a small bowl, whisk together the remaining 2 tablespoons sugar and the cornstarch. Whisk in the remaining ¼ cup milk.

When the milk mixture comes to a boil, remove it from the heat and slowly whisk about a cup of the hot liquid into the cornstarch mixture in a steady stream, whisking constantly, to temper it. Pour the contents of the bowl back into the saucepan and bring to a boil over medium heat, whisking constantly; be sure to get into the edges of the pan to keep the mixture from sticking or burning. Boil for a full minute, whisking constantly, then transfer the sherbet base to a large bowl and let cool.

Cover the sherbet base and refrigerate until thoroughly chilled, or preferably overnight.

Process the blackberries in a blender until smooth. Pass through a fine-mesh strainer into a bowl and measure out ¼ cup of puree.

Stir the blackberry puree and lime juice into the sherbet base. Pour into an ice cream maker and freeze according to the manufacturer's directions. Transfer the sherbet to a freezer container, cover, and freeze until firm enough to scoop.

BLUEBERRY-SWEET CORN ICE CREAM SUNDAE

SERVES 8

This dessert has a special place in our hearts—it is the first one that Nancy put on the menu in August 2006, when she became the pastry chef. In fact, she made it for Kevin Mahan, Gramercy's managing partner, for the tasting portion of her job interview. Served accompanied by small corn bread muffins, it's been on our late-summer menu ever since. Don't be put off by the length of the recipe: everything but the black pepper whipped cream can be made at least a day ahead.

2½ cups blueberries

6 tablespoons sugar

1 cup corn kernels (from about 2 ears)

4 tablespoons (½ stick) unsalted butter

2 tablespoons popcorn kernels

1 teaspoon canola oil

⅓ cup sugar

2 tablespoons light corn syrup

¼ teaspoon vanilla extract

⅛ teaspoon salt

½ cup heavy cream

2 teaspoons confectioners' sugar

⅛ teaspoon freshly ground black pepper

Sweet Corn Ice Cream (page 180)

Make the blueberry compote. In a small saucepan, combine 1½ cups of the blueberries and the sugar, and cook over medium-high heat, stirring constantly and pressing on the berries with a heatproof spatula, until the berries pop and the mixture begins to look syrupy. Stir in the corn kernels, remove from the heat, and stir in the remaining 1 cup blueberries. Transfer to a container and let cool, then cover and refrigerate the compote until completely chilled.

Lightly coat a large heatproof bowl and a baking sheet with 1 tablespoon of the butter. Pop the popcorn kernels, using the canola oil, and put in the buttered bowl.

In a small saucepan, combine the remaining 3 tablespoons butter, the sugar, and corn syrup and heat over low heat, stirring occasionally with a heatproof spatula, until the butter melts. Increase the heat to medium and cook, stirring constantly, until the toffee is about the color of Cracker Jacks. (The toffee will darken a bit after you remove it from the heat.) Remove from the heat and stir in the vanilla and salt—the toffee will sputter, so be careful.

Immediately pour the toffee over the popcorn and stir quickly to coat the popcorn before the toffee hardens. Turn the coated popcorn onto the buttered baking sheet and use two wooden spoons to quickly separate the popcorn. (Once cooled, the toffee popcorn can be stored, covered, for up to a week—assuming no one devours it first.)

Just before you're ready to serve the sundaes, make the whipped cream. In a large bowl, whip the cream with the confectioners' sugar and pepper until soft peaks form.

Put a few pieces of toffee popcorn in each parfait glass. Top with 2 small scoops of the ice cream and 2 spoonfuls of the blueberry compote. Add a large handful of popcorn, another small scoop of ice cream, and another spoonful of compote. Top each sundae with a dollop of the whipped cream.

SWEET CORN ICE CREAM

MAKES ABOUT 1½ QUARTS

Using the sweetest corn and letting the ice cream base infuse and chill overnight creates the most flavorful ice cream.

6 medium ears corn, kernels removed, cobs trimmed and reserved

1 quart whole milk

2 cups heavy cream

6 tablespoons light corn syrup

1 cup plus 2 tablespoons sugar

1 vanilla bean, split lengthwise

12 large egg yolks

1½ teaspoons vanilla extract

½ teaspoon salt

In a large pot, combine the corn kernels, 3½ cups of the milk, the cream, corn syrup, and sugar. With the tip of a paring knife, scrape the seeds from the vanilla bean into the pan, then add the bean and corncobs. Bring the mixture just to a boil, stirring until the sugar dissolves. Remove from the heat and remove and discard the corncobs and the vanilla bean.

In a medium bowl, whisk together the remaining ½ cup milk and the egg yolks. Slowly whisk 2 cups of the hot milk mixture into the yolk mixture to temper it, then pour the contents of the bowl back into the saucepan. Cook over medium-low heat, stirring constantly with a wooden spoon until the custard thickens enough to hold a line drawn with a finger down the back of the spoon, 3 to 5 minutes.

Remove from the heat and stir in the vanilla and salt, then pour the ice cream base into a large bowl, set it in an ice bath, and let cool, stirring occasionally.

Process the ice cream base in batches in a blender until smooth and creamy, then pass through a fine-mesh strainer into a large bowl. Cover and refrigerate until thoroughly chilled, or preferably overnight.

Pour the base into an ice cream maker and freeze according to the manufacturer's directions. Transfer to a freezer container, cover, and freeze until firm enough to scoop.

ROASTED ALMOND PANNA COTTA
WITH CHERRIES

SERVES 8

Cherries and almonds taste wonderful together: here the roasted almonds go well with the cream and the refreshing cherries balance the whole dessert. We make and serve this panna cotta in 4-ounce jam jars, but it's also lovely in a single big bowl.

1 cup skin-on whole raw almonds

One ¼-ounce packet (about ¾ tablespoon) unflavored gelatin

2 cups whole milk

1 cup heavy cream

½ cup sugar

1½ cups cherries, halved lengthwise and pitted

Leaves from 1 sprig lemon thyme, chopped

Almond oil (optional)

Preheat the oven to 350°F, with a rack in the middle position.

In a food processor, pulse ½ cup of the almonds a few times until they are pebbly. Spread them out on a small baking sheet and toast in the oven until deep golden brown, about 20 minutes. At the same time, toast the remaining ½ cup almonds on another small baking sheet until fragrant, 10 to 15 minutes.

Meanwhile, in a small bowl, sprinkle the gelatin over ¼ cup of the milk.

In a medium saucepan, combine the pebbly almonds, the remaining 1¾ cups milk, the cream, and sugar and bring to a boil, stirring until the sugar is dissolved. Remove from the heat, stir in the gelatin mixture, and let steep for 30 minutes.

Process the milk mixture in a blender until smooth, then pass through a fine-mesh strainer into a large bowl. Set the bowl in an ice bath and gently stir the mixture until it's cool. (You may be tempted to skip this step, but cooling the mixture before pouring it into the molds yields fewer air bubbles and a smoother texture and reduces the risk that the milk and cream will separate.) Pour the mixture into eight 4-ounce containers. Cover with plastic wrap and refrigerate until set, 3 to 4 hours. (The panna cotta can be refrigerated for up to 2 days.)

Cut the toasted whole almonds crosswise in half. Combine them with the cherries and thyme in a small bowl, and dress with almond oil, if you like. Top the panna cottas with the cherry mixture and serve.

AUTUMN

RED KURI SQUASH SOUP WITH BRUSSELS SPROUTS AND APPLES

SERVES 6

I love the heirloom squash called kuri for its vivid color and dense texture. Other heirlooms—like Cinderella (rouge vif d'Etampes), kabocha, and cheese pumpkin—have distinctive names and distinctive flavors, too. Each makes a wonderful soup.

1 bay leaf

1 sprig thyme

2 cloves

1 teaspoon coriander seeds

3 tablespoons olive oil

2 medium leeks (white parts), halved lengthwise and thinly sliced

5 shallots, thinly sliced

1 garlic clove, minced

6 cups peeled, seeded, and cubed red kuri squash, plus 1/2 cup finely diced

2 medium carrots, sliced

Salt and pepper

1/2 cup orange juice

6 cups Vegetable Broth (page 118) or water

1/8 teaspoon ground allspice

1/8 teaspoon ground cinnamon

3 1/2 tablespoons unsalted butter

1 tablespoon honey

Fresh lemon juice

Large leaves from 6 Brussels sprouts

1/2 cup peeled, cored, and finely diced sweet firm apple, such as Honeycrisp, tossed with a little lemon juice

Tie up the bay leaf, thyme, cloves, and coriander in a piece of cheesecloth to make a sachet.

In a large pot, heat 2 tablespoons of the oil over medium-low heat. Add the leeks, shallots, and garlic and cook, stirring occasionally, until the leeks are softened, 5 to 7 minutes. Add the cubed squash and carrots, season with salt and pepper, and cook, stirring, for a few minutes.

Increase the heat to high, add the orange juice, and simmer until reduced by half. Add the broth, allspice, cinnamon, and sachet, bring to a simmer, and cook until the squash and carrots are very tender, about 35 minutes. Remove from the heat.

In a small saucepan, cook 3 tablespoons of the butter over medium heat until it melts and the milk solids turn golden brown, about 2 minutes. Stir the browned butter into the soup, along with the honey.

Discard the sachet and set aside 1 1/2 cups of the soup broth. Process the remaining soup in batches in a blender until very smooth and creamy, then pass through a fine-mesh strainer back into the pot. Thin the soup as needed with the reserved liquid; I prefer a thin consistency. Season with salt, pepper, and lemon juice, cover, and keep hot.

In a very small saucepan, cover the finely diced squash with an inch of water, bring to a simmer, and cook until just tender, about 3 minutes. Drain the squash, toss with the remaining 1/2 tablespoon butter, and season with salt.

Meanwhile, in a small skillet, heat the remaining 1 tablespoon oil over medium-high heat, then add the Brussels sprout leaves and toss for a minute. Add a splash of water and continue to cook for 1 to 2 minutes. Drain and season with salt.

Ladle the soup into bowls, then top with the diced squash, apples, and Brussels sprout leaves.

SMOKED TOMATO SOUP

SERVES 6

While we associate tomatoes with summer, their season in the Northeast extends through the end of September and even into October. As their sweetness begins to fade, we search for ways to add flavor to them, and smoking is a wonderful way to do that—a few minutes on a backyard grill or in a stovetop smoker is all it takes.

4½ pounds beefsteak tomatoes (about 7), cored and quartered

¼ cup olive oil, plus more for seasoning

Salt and pepper

1½ cups thinly sliced fennel

1 cup thinly sliced onion

1 cup thinly sliced shallots

4 garlic cloves, smashed

1 scant teaspoon pimentón

2 tablespoons sherry vinegar

2 tablespoons white balsamic vinegar

¼ cup white wine

1 sprig thyme

1 sprig rosemary

2 tablespoons unsalted butter

3 sprigs basil, plus 20 small leaves

¼ cup diced Pickled Swiss Chard Stems (page 188)

1 cup applewood chips

Prepare a stovetop smoker or an outdoor grill for smoking with the applewood chips; maintain a temperature of about 140°F.

In a large bowl, season the tomatoes with oil, salt, and pepper. When the wood chips are mostly gray, put the tomatoes skin side down on the grate (over indirect heat if using an outdoor grill) and smoke for 10 minutes. Transfer the tomatoes to a platter.

In a large pot, heat the ¼ cup oil over medium heat. Add the fennel, onion, shallots, and garlic and cook, stirring often, until softened, about 10 minutes. Add the pimentón and stir for a few seconds, then add the sherry and balsamic vinegars and simmer until they are almost gone. Add the wine and simmer until it is almost gone. Add the smoked tomatoes, with their juices, the thyme, rosemary, and butter, cover the pot, and simmer, stirring often and breaking up the tomatoes with a wooden spoon, until the tomatoes are cooked down and the vegetables are completely soft, about 30 minutes. Add the basil sprigs and simmer for 5 minutes more.

Discard the thyme, rosemary, and basil. Process the soup in a blender in batches until smooth, then pass through a fine-mesh strainer. Season with salt and pepper. Serve the soup topped with the pickled Swiss chard stems and basil leaves.

PICKLED SWISS CHARD STEMS

MAKES ABOUT 1 PINT

Stems from 3 bunches Swiss chard,
cut into thin pieces (about 1½ cups)

¾ cup rice vinegar

¼ cup water

¼ cup sugar

1 tablespoon kosher salt

1 small beet, peeled and quartered

While the leafy part of Swiss chard is easy to use by cooking it just like
spinach, the stems perplex most cooks. When young, Swiss chard stems are
not yet very fibrous, but as they get longer and thicker (as below), they require
peeling before cooking. Try sautéing the stems with a clove of garlic and olive
oil. Another great way to use every bit of this amazing plant is to pickle the
stems. This pickle has a vibrant color and adds a great pop of acidity to soups,
salads, and vegetable dishes.

Follow the Basic Pickling Recipe (page 86), substituting these ingredients.
Remove the beet (which gives a lovely color to the pickles) before transferring
the pickles to a container. Because the stems are cut so thin, these pickles are
ready after about an hour in the refrigerator.

PETER BENTEL

BENTEL & BENTEL ARCHITECTS •
SINCE 1993

When we got the call from Danny Meyer to do some work on Union Square Cafe, my first thought was, "We went to a very nice graduate school of architecture. We don't do restaurants!" Twenty-some years ago, restaurants seemed insubstantial to us in design terms. Pure theater. But of course we were just being high-culture idiots. Our parents, Maria and Fred Bentel, started our firm, and my mother, ever the optimist, said, "Wait! This could be interesting." In fact, it went further. It was Whitmanesque, in the sense that anything can contain multitudes. Well, it did. We met Danny and were impressed with his commitment to hospitality. He wanted us to think about making the guest experience better through design. Union Square turned out to be just a minor renovation, but it was our baptism by waitstation.

In 1993, Danny told us about his inspiration from the country trattorias of Italy for what would become Gramercy Tavern. My brother, Paul, and I had deep roots there—we had carved marble for a year in Pietrasanta, in northern Tuscany. Danny also spoke about bed-and-breakfasts in Bucks County and taverns in New England and a three-star restaurant in Paris. Even a nonrestaurant, the Pantheon, was on his list! After graduate school, Paul; his wife, Carol; and I went to MIT to study architectural history and theory (along with my wife, Susan; we all practice together). It was the heyday of postmodernism, which is to say "historicism." Needless to say, research is part of the culture of our office. So we looked at the basket of fruit (and nuts) Danny had presented us and said, "No problem. We'll just tease out all of these threads and discover the common link!"

Susan and I followed Danny's list of favorite restaurants on our honeymoon in Italy: Cibrèo in Florence, Antica Osteria del Ponte outside

As were their parents, Frederick and Maria, before them, the architect brothers Paul *(far left)* and Peter are partners with their wives in Bentel & Bentel. Susan Nagle Bentel *(center)* is an interior designer and Peter's wife. Carol Rusche Bentel *(near right)* is an architect.

Milan, Dodici Apostoli in Verona. And we discovered that all the places he liked had dining rooms with no corridors between them; they shared the cellular idea of passing from one room to another. We learned by pacing the rooms that they were of similar size: about twenty feet wide and forty feet long, allowing for deuces or 4-tops against the walls, with tables for 4, 6, or 8 in the center. We were young architects, and we didn't go to a lot of high-end restaurants, but we began to see how hospitality can be characterized by furniture. (And we learned that those Italian dining rooms were never much wider than twenty feet because the beams were made from chestnut trees that only grow that high!)

Our practice had been devoted to public spaces: university libraries, religious buildings, community spaces where people gathered and socialized. Well, we thought, a tavern is a community, too. So this is not a stretch at all. And, suddenly, in the office, it was OMG!: restaurant design is a rich, completely unmined vein running through the architecture mountain that none of our friends are onto. Danny wanted the Tavern to be a long-term commitment, an institution, and it was incredibly exciting to see how a restaurant could play that role in the community. Some people may use a restaurant as a way to forget about life, but we liked Danny's idea that the Tavern would be an extension of life. We were intrigued with the way a restaurant can function as a cultural institution, in the highest sense of the word.

We researched taverns in New England, and we visited classic 1600s saltbox houses with central fireplaces, which gave us the idea of a working hearth in the dining room where cooking could happen. In the GT space on 20th Street, we demolished interior walls and wound up with a wide-open space, about eighty feet square. The space was crazy good—very unlike typical New York restaurants, which are usually long and narrow with no natural light.

Scale is crucial at Gramercy Tavern. You enter the vestibule and gaze up at those high ceilings through a chandelier that gets the candles way the heck out there on the thinnest branches of wrought iron. There's a Yankee frugality to it. That entryway has an exalted

feeling (if that's not an overblown term); light goes clear up to the ceiling. Those big windows, part of the existing facade, make the restaurant part of the street. Above the clear-glass windows there are two sets of prismatic glass, which were originally used to literally bend light into the farthest corners of dark rooms.

So we kept the entry ceiling high, then dropped it by the maître d' desk and along the corridor. What we wanted was a sense of compression and then release into the Tavern and back to the dining rooms. That hallway, where the Tavern table sits, has a wall on one side only and really functions like a porch. It looks in on the Tavern in the same way a porch relates to the street— the lowered ceiling leads to the quiet boisterousness of the Tavern, with its

The big window in Gramercy's vestibule makes the restaurant part of the street. The clear prismatic glass squares on top were part of the original building, used to illuminate once dark interiors. The grillwork on archways, reminiscent of the old Italian restaurants Danny loves, provides transitions (opposite).

THE FLOOR PLAN

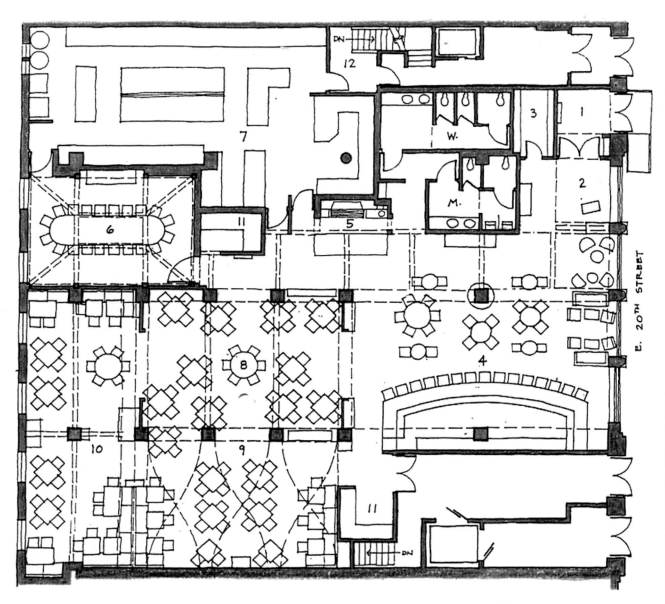

GRAMERCY TAVERN - PLAN KEY

1. Entry Vestibule
2. Maître d'/Greeting
3. Coat closet
4. Tavern/Bar
5. Rotisserie/Exhibition Cooking
6. Private Dining Room
7. Kitchen
8. First Dining Room
9. Second Dining Room
10. Third Dining Room
11. Waiter stations
12. Stair down to basement

ABOVE: You probably would not guess that the restaurant is roughly 80 feet square, so deftly is it divided into welcoming rooms. The long entry hallway, with its lowered ceiling, functions as a kind of "porch." Guests passing through can peek in at the bustling activity in the Tavern and dining rooms.

OPPOSITE: The architects wanted the walls to age with grace. Susan Bentel prototyped dozens of solutions before settling on plaster burnished with beeswax, which, over time, would acquire a unique luster.

fifteen-foot ceilings. Just as at home, you can peek into the rooms, see what other family members are doing. The porch is a transition space that lets you gather your thoughts and then move on to the bar or to your table.

Danny's idea was that, unlike the hierarchy of great old restaurants, where if you were nobody, you'd have the table back by the kitchen, here every seat would be a winner. He wanted Gramercy Tavern to be egalitarian. But the problem with egalitarianism is that it can get boring because it is *all the same!* We didn't want that. So we built small rooms like those in the Italian restaurants and Early American inns, where rooms are narrow as a way to anchor people. And look up the next time you go to Gramercy—the ceiling in each dining room is totally different.

When you design institutions, you must choose materials that will age with grace: like the light fixtures of copper that will oxidize. Sometimes the right material is the oldest one, such as the chestnut beams in the old trattorias. Sometimes you can't get that, so what would you use instead? The Parson Capen house in Topsfield, Massachusetts, built in the late 1600s, has its original oak floors and they still look great. Cheap pine would look good, but it is too soft, so we knew we needed quarter-sawn oak. And it had to be red oak. Gramercy's floors are not polyurethaned; they're just polished regularly and waxed twice a year. That space benefits mightily from the reverent treatment by the staff.

The walls had to age with grace, too. Susan did lots of research and we made prototypes, getting in tons of samples that we winnowed down to a set of materials that are basic and true and resonate with the idea of a tavern. Some fifty samples later, we found the plaster for the walls. And then the beeswax finish. First we tried carnauba car wax, but we felt confident that the plaster walls, after years of burnishing with beeswax, would acquire the kind of luster that you just cannot fabricate.

A word about nostalgia. As effective a driver of character development in architecture as it might be, we said, "*Forget it!* We do not want this place to be *nostalgic.*" It had to be of its time and place, because ultimately nostalgia is just a way to dismiss contemporary life

and its vagaries. Danny always spoke about a tavern as a contemporary social setting where politics were discussed. You could argue that the Declaration of Independence was written in a tavern. It was not as if people in taverns just wanted to get drunk and forget about life out there.

By the time we dove into Gramercy Tavern, we were totally convinced about the worthiness of restaurant design. And look what it has wrought! We did Eleven Madison Park, and Tabla, The Modern and Café 2 at MoMA, Blue Smoke, North End Grill, and the renovation of Le Bernardin. We get calls every five minutes to do restaurants. After Gramercy Tavern, we could have said that's it, we're done. But we saw promise because we had developed a think-tank studio mentality that sees restaurants as cultural institutions. Now with every space we walk into—a phone booth, a broom closet, or a basement—we say to each other, "Hey, this could make a great restaurant."

MARINATED BLACK SEA BASS
WITH PICKLED AJI DULCE PEPPERS

SERVES 4

This recipe is in the style of Japanese sashimi, where the fish cures lightly on the plate as it comes in contact with lime juice and vinegar. This dish tastes best when the bass is thinly sliced, but don't worry about making perfect cuts—it can be even better if it shreds, picking up more of the marinade. Ají dulce is an excellent pepper that's harvested in the fall; I like it because it's very aromatic, not too spicy, and makes a wonderful pickle.

2 tablespoons extra-virgin olive oil

1 tablespoon fresh lime juice

½ tablespoon white balsamic vinegar

One ¾-pound skinless sushi-quality black sea bass fillet, thinly sliced

Aleppo pepper

Sea salt

3 Pickled Ají Dulce Peppers (opposite), halved lengthwise, seeded, and very thinly sliced

Greens from 1 scallion, julienned

6 Sun Gold or other small cherry tomatoes, halved

In a small bowl, combine the oil, lime juice, and vinegar. Lay the fish slices on plates and then spoon the marinade over them. Sprinkle with a little Aleppo pepper and sea salt and top with the pickled peppers, scallion greens, and tomatoes.

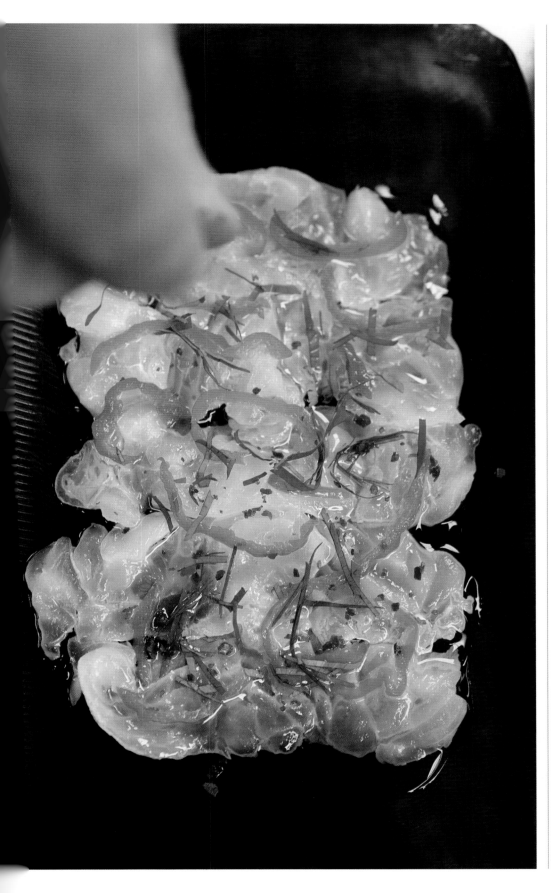

PICKLED AJI DULCE PEPPERS

MAKES ABOUT 1 PINT

Every pepper has its own unique aroma and heat. This preparation will enhance those qualities, whether the pepper is mild, like ají dulce, or rippingly hot, like a jalapeño. The pickle will have the same character as the pepper it's made from.

Follow the Basic Pickling Recipe (page 86), substituting these ingredients.

2 cups ají dulce or other small red peppers, stemmed

3/4 cup rice vinegar

1/4 cup water

1/4 cup sugar

1 tablespoon kosher salt

ROBERT KUSHNER

ARTIST, *CORNUCOPIA*, THE TAVERN MURAL • SINCE 1993

My studio is right next to Union Square Cafe, and I was sitting at the bar eating lunch sometime in 1986 or '87 when I first met Danny Meyer, who was then maître d'. He visited my studio and said, "Your work is far better than what's at the restaurant," and then he bought a piece. A few years later, he approached me: "I know you are a serious painter and your work is collected in the best museums, but would you consider doing something for the new restaurant we're planning. Something bold?" From seeing my work, Danny assumed I'd choose flowers. But I wanted to do food—vegetables and fruit. Art and food go very well together: I thought of Sandro Chia's mural at the old Palio in Midtown, of the Kronenhalle in Zurich, of Matisse's Still Life with Oysters.

The commission came at a remarkably good time. I was about to sell my house upstate, and I really needed something to throw myself into. Danny gave me the guidelines: this would be a country inn that had been in the family for several generations, transported to New York City. I came up with the idea to use colors that would have been used in colonial America. The project was huge: twenty canvases, each five feet square. It was so big that just one wall of the painting took up a wall and a half of my studio.

I began sketching to guide myself. It was summer. I drew vegetables from my garden. I wanted things that could grow in this region, but a little off: a persimmon, black radishes. I only work from life: I need to draw the thing. But there's not a seasonal theme: asparagus, in the painting, are black. Bold browns, fuschia, and turquoise were my inevitable rebellion against Early American. I love the pineapple, a symbol of hospitality that ship captains returned with from the Caribbean and put in front of their houses, a classic New England trope.

I worked every day for a year. I wanted the touch to be the same. I was totally warmed up. If you look very closely at the painting, you can see that I used quite a few layers of paint; that I embedded leaves from the neighborhood in the paint; that I extended objects across the canvases;

and that there is no shading. It is very flat, Asian, a Matisse-like drawing that suggests volume.

I was excited when the painting was installed, eight panels each on the east and west walls, four across the back. It looked better than I had hoped. Afterward, I had dozens of phone calls from restaurants. My answer: "I won't be rushed and I am very expensive!" Today, when I walk over to the bar at Gramercy to have a drink with an out-of-town dealer and sit under the painting, well, that's one of the perks.

Robert Kushner painted the Tavern mural, *Cornucopia* (top), in his Union Square studio in 1993–94. At right, he sits in the same spot beneath a more recent piece: *Pear Pavane*, 2011, is richly layered with oil, acrylic, and gold and copper leaf.

OUR AMERICAN
PASTA PROGRAM

Old-fashioned attention to detail
happens every single morning at
our pasta station. FROM LEFT: sheets
of squid-ink pasta are folded into
cappelletti; rounds of basic pasta
dough ready for open ravioli;
spinach fettuccine; and nests of
buckwheat spaghetti.

FRESH PASTA DOUGH

MAKES ABOUT 1½ POUNDS

We use this basic pasta dough recipe for most of our pastas. To make the Mushroom Lasagna (page 207), you'll use three-quarters of the recipe; Open Ravioli of Beef and Carrots (page 213) requires a quarter. But extra dough won't be wasted: it can be frozen, tightly wrapped in plastic and placed in a freezer bag, for several months. So if you make a batch for one dish, you can have the rest ready to go for the next one.

It's worth looking for the specific combination of flours we use in this recipe: Italian "oo" flour, which is white, soft, and finely ground, and semolina, which is yellow, hard, and coarse. I like to make the dough by hand, but you can make it in a stand mixer with the paddle, or a food processor.

We have a full-time line cook in charge of our pasta station, which is unusual for a restaurant that's not Italian. I invested in a machine that's the best of the best for rolling pasta (made by Emilio Mitdiero), and from 8 a.m. to 5 p.m., we run it at maximum capacity. At home, inexpensive hand-cranked machines work just fine; I still use my grandfather's old cavatelli crank.

2½ cups Italian "OO" flour, plus more for kneading

½ cup semolina flour

½ teaspoon salt

4 large eggs

In a large bowl, combine the flours and salt. Make a well in the center of the flour and add the eggs. With a fork, beat the eggs in the well, then begin slowly incorporating the flour, working in circles toward the edges of the bowl. Add cold water slowly only as needed to help the dough come together (up to about ¼ cup).

Transfer the dough to a floured work surface and knead until smooth and no longer sticky, about 10 minutes. Wrap tightly in plastic wrap and refrigerate for at least an hour. The dough can be refrigerated for up to 2 days.

NICK AND PASTA

When I joined the kitchen at Gramercy in 2006 as executive chef, Nick Anderer was a sous chef. We hit it off immediately—even though we'd never worked together. I felt like a kid at summer camp meeting my new best friend. He has had such an impact on the evolution of the restaurant, and he deserves a lot of credit for Gramercy's transformation. Among Nick's many talents are a passion for and deep knowledge of Italian cooking, pasta in particular. He did an amazing job in creating the pasta program at Gramercy; no wonder he's had so much success in such a short time as the executive chef at our sister restaurant Maialino.

FRESH SPINACH FETTUCCINE

MAKES ABOUT 1 POUND

I think of pasta as a canvas for delicious seasonal flavors, not in the traditional Italian style, where it's more a study of noodles. Instead, our pasta recipes open the door for endless fresh combinations. Use the farmers' market to help you imagine which ingredients would taste best with this fettuccine. Try Sun Gold tomatoes and baby artichokes or shiitake mushrooms and Swiss chard. Or serve it with Duck Ragout (page 204) or Corn and Basil (page 205). I like a luxurious amount of these seasonal ingredients, keeping the sauce loose so that the last bite is as moist and satisfying as the first. If there's a little sauce left in the bottom of the bowl after the pasta is gone, that's perfect.

5 ounces spinach (about 8 packed cups)

2 large eggs

1 large egg yolk

1½ cups Italian "00" flour, plus more for kneading and rolling

¼ cup semolina flour, plus more for dusting

½ teaspoon salt

Steam the spinach in a steamer insert over boiling water until bright green and wilted, about a minute. Let cool slightly, then squeeze out all the liquid.

Process the spinach in a food processor until finely chopped, scraping down the sides as needed. Add the eggs and egg yolk and process until well combined; it's fine to have flecks of spinach.

Follow the instructions for making the dough (opposite), using the ingredients in this recipe.

Cut the dough into thirds. Keeping the remaining dough covered, run one piece through a pasta machine, flouring the dough as needed, until you have a sheet roughly ¹⁄₁₆ inch thick. (At home, the Deluxe Atlas Pasta Queen is a great tool.) Trim the sheet and cut it into pieces about 10 inches long; don't worry if some of the pieces aren't perfect. Lay the sheets on a drying rack or floured baking sheet and let dry for about 10 minutes. Repeat with the remaining dough.

Using a pasta machine or a knife, cut the sheets into strips about ¼ inch wide. Dust the strips with a little semolina and transfer to the drying rack or baking sheet. If you're not using the pasta immediately, form it into loose nests on a floured baking sheet, cover tightly with plastic wrap, and refrigerate for up to 12 hours.

SPINACH FETTUCCINE
WITH CORN AND BASIL
(PAGE 205)

SPINACH FETTUCCINE
WITH TOMATO AND DUCK RAGOUT
(PAGE 204)

GARLIC CONFIT AND GARLIC OIL

Garlic confit adds a distinctive sweet flavor to vegetable stir-fries and a light body to broths. And that's the real reason a confit is worth doing. We add it to Spinach Fettuccine with Tomato and Duck Ragout, and it's great in Braised Beef (page 97). We also make super-smooth Garlic Puree (page 231) to flavor many dishes. The garlic confit can be refrigerated for up to several weeks.

Separate 2 or 3 heads of garlic into cloves and peel. Put the garlic in a saucepan, cover with cold water, and bring to a boil, then immediately drain. Return the garlic to the saucepan, cover with peanut or grapeseed oil, and let steep for 2½ hours over low heat. You know the garlic is ready when you can smash a clove with gentle pressure. Strain out the garlic and save the flavored oil to cook with later.

SPINACH FETTUCCINE WITH TOMATO AND DUCK RAGOUT

SERVES 4 GENEROUSLY

Duck confit is a beautiful way to use and preserve duck legs. Here we pair the rich duck meat with acidic fresh tomatoes (baked to intensify the flavors), which perfectly balance the dish and make a surprisingly sensuous sauce for pasta. Make the Duck Confit (page 305), or just buy it!

6 plum tomatoes, peeled, halved, and seeded

2 tablespoons olive oil

2 garlic cloves, fresh or Garlic Confit, smashed

Salt and pepper

2 cups Brown Duck Sauce (page 310)

1⅓ cups small pieces Duck Confit meat (page 305; from 2 to 3 legs)

3 tablespoons unsalted butter

2 tablespoons red wine vinegar

1½ tablespoons finely chopped basil

1 tablespoon finely chopped flat-leaf parsley

Salt and pepper

Fresh Spinach Fettuccine (page 201)

1 tablespoon extra-virgin olive oil

8 Sun Gold or other small cherry tomatoes, halved

Sea salt

Freshly grated Parmigiano cheese

1½ tablespoons finely chopped chives

Preheat the oven to 225°F.

In a medium bowl, gently toss the plum tomatoes with the olive oil and garlic. Season with salt and pepper. Arrange the tomatoes cut side down on a baking sheet and bake until soft and slightly shriveled, 3½ to 4 hours, flipping once about halfway through.

Bring a large pot of water to a boil.

Meanwhile, in a large saucepan, bring the duck sauce to a simmer. Add the duck confit and gently heat through. Stir in 2 tablespoons of the butter, the vinegar, basil, and parsley and season with salt and pepper. Set the ragout aside.

Salt the boiling water, add the fettuccine, and cook until al dente, about 5 minutes. Drain the pasta and transfer it to the saucepan with the ragout. Add the remaining 1 tablespoon butter and the extra-virgin olive oil, season with salt and pepper, and gently toss to combine. Serve in bowls topped with the roasted tomatoes, Sun Gold tomatoes, sea salt, cheese, and chives.

SPINACH FETTUCCINE WITH CORN AND BASIL

SERVES 4 GENEROUSLY

This dish is a snapshot of a walk through the garden—light, crunchy, sweet corn kernels spilled over soft green noodles. The corn soup adds creaminess without any actual cream.

2 cups Chilled Corn Soup (page 123)

2 tablespoons unsalted butter

Fresh lemon juice

1 tablespoon olive oil

1 shallot, minced

$\frac{1}{2}$ garlic clove, minced

1$\frac{1}{3}$ cups corn kernels (from about 2 ears)

Salt and pepper

Fresh Spinach Fettuccine (page 201)

1 tablespoon extra-virgin olive oil

Freshly grated Parmigiano cheese

12 basil leaves, sliced

Bring a large pot of water to a boil. Meanwhile, in a small saucepan, gently heat the corn soup. Stir in 1 tablespoon of the butter and a squeeze of lemon juice. Keep warm.

In a medium skillet, heat the olive oil over medium-low heat. Add the shallot and garlic and cook, stirring, until softened, about 3 minutes. Increase the heat to medium-high, add the corn, and cook, stirring often, until crisp-tender, about 3 minutes. Season with salt and pepper; keep warm.

Salt the boiling water, add the fettuccine, and cook until al dente, about 5 minutes. Drain the pasta, reserving $\frac{1}{3}$ cup of the pasta water, and return the pasta to the pot. Add the $\frac{1}{3}$ cup pasta water, the remaining 1 tablespoon butter, and the extra-virgin olive oil, season with salt and pepper, and gently toss to combine. (The oil and pasta water will keep the pasta loose and shiny and give it extra flavor.)

Spoon the corn soup into bowls. Top with the fettuccine, followed by the corn mixture, cheese, and basil.

It's important to cut shallots or onions with a sharp knife. With my hand in a safe position, I make horizontal slices, root intact (top); then vertical slices (center); I finish by mincing the pieces in a smooth, rocking motion (bottom).

MUSHROOM LASAGNA

SERVES 8 TO 10

To stay true to my vision of the restaurant, it became obvious to me that we had to infuse pasta dishes with our own distinctive American perspective. This mushroom lasagna was born from the impulse to show off the magic of the Tavern's wood-burning grill, which gives the lasagna its signature smoky flavor and charred edges. No other cooking method replicates that slow-burn flavor. This lasagna is a wonderful vegetarian option on our menu: hearty, luxurious, and filling. At home, it's convenient to make in advance; it only gets better after the flavors have melded, and it's a cinch to warm up and serve. At the restaurant, we add layers of flavor with a mushroom vinaigrette and Garlic Chips, but at home, a simple drizzle of balsamic vinegar is a great alternative.

BÉCHAMEL SAUCE

4 tablespoons (1/2 stick) unsalted butter

1/4 cup all-purpose flour

1 1/2 cups whole milk

1 1/2 cups Mushroom Broth (page 208) or Chicken Broth (page 59)

Pinch of freshly grated nutmeg

Salt and pepper

FILLING

6 tablespoons olive oil

1 1/2 onions, thinly sliced

2 leeks (white parts), thinly sliced

5 garlic cloves, minced

4 sprigs thyme

Salt and pepper

2 cups thinly sliced Swiss chard leaves

3 pounds white mushrooms, thinly sliced

1/2 cup mascarpone cheese

3 tablespoons sherry vinegar

1 tablespoon balsamic vinegar

3/4 recipe (about 18 ounces) Fresh Pasta Dough (page 200)

All-purpose flour for rolling

Salt

Butter for the pan

2 cups ricotta cheese

1 1/3 cups coarsely grated Parmigiano cheese

Garlic Chips (page 208; optional)

Make the béchamel sauce. In a medium saucepan, melt the butter over medium heat. Add the flour and cook, stirring constantly, for 2 minutes; don't let the mixture brown. Slowly add the milk and broth, whisking until smooth. Simmer, whisking occasionally, until the sauce resembles thick cream, about 10 minutes. Remove from the heat, add the nutmeg, and season with salt and pepper. Cover the surface of the béchamel with plastic wrap to prevent a skin from forming.

Make the filling. In a large skillet, heat 2 tablespoons of the oil over medium-low heat. Add the onions and cook, stirring often, until soft, about 10 minutes. Add the leeks, garlic, and thyme and cook, stirring often, until the leeks are soft, about 7 minutes. Season with salt and pepper, then stir in the chard and cook until wilted, about 2 minutes. Remove the thyme sprigs and transfer the mixture to a food processor. Pulse until finely chopped, then transfer to a large bowl.

In another large skillet, heat 1 tablespoon of the olive oil over high heat. When the oil is very hot, add one-quarter of the mushrooms and cook, stirring often, until they are well browned and all the liquid they release has evaporated, about 8 minutes; season with salt and pepper about halfway through. Transfer the mushrooms to a food processor, and repeat with the remaining oil and mushrooms in three batches. (The number of batches will vary depending on the size of your pan; the important thing is not to crowd the mushrooms.)

Pulse the mushrooms several times (they should still have some texture), then transfer to the bowl with the onion mixture. Add the béchamel sauce, mascarpone, and sherry and balsamic vinegars and stir until thoroughly combined. Season with salt and pepper.

RECIPE CONTINUES

Preheat the oven to 400°F.

Bring a large pot of water to a boil. Meanwhile, cut the pasta dough into quarters. Keeping the remaining dough covered, run one piece through a pasta machine, flouring the dough as needed, until you have a sheet roughly 1/16 inch thick and 4½ x 23 inches long. (At home, the Deluxe Atlas Pasta Queen is a great tool.) Trim the sheet into two pieces roughly 4 by 11 inches. (Don't worry if some of the pieces aren't perfect; just save the 2 best pieces for the top layer. Lay the sheets on a drying rack or floured baking sheet. Repeat with the remaining dough.

Salt the boiling water, add the noodles and cook until just tender, about 4 minutes. Drain and shock in a bowl of ice water. Carefully remove the noodles from the bowl, letting the excess water drip off, and lay in a single layer on plastic wrap.

Butter a 9-by-13-inch baking pan. Lay 2 noodles in the bottom of the pan. Top with one-quarter of the mushroom filling, one-quarter of the ricotta, and one-quarter of the grated cheese. Repeat 3 times with the remaining noodles, filling, ricotta, and grated cheese (there isn't a layer of noodles on the top).

Bake the lasagna until the center is very hot and the top is browned, 35 to 45 minutes. Let rest at room temperature for at least 15 minutes before serving so it's easier to cut. Scatter some garlic chips on top, if you like.

MUSHROOM BROTH

MAKES ABOUT 2 CUPS

This is the easiest stock there is, and it adds great flavor to the mushroom recipes in this book. Use it, too, as a base for almost any soup or a stew.

1 pound white mushrooms, thinly sliced

Salt and pepper

In a medium pot, combine the mushrooms and 4 cups water, bring to a simmer, and cook for 1 hour. Pass the broth through a fine-mesh strainer into a container and season with salt and pepper.

GARLIC CHIPS

MAKES ABOUT ½ CUP

Fried garlic chips give crunch when scattered over the Mushroom Lasagna and are fun to toss on a salad or just to snack on.

10 large garlic cloves, sliced lengthwise paper-thin (use a mandoline)

1 cup peanut or grapeseed oil

Salt

Fill a small saucepan halfway with cold water, add the garlic, and bring to a boil over high heat. Immediately remove from the heat and drain the garlic. Lay the garlic on a baking sheet and pat dry with paper towels.

In a small saucepan, heat the oil over medium-high heat. Add the garlic slices in two batches and fry, stirring the oil with a wooden spoon so the slices don't stick together, until they are crisp but have taken on very little color, just a few seconds. With a slotted spoon, transfer the garlic chips to a paper towel–lined plate to drain and cool. Lightly salt them. The oil can be strained and reused for frying.

Lasagna is a simple preparation, but it does require planning and organization. **CLOCKWISE FROM TOP LEFT:** Our production schedule is set for the entire week; sous chef Suzanne Cupps inspects a mushroom delivery; shiitake mushrooms cultivated in Pennsylvania; we require so much filling, we roast the mushrooms and chop them in a food processor; a pasta cook's notebook; and assembled lasagna just before baking.

SHOULD I GO TO COOKING SCHOOL?

So many people from so many different backgrounds have become enthusiastic about cooking professionally. Many inevitably ask me the best way to start. Cooking school? An apprenticeship in a restaurant? Travel? My answer is all of the above. There is no one way to get into the restaurant business. The decision is different for everyone. As long as you commit yourself completely, you'll find important learning experiences. For me, after graduating from college and working for a year and a half in Tokyo, I decided to follow the advice of my first chef and go to vocational training school, L'Ecole Technique Jean Ferrandi in Paris. Since I'd lived in France as a college student and worked summer jobs there, I was fluent in French—but I had no basis in technical language or the slang cooks use.

At Ferrandi the professional culinary course of study is stratified: in the same chaotic school building, there is one floor for woodworking, another for charcuterie; there are fishmongers in training and apprentice pastry chefs, all alternating between their classes and working in restaurants. Each group has its own set of tools, uniforms, and professional jargon. There were different crafts and camps and nobody mixed. But for all of its challenges, I looked up and realized this was the real deal: I was both in deep and in heaven. I wasn't just in a culinary class, I was in a different world. Ferrandi is just one of three major vocational schools in Paris that prepare people to enter the workforce—that's what it's designed for, not to produce superstar chefs. It wasn't a welcoming place. It was tough. On day one, they told our class of thirty that in ten years, only one of us would be cooking for a living.

For me, this practical training for the real business of cooking was indispensable. I was immersed in the culture, far from the distractions of family and friends, and I graduated with a solid understanding of the fundamentals of cooking. So, for me, the answer was yes!

OPEN RAVIOLI OF BEEF AND CARROTS

SERVES 4

We have to use every ounce of a 400- to 600-pound side of beef, because that's the way we buy our sustainably raised meat. So for us, cooking the delicious secondary cuts is both imperative and delicious and it should be for you, too. Here we opt for the flatiron steak, an interesting lesser-known cut that braises beautifully: moist, tender, flavorful. This steak (which comes off the shoulder) has connective tissue that melts succulently into the braise.

BEEF FILLING

1 tablespoon olive oil

½ onion, thickly sliced

1 garlic clove, minced

1 tablespoon tomato paste

¼ cup red wine vinegar

½ cup red wine

1 pound Braised Beef (page 97), shredded

4 cups Braised Beef liquid (page 97), strained

6 cups thickly sliced Swiss chard leaves

½ cup freshly grated Parmigiano cheese

¼ teaspoon Aleppo pepper

8 large basil leaves, julienned

¼ cup finely chopped flat-leaf parsley

¼ cup thinly sliced chives

2 tablespoons unsalted butter

Salt and pepper

Red wine vinegar

¼ recipe (about 6 ounces) Fresh Pasta Dough (page 200)

All-purpose flour for rolling

CARROTS

2 cups carrot juice

¼ cup orange juice

5 medium carrots, sliced on the diagonal into ⅓-inch pieces

1 teaspoon honey

1 tablespoon unsalted butter

Salt and pepper

Fresh lemon juice

Salt

1 tablespoon extra-virgin olive oil

1 tablespoon unsalted butter

1 garlic clove, smashed

1 sprig rosemary

Pepper

Start the beef filling. In a medium pot, heat the olive oil over medium-low heat. Add the onion and garlic and cook, stirring often, until softened, 6 to 8 minutes. Add the tomato paste and cook, stirring, for a minute. Increase the heat to high, add the vinegar and wine, and simmer to reduce the liquid by half. Add the braised beef, then pour in the braising liquid. Bring the mixture to a simmer, stirring occasionally, and cook until the liquid is reduced to about a cup, about 1 hour.

Meanwhile, run the pasta dough through a pasta machine, flouring it as needed, until you have a sheet roughly ¹/₁₆ inch thick and 4 x 26 inches long. Cut eight 3-inch circles from the dough, lay them on a floured baking sheet, and cover with a towel.

Make the carrots. In a small saucepan, combine the carrot and orange juices and bring to a boil over high heat, then add the carrots and simmer until just tender, about 8 minutes. Transfer the carrots to a small bowl, and continue to simmer the liquid until it is reduced to about ½ cup, about 20 minutes more.

Return the carrots to the pan, stir in the honey and butter, and season with salt and pepper and a drop or two of lemon juice. Cover and keep warm.

Bring a pot of water to a boil. Salt well, add the pasta circles, and cook until al dente, about 5 minutes.

Meanwhile, finish the filling by folding the chard into the braised beef, stirring until it wilts. Add the cheese, Aleppo pepper, basil, parsley, chives, and butter, then season with salt and pepper and vinegar; keep warm.

Transfer ⅓ cup of the pasta water to a large saucepan, add the extra-virgin olive oil, butter, garlic, and rosemary, season with salt and pepper, and gently heat. Drain the pasta, add it to the saucepan, and turn gently to coat.

Put a pasta circle in each shallow bowl and spoon the braised beef mixture and juices over them. Cover with the remaining pasta and then the carrots and their juices.

CAULIFLOWER WITH QUINOA, PRUNES, AND PEANUTS

SERVES 4

This dish came about when I was trying to make my wife, Mindy, fall in love with cauliflower (and me!). Although an adventurous eater, she wasn't excited about this particular vegetable. I've found that by browning cauliflower, you can win over even the most skeptical eater. And she married me, after all.

Pairing grains with vegetables is a fascinating way to make inspiring new combinations that are distinctly American. Not only is such a combination healthy, sensible, and less protein-driven, it can make a meal in itself. Seeds and grains are easy to cook: no soaking or special techniques, just add water and salt and boil. Whether you use the red quinoa seed, as here, or another grain like farro, emmer, or spelt, its texture is a welcome surprise. In South America, the Incas considered quinoa the mother of all cereals. Now we call it a superfood.

3 tablespoons olive oil

¼ red onion, minced

1 shallot, minced

1 garlic clove, minced

½ cup quinoa

2 cups Vegetable Broth
(page 118) or water

1 sprig thyme

Salt and pepper

1 head cauliflower

⅓ cup finely diced prunes

2 tablespoons chopped unsalted
roasted peanuts, plus 1 tablespoon
crushed nuts

1 tablespoon Onion Puree

1 tablespoon unsalted butter

2 tablespoons finely chopped
cilantro, plus a handful of whole
leaves for garnish

1 tablespoon finely chopped chives

Preheat the oven to 400°F.

In a small saucepan, heat 1 tablespoon of the oil over medium-low heat. Add the onion, shallot, and garlic and cook, stirring often, until the onion is softened, about 5 minutes. Add the quinoa and toast, stirring constantly, for about a minute.

Increase the heat to high, add 1 cup of the broth and the thyme, season with salt and pepper, and bring to a simmer. Cook, covered, until almost all the liquid has been absorbed, about 15 minutes. Remove from the heat and let stand for 5 minutes. Discard the thyme sprig.

Trim the stem of the cauliflower so that the head sits flat on a cutting board. Cut down through the center of the head, making 4 thick slices. Most of the slices will still have a bit of stem still attached and that's good.

Heat 2 tablespoons of the olive oil over medium-high heat in the largest skillet you have. Working in batches, brown the cauliflower slices on both sides, about 3 minutes per side. Transfer to a baking pan.

Season the cauliflower with salt and pepper, transfer to the oven, and roast until tender, about 15 minutes.

Meanwhile, add the prunes, chopped peanuts, and onion puree to the quinoa and gently heat through, stirring. Add the remaining 1 cup broth to moisten the quinoa, then stir in the butter and chopped cilantro. Season with salt and pepper.

Lay the cauliflower slices on plates and spoon the quinoa on top. Sprinkle with the crushed peanuts, chives, and cilantro leaves.

ONION PUREE

MAKES ABOUT ½ CUP

There is a reason to make this subtle and delicious puree for the cauliflower recipe and other dishes: like butter, the puree binds the ingredients together and coats the cauliflower, quinoa, prunes, and peanuts.

2 tablespoons olive oil

1 onion, very thinly sliced

1 tablespoon sherry vinegar

Salt and pepper

In a medium saucepan, heat the oil over medium-low heat. Add the onions and cook, stirring often, until they are completely soft but have not taken on any color, 15 to 20 minutes. A bit of water helps here.

Add the vinegar and cook for 5 more minutes. Season with salt and pepper. Transfer to a blender and process until satiny-smooth. The puree can be cooled, covered, and stored in the refrigerator for up to 2 days.

HOW WE PAN-ROAST FISH

Don't be put off by cooking fish at home; it just takes a little practice. Begin with a skinless and boneless fillet, and season it generously with salt and pepper on both sides. Preheat a small skillet with a drizzle of olive oil. Lay the fish flat in the hot pan. At the same time, heat up any vegetables or sauce you plan to serve with the fish. After about 3 minutes (depending on the thickness of the fillet), use a spatula and your other hand to delicately flip the fish. Cook for about 2 minutes more. Add a smashed clove of garlic, a sprig of thyme, and a tablespoon of butter to the pan. As the butter melts, use a squeeze of lemon juice to emulsify the melted butter. You may need a drop of water or stock to keep the butter from separating. Baste the fish with the butter until just cooked through—it'll help to keep the fish moist and to cook it evenly. The goal is to use the butter as a very thin glaze. Most of the butter will never make it to the plate; it is just a medium in which to gently cook the fish.

PORGY WITH SPAGHETTI SQUASH AND SHERRY SAUCE

SERVES 4

Porgy is a sweet fish in the sea bream family that a lot of people in the Northeast remember fondly from fishing in their childhoods, but it tends to be overlooked by chefs. Despite its modest reputation, porgy is a smart, sustainable choice today—abundant (wild), small (low on the food chain), and local (on the East Coast). The starting point for this dish is the lovely flavor combination of sherry and walnuts, taken to new heights when layered with spaghetti squash.

1 small spaghetti squash (about 2 pounds), halved lengthwise and seeded

5 tablespoons olive oil

Salt and pepper

1 cup thinly sliced shallots

1/4 cup minced garlic, plus 1 clove, smashed

1 1/4 teaspoons turmeric

1/2 teaspoon mild curry powder

1/2 teaspoon saffron threads

1 1/2 cups Amontillado sherry

1/2 cup plus 1/3 cup Vegetable Broth (page 118) or water

5 tablespoons unsalted butter, cubed, plus 1 tablespoon

Fresh lime juice

1/3 cup walnuts, roughly chopped

1 tablespoon honey

Fresh lemon juice

Four 6-ounce skinless porgy fillets

1 sprig thyme

1/4 cup roasted, salted pumpkin seeds

1/2 cup peeled and finely diced sweet firm apple, such as Honeycrisp, tossed with a little lemon juice

1 tablespoon finely chopped chives

Preheat the oven to 375°F.

Coat the squash with 1 tablespoon of the oil and season with salt and pepper. Put cut side down in a baking pan and roast until the flesh pulls away from the skin but is still a little crunchy, about 35 minutes. After the squash has cooled slightly, scrape out the flesh with a fork; discard the skin.

Meanwhile, in a small saucepan, heat 2 tablespoons of the oil over medium-low heat. Add the shallots and minced garlic and cook until the shallots are softened, 5 to 7 minutes. Add the turmeric and curry powder and stir for about a minute, then add the saffron, sherry, and 1/2 cup of the broth. Simmer the liquid until reduced to about 1/2 cup, about 20 minutes.

Transfer the sauce to a blender and process until smooth. Pass through a fine-mesh strainer into a small saucepan. Set over low heat and add the 5 tablespoons cubed butter, one cube at a time, stirring until completely incorporated. Season with salt, pepper, and lime juice and keep warm.

In a large skillet, heat 1 tablespoon of the oil over medium heat. Add the walnuts and cook, stirring occasionally, until lightly browned, about 3 minutes. Add the honey and stir to coat the walnuts, then add the spaghetti squash and heat through. Season with salt, pepper, and lemon juice and keep warm.

In a large skillet, heat the remaining tablespoon of oil over medium-high heat. Season the porgy with salt and pepper. Lay the fillets in the pan and cook until light brown on the bottom, about 3 minutes. Flip the fillets and cook until almost cooked through, about 2 minutes more. Add the remaining tablespoon of butter, the smashed garlic clove, thyme, the remaining 1/3 cup broth, and a splash of lemon juice, baste the fillets with the pan juices (see page 216), and continue to cook, basting regularly, until just cooked through, a minute or 2 more.

Add the pumpkin seeds, diced apple, and chives to the sherry sauce. Mound some of the squash mixture in the middle of each plate and top with a porgy fillet. Spoon the sherry sauce over the fillets.

CARROT AND CALAMARI SALAD

SERVES 4

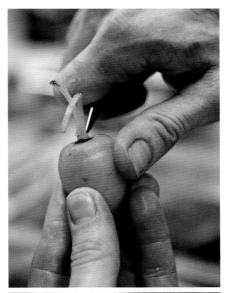

Paul Cézanne once said, "The day is coming when a single carrot, freshly observed, will set off a revolution." It was in that spirit that I created this dish after I'd worked at Gramercy for only three months. What's beautiful about the salad is while it's relatively easy to make, it has complex textures and flavors. I like to let the vegetable be the star and the calamari the supporting actor. It's amazing that it has taken us so long to begin to shift the focus of a dish from the protein to the vegetable. We are so used to giving meat, fish, or poultry the spotlight because we usually think about food from a European point of view. Other cultures, mainly Asian, consider vegetables first.

In the restaurant we use a combination of citrus flavors, including lemon oil, lemon vinaigrette, and cured Meyer lemons, because we always have them on hand. I love the lemon vinaigrette, but feel free to season with a good squeeze or two of lemon juice and your favorite olive oil instead.

LEMON VINAIGRETTE

1/3 cup fresh lemon juice

1 tablespoon white wine vinegar

1 tablespoon Onion Puree (page 215)

1/2 tablespoon honey

1/2 cup Lemon Oil (page 222)

2 tablespoons olive oil

Salt and pepper

1 tablespoon wasabi tobiko (wasabi-infused flying-fish roe)

2 tablespoons olive oil

3/4 pound cleaned calamari

Salt and pepper

5 carrots, julienned

1/8 cup pine nuts, toasted

1/4 Cured Meyer Lemon (page 222; optional), rinsed, pulp removed and discarded, peel minced

2 tablespoons finely chopped chives

A small handful of flat-leaf parsley leaves

Make the lemon vinaigrette. Combine the lemon juice, vinegar, onion puree, and honey in a blender. With the blender running, drizzle in the lemon oil, followed by the olive oil. Season with salt and pepper.

Mix a few tablespoons of the vinaigrette with the tobiko. Set the rest of the vinaigrette aside.

In a large skillet, heat the olive oil over high heat. Season the calamari with salt and pepper and cook until just opaque, 1 to 2 minutes per side. Transfer the calamari to a cutting board. Cut the bodies and tentacles into strips about the same size as the carrots.

In a large bowl, combine the calamari, carrots, and pine nuts. Toss with some of the reserved vinaigrette. Stir in the cured lemon, if using, and chives and season with salt and pepper. Mound the salad onto plates, drizzle with the tobiko vinaigrette, and scatter the parsley on top.

LEMON OIL

MAKES 1 CUP

Making lemon oil requires a small investment of time to infuse the flavors, but this can happen overnight. It is such a flavorful addition to a salad dressing, sautéed vegetables, or a pan sauce for fish.

1 cup grapeseed or other neutral vegetable oil

Peel of 1 lemon

Peel of 1 lime

1 lemongrass stalk, bruised with the side of a chef's knife and roughly chopped

One ½-inch piece of ginger, peeled, smashed, and roughly chopped

1 sprig lemon thyme or thyme

In a jar or other container, combine the oil, lemon and lime peel, lemongrass, ginger, and thyme. Cover and refrigerate overnight; strain. The lemon oil will keep, covered, in the refrigerator for up to a week.

CURED MEYER LEMONS

MAKES 4

When Meyer lemons are in season, we make batches of cured lemons to use all year round. They show up unexpectedly to accentuate the fresh ingredients in a salad or to brighten the rich flavors of a meat braise.

1 star anise

1 cardamom pod

¼ teaspoon black peppercorns

¼ teaspoon fennel seeds

¼ teaspoon cumin seeds

¼ teaspoon coriander seeds

4 Meyer lemons

½ cup kosher salt

⅛ cup sugar

Pinch of red pepper flakes

Fresh lemon juice to cover

In a small skillet, combine the star anise, cardamom, peppercorns, and fennel, cumin, and coriander seeds and toast over medium heat, stirring often, until fragrant, about 3 minutes. Let the spices cool completely.

Meanwhile, deeply score the lemons from top to bottom, leaving about ½ inch of the base of each one intact so the fruit stays in one piece. Put in a large bowl, add the salt, and pack the salt into the lemons.

Add the sugar, pepper flakes, and toasted spices to the lemons and toss until thoroughly combined. Transfer the contents of the bowl to a pint jar, evenly distributing the salt mixture and pushing down on the lemons to fit them in. Add enough lemon juice to cover the lemons, leaving a little room at the top of the jar.

Seal the jar and refrigerate for a month, shaking it frequently to distribute the salt mixture and juices. The cured lemons will keep, tightly covered, in the refrigerator for many months. Rinse thoroughly before using.

GRILLED POLE BEANS, CHORIZO, AND MUSSELS

SERVES 4

I love these long, flat pole beans (also called Romano)—especially those grown by Zaid Kurdieh on his Norwich Meadows Farm in central New York—not just because they taste so magical, but because their season extends well into the fall. We char them over the open fire on the Tavern grill and serve them with mild short green shishito or padrón peppers.

3/4 pound pole beans, trimmed

1/4 cup olive oil

Salt and pepper

3 garlic cloves, 2 minced, 1 smashed

2 shallots, minced

1 cup white wine

2 pounds mussels, cleaned

1/2 cup cilantro leaves

6 cipollini onions, sliced

6 shishito or padrón peppers, stemmed, seeded, and sliced

3 ounces Mexican chorizo, casing discarded

Pinch of Aleppo pepper

Fresh lemon juice

Preheat a charcoal or gas grill to medium. (Alternatively, if you'd rather not grill the beans, blanch them in boiling salted water until tender.)

In a large bowl, toss the beans with 2 tablespoons of the oil and season with salt and pepper. Grill until charred on the outside and tender, about 4 minutes per side. Transfer the beans to a cutting board and slice on the diagonal into small pieces.

In a large pot, heat 1 tablespoon of the olive oil over medium-low heat. Add the minced garlic and shallots and cook, stirring often, until softened, about 3 minutes. Increase the heat to high, add the wine and 1 cup water, and bring to a boil. Add the mussels, cover the pot, and steam them until they just open wide, 3 to 4 minutes.

Using a slotted spoon, transfer the mussels to a medium bowl, leaving the broth in the pot. Remove the mussels from the shells. Discard the shells and any mussels that haven't opened. Strain the broth into a blender; add the cilantro and puree.

In a large skillet, heat the remaining 1 tablespoon olive oil over medium heat. Add the onions and cook for 3 minutes, then add the peppers and smashed garlic and cook, stirring often, until the vegetables are softened and slightly caramelized, about 3 minutes more.

Add the chorizo and cook, breaking up any lumps, for about 3 minutes. Add the mussel broth and bring to a simmer. Add the pole beans and heat through, then add the mussels and remove the skillet from the heat.

Season with the Aleppo pepper, salt, and a few drops of lemon juice, and serve in bowls.

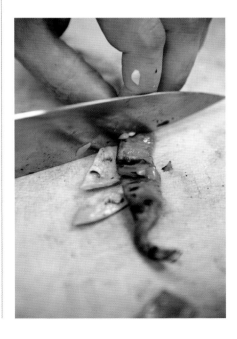

THE RESTAURANT AS TEACHER

Each of Danny's restaurants has a vision: it belongs first to its geographical location, then to its community, and finally to the city as a whole. It was important for me to decide how Gramercy Tavern should fulfill that vision. The thought made me look inside, to what's important to me, and it became clear that Gramercy should be an educator. And, since local food is the backbone of our menu, local food should be our mission. We decided to use our passion and devotion to local ingredients as a way to influence the way our community approaches good cooking and good living.

I'm a dad (and my parents were both teachers), and it has always been important to me that my kids learn about food. Of course, they say, "Yuck!" too. Everyone, no matter their family story, has a chasm between the way they live and the way they wish to eat. At Gramercy, we made a decision to focus on children, since they are a blank canvas. Restaurants like ours have a responsibility and the luxury to be able to share our practical knowledge and our enthusiasm. We have made education part of the DNA of the restaurant. At first we had to get our own people behind the idea that we don't just cook food, serve food, and create enlightened hospitality. Gramercy's goal is to teach. It is not an extracurricular activity or something we do only when we have time—teaching has become part of the restaurant's identity.

So, whom do we teach? First, we train cooks and servers and set a high standard. Then what? Schools are a perfect place to share our food enthusiasm with children while their ideas and palates are developing. Part of the first-grade curriculum in the public schools is to introduce children to the world around them, so they meet firemen and policemen and go to museums. Our goal is to open kids' eyes to the natural world around them, to show them how tasting local foods reconnects us to the environment and opens our eyes to a world of decisions. Every school, every community, every family (mine, too) can use help putting good food on the table.

The photographs on these pages show the staff interacting with PS 41 in Greenwich Village, in an elementary school program that has been in place since 2007. We have forged a great relationship with the kids, teachers, administrators, and parents, and we've found that the influence on the adults (including us) is as profound as what the kids walk away with.

Two other community ideas intrigue us: One is providing cooking lessons. How to reorganize the home kitchen for people who want to live and eat better. A kind of Home Ec for adults with strategies and practical information. What equipment do you really need? How to make a kitchen the center of the home. Second, we want to cook for people who are not healthy. We'll address disease-specific diets with plant-based, whole-grain recipes. This is the future of GT's community efforts.

Our year-long plan for food studies features restaurant visits—touching and tasting food. Here, first graders are introduced to bean soup and get a recipe and ingredients to take home.

TOASTED GREEN WHEAT AND WARM BEETS

SERVES 4

The idea of basing a meal on a whole grain has inspired a new generation of chefs to use farro, spelt, or green wheat as the foundation of a dish, or even of a complete meal. Using whole grains in the United States goes beyond making ethnic foods. Whole grains impact baking, too, because we can grind these unrefined and more flavorful grains for flour. In the brewing industry, using whole grains has helped revive local craftsmanship and the local economy.

Green wheat, or frik or freekeh, is originally from the Middle East and has a distinctive smoky flavor. This is *not* risotto, nor is it a side dish—it is a main attraction: a hearty dinner for all beet lovers. I use the unusual toothsome texture of frik to complement the meaty texture of Forona beets, my favorite (below). To me, this dish is as satisfying and seductive as rice and beans.

6 small beets (about 1 pound), red and golden

¼ cup olive oil

Salt and pepper

1 cup toasted green wheat (frik or freekeh)

1 tablespoon red wine vinegar

¾ cup Vegetable Broth (page 118) or water, or more if needed

1½ tablespoons Garlic Puree (page 231)

1 tablespoon finely chopped flat-leaf parsley

1 tablespoon finely chopped chives

1 teaspoon finely chopped tarragon

Fresh lemon juice

2 tablespoons roasted, salted pistachios

Preheat the oven to 375°F.

Coat the beets with 1 tablespoon of the olive oil, season with salt and pepper, and wrap in aluminum foil. Put in a baking pan and roast until tender, about 50 minutes.

Meanwhile, in a small saucepan, combine the green wheat with 2 cups water and season with salt and pepper. Cover, bring to a simmer, and cook until almost tender, about 30 minutes. Drain, if needed, and return to the saucepan.

As soon as the beets are cool enough to handle, peel and trim them, then cut into small wedges. In a medium bowl, toss the beets with 2 tablespoons of the olive oil and the vinegar; season with salt and pepper.

Moisten the cooked wheat with the broth and heat through. Stir in the remaining tablespoon of olive oil, the garlic puree, parsley, chives, tarragon, and a squeeze of lemon juice. The green wheat should be fairly loose and creamy; stir in a little more broth or water if needed. Season with salt and pepper. Spoon the green wheat onto plates and top with the beets and pistachios.

ANTHONY GARLIC

At Gramercy Tavern, we are constantly in search of distinctive ingredients. In the process, I realized that there was a great example of heirloom garlic right in my Uncle Paul's garden in Syracuse, New York. I asked my uncle to send me a box of the garlic he grows every year, knowing that his seed came from my grandfather's garden and *that* seed came from his father's garden. It was probably the only thing that farmer from Naples brought to this country when he immigrated from Italy around 1908.

A century later, I took the garlic to Jim Wrobel (above right, in 2012), a passionate professional grower and garlic fanatic who, on his farm in upstate New York, outside Utica, also grows American hops for brewing. I asked Jim if he could try to grow my family's garlic on a larger scale. In his skillful hands, each year that crop has grown exponentially. Now we buy more than 450 pounds of Anthony garlic a year! By carefully selecting the best and the biggest heads each year to replant, Jim was able to increase the size of the garlic bulbs, but the flavor of this heirloom variety remains true. We use our own garlic (below right) to make Garlic Confit and Garlic Oil (page 204), Garlic Puree (opposite), and Garlic Chips (page 208).

GARLIC PUREE

MAKES ABOUT ½ CUP

Most chefs can't imagine cooking without fresh garlic. Raw and roughly chopped, garlic gives its distinctive angular fiery flavor to a dish; minced and discreetly used, it adds a refined touch. But garlic goes through a real transformation when made into a puree, becoming so mellow, it's a thing of sweet earthiness. Spread on or under a piece of fish, it delivers another layer of flavor. Combined with a vegetable like beets, the puree lends the root vegetable a dynamic richness without overwhelming it the way raw garlic would. A touch of garlic puree in a soup or a sauce acts like butter, giving it creaminess and body.

½ cup peeled garlic cloves (about 20 cloves)

1 cup whole milk

Salt

Put the garlic in a small saucepan and add enough cold water to just cover it. Bring to a boil over high heat; immediately drain the garlic. Return the garlic to the pan, cover with cold water, and repeat the process five more times. Sure, it's repetitive, but it's easy, and this process takes away the garlic's bitterness and amplifies its sweetness.

After draining the garlic the last time, return it to the pan, cover with the milk, and add a pinch of salt. Bring to a simmer and cook until the garlic is completely soft, about 15 minutes.

Transfer the garlic to a blender and process with just enough of the milk to create a satiny and very light puree. Season with salt. Once cool, the puree can be covered and refrigerated for up to 5 days.

SEA SCALLOPS WITH GRAPES AND VERJUS

SERVES 4

One of the defining elements of contemporary American cooking is to use a variety of acidic high notes from citrus, verjus, wine, or vinegar. These are ingredients we instinctively reach for, both during cooking and as a final touch, to make our food taste brighter. Verjus is unfermented grape juice and it brings a much softer acidity to a dish than wine or vinegar. It belongs in the home cook's basic pantry. Here it enlivens the flavor of raw scallops without overpowering the dish.

½ cup white verjus

1 tablespoon white balsamic vinegar

Grated zest of ⅓ lemon

1 teaspoon fresh lemon juice

5 basil leaves, roughly torn

Salt

¾ pound sea scallops, thinly sliced horizontally

Extra-virgin olive oil

Sea salt

20 seedless grapes, thinly sliced

A handful of small basil leaves

In a small bowl, combine the verjus, vinegar, lemon zest, juice, torn basil, and 1 tablespoon water. Let the mixture steep for 20 minutes.

Strain the verjus mixture into another small bowl. Season with salt, stirring until it dissolves. Refrigerate until chilled.

Divide the scallops among plates, then spoon the cold verjus mixture over the top. Drizzle with extra-virgin olive oil, sprinkle on a little sea salt, and top with the grapes and basil leaves.

AUTUMN
HARVEST DINNER

AUTUMN HARVEST DINNER

Danny Meyer and Gramercy Tavern have had a long relationship with Share Our Strength and its founder, Billy Shore *(below, far left),* uniting to help fight childhood hunger in America. Every fall we invite outstanding chefs from around the world to cook a dinner together in our kitchen *(following pages)* to raise money for SOS. Each chef creates a dish for a seven-course tasting menu. Generous friends contribute wine, travel, and gifts to a special auction. This event defines the powerful symbiotic relationship between the restaurant community and the not-for-profit sector, bringing together great friends and talent.

HALIBUT WITH RED CABBAGE AND HAZELNUT-YOGURT SAUCE

SERVES 4

I believe restaurants that shine at preparing fish prove their cooking finesse, and I'm extremely proud of our fish dishes at Gramercy. By using a variety of techniques, most done at the last moment, we showcase the careful nature of our fish cooking. This dish celebrates the pillowy, seductive side of halibut. There are two ways I like to prepare this fish: At the restaurant, we cook it very slowly at a low temperature. Ingredients like the tart marinated red cabbage, aromatic toasted hazelnuts, and mouthwatering tangy Greek yogurt provide a contrast with the soft, moist halibut. But there's another way: At home, and in this recipe, I raise the temperature and cook it hotter, because it is faster and easier, and the light caramelization on the fish is irresistible.

CABBAGE

½ red cabbage, cored and thinly sliced

½ red onion, thinly sliced

1 cup orange juice

½ cup fresh lemon juice

½ tablespoon salt

1 star anise

½ cinnamon stick

2 cloves

1 cup red wine

1 cup port

Pepper

2 tablespoons red wine vinegar, or more if needed

1 tablespoon raspberry vinegar

2 teaspoons honey, or more if needed

YOGURT SAUCE

½ cup Greek yogurt

1 teaspoon extra-virgin olive oil

1 tablespoon fresh lemon juice

1 tablespoon olive oil

Four 6-ounce skinless halibut fillets, about 1 inch thick

Salt and pepper

1 tablespoon unsalted butter

1 garlic clove, smashed

1 sprig thyme

⅓ cup Vegetable Broth (page 118) or water

Fresh lemon juice

⅓ cup hazelnuts, toasted, skinned, and roughly chopped

Marinate the cabbage. In a large bowl, combine the cabbage, onion, orange juice, lemon juice, and salt. Marinate for 1 hour.

Meanwhile, make the yogurt sauce. In a small bowl, combine the yogurt, extra-virgin olive oil, lemon juice, and ¼ cup water. The mixture should be loose enough to pour. Refrigerate.

To finish the cabbage, tie the star anise, cinnamon, and cloves in a piece of cheesecloth to make a sachet.

Drain the cabbage, discarding the marinade, and transfer to a large saucepan. Add the wine, port, sachet, and 1 cup water, season with pepper, and bring to a simmer. Cook, stirring occasionally, until the cabbage is very soft, about 40 minutes.

Discard the sachet, then add the vinegars and honey to the cabbage and cook for 5 minutes more. The liquid should be medium-bodied and full-flavored; if needed,

increase the heat and reduce it further. The cabbage should have a nice sweet/tart balance. Add a drop of red wine vinegar and/or honey to heighten the flavor, if you like. Keep warm.

In a large skillet, heat the olive oil over medium-high heat. Season the halibut with salt and pepper. Lay the fillets in the pan and cook until light brown on the bottom, about 4 minutes. Flip the fillets and cook until almost cooked through, about 4 minutes more. Add the butter, garlic, thyme, broth, and a splash of lemon juice to the pan. Baste the fillets with the butter and continue to cook, basting regularly, until just cooked through, a minute or 2 more.

Stir the nuts into the chilled yogurt sauce and season with salt and pepper. Spoon some sauce into the center of each plate and top with a mound of the warm cabbage and then a halibut fillet.

LOBSTER WITH FENNEL SAUCE AND SALSIFY

SERVES 4

This technique of handling a lobster may be new to you, but it is the best way to keep the lobster tender. The idea is to cook it first, briefly, in salted boiling water, then remove the shell and finish the meat very gently over low heat in a well-seasoned butter sauce. Don't let the amount of butter put you off. It acts as a medium to slowly transfer the heat, but it doesn't make its way to the plate! The result is fantastic, succulent lobster that elevates its simple vegetable companions: salsify, leeks, and fennel.

Four 1¼-pound live lobsters

FENNEL SAUCE

½ cup flat-leaf parsley leaves

¼ cup dill fronds

¼ cup tarragon leaves

2 tablespoons unsalted butter

1 cup thinly sliced leeks (white parts, halved lengthwise)

1 cup thinly sliced fennel (fronds reserved for garnish)

1 small garlic clove, smashed

Leaves from 1 sprig thyme

Salt and pepper

1 cup cold Vegetable Broth (page 118) or water

Fresh lemon juice

SALSIFY

Fresh lemon juice

¾ pound salsify

1 tablespoon unsalted butter

1 teaspoon sugar

Salt and pepper

BUTTER SAUCE

1 shallot, thinly sliced

⅓ lemongrass stalk, thinly sliced

3 sprigs tarragon

1 sprig thyme

¼ cup white wine

¼ cup white wine vinegar

¼ cup heavy cream

½ pound (2 sticks) unsalted butter, cubed and chilled

Juice of 1 lemon

Salt and pepper

Bring a large pot of salted water to a boil. Have ready a large bowl of ice water. Remove the claws from the lobsters. Put the claws and bodies in the boiling water. Cook the tails for 3 minutes and the claws for 4 minutes, then shock in the ice water. Drain and remove the meat from the shells. Cut the bodies lengthwise in half.

Make the fennel sauce. In a small saucepan of boiling water, blanch the parsley, dill, and tarragon for 10 seconds. Drain and shock in ice water, then remove and gently squeeze out the water.

In a medium saucepan, melt the butter over medium heat. Add the leeks, fennel, garlic, thyme, and ¼ cup water, season with salt and pepper, and cook, stirring often, until the vegetables are very soft, about 15 minutes.

Transfer the vegetable mixture to a blender, add the blanched herbs and broth, and process until smooth and creamy. Pass the sauce through a fine-mesh strainer into a small saucepan. Season with a couple of drops of lemon juice, salt, and pepper. Set aside.

Make the salsify. Fill a bowl with cold water and add a generous splash of lemon juice. Peel the salsify, cut it into 3-inch lengths, and then quarter the pieces; keep the peeled salsify in the lemon water as you work.

Drain the salsify and combine it with the butter and sugar in a small saucepan. Add enough water to just cover the salsify and season with salt and pepper. Bring the water to a boil over high heat and cook until the salsify is just tender and the liquid has reduced to a glaze, 6 to 7 minutes.

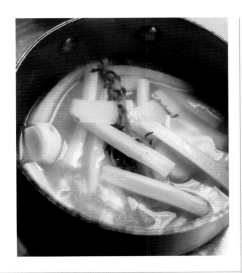

Make the butter sauce. In a small saucepan, combine the shallot, lemongrass, tarragon, thyme, wine, and vinegar and simmer until the liquid is reduced to about 2 tablespoons. Add the cream and reduce briefly.

Over low heat, whisk in the butter 1 piece at a time, adding each piece before the previous one has completely melted. Remove from the heat, stir in the lemon juice, then season with salt and pepper. Pass the butter sauce through a fine-mesh strainer into a saucepan large enough to hold the lobster. Heat over very low heat. When the butter is just warm to the touch, add the lobster meat and warm gently for 3 minutes; you want the lobster meat to be just slightly above room temperature.

Spoon the fennel sauce into bowls, arrange the lobster, and top with the salsify and fennel fronds.

ARCTIC CHAR WITH GREEN CABBAGE, CAULIFLOWER, AND AMERICAN CAVIAR

SERVES 4

The caviar that we use in the restaurant comes from domestic paddlefish (a relative of sturgeon) taken from the fresh waters of the Mississippi and Missouri rivers. It's produced using the same techniques as the fast-disappearing Russian caviars and the harvest is supervised by marine biologists, ensuring the caviar's sustainability. Combining the briny fish roe with creamy cauliflower makes a wonderful sauce and an elegant presentation when napped over the Arctic char.

½ head cauliflower

6 tablespoons olive oil

¼ cup minced onion

¼ cup thinly sliced leek (white and pale green parts, halved lengthwise)

1 shallot, minced

1 garlic clove, minced

1 cup Vegetable Broth (page 118) or water

1 cup whole milk, or more

Salt and pepper

4 cups very thinly sliced savoy cabbage

1 tablespoon unsalted butter

2 teaspoons white balsamic vinegar, or more if needed

Fresh lemon juice

Four 6-ounce skinless Arctic char fillets

1 heaping tablespoon American paddlefish caviar

1 tablespoon finely chopped chives

Make the cauliflower sauce. Cut the cauliflower into florets and then slice vertically into thin pieces. You'll need about 12 slices. (These slices will be used for garnish.) Chop the scraps into small pieces and reserve.

In a medium saucepan, heat 1 tablespoon of the oil over medium-low heat. Add the onion, leek, shallot, and garlic and cook until the onion is softened, about 6 minutes. Add the cauliflower scraps, broth, and milk, season with salt and pepper, and bring to a simmer. Cook until the cauliflower is completely soft, about 10 minutes.

Transfer the solids to a blender, reserving the liquid. Process to a light, creamy consistency, adding the liquid to thin the sauce as needed. Pass the sauce through a fine-mesh strainer into a large measuring cup. Pour 1 cup into a very small saucepan, cover, and keep over very low heat.

In a large skillet, heat 2 tablespoons of the oil over medium-high heat. Add the cabbage and cook, stirring often, until it's half-wilted, about 2 minutes. Add the butter and vinegar and continue to cook and stir until the cabbage is just barely tender, about 2 minutes more. Season with salt and pepper. The cabbage should have a slight vinegary tang; if needed, add more vinegar. Keep warm.

In a large skillet, heat 2 tablespoons of the oil over medium heat. Add the cauliflower pieces and cook until just tender and slightly caramelized on both sides, 2 to 3 minutes per side. Squeeze a little lemon juice over the pieces and then season with salt and pepper.

Meanwhile, in a large skillet, heat the remaining 1 tablespoon olive oil over medium-high heat. Season the char on both sides with salt and pepper. Lay the fillets in the pan and cook until just barely brown on the bottom, about 3 minutes. Flip the fillets and cook until just cooked through, about a minute more.

Put the cauliflower pieces in a single layer on each plate and top with some cabbage, followed by a char fillet. Stir the caviar into the warm cauliflower sauce (make sure it's not hot, or it will cook the caviar!), spoon the sauce evenly over the fillets, and top with the chives.

THE BARISTA AND THE GLASS POLISHER

Hassan Ahmed, originally from Bangladesh, has found his medium drawing fanciful patterns and even complicated portraits in the soft foam of beautiful cappuccinos.

Our guests might think that there is a set way of running this restaurant that has always existed, but the fact is that every decision to add a staff position is full of drama. A prime example is the barista. In early Gramercy days, the coffee machine was behind the bar and it was a dreaded sight for most bartenders: I've never met a bartender who wanted to be a barista! The bar was never designed to be a coffee station. The bartenders didn't have the time to make coffee; servers dreaded bothering them with coffee orders. After too many years, we decided to move coffee into its own station, created the position of barista, and all of a sudden, the staff *loved* selling coffee! In fact, they encouraged it, because now we had somebody who actually liked making it. And at the end of a big dinner, you would have six people all ordering coffees and cappuccinos, which prompted orders of after-dinner drinks. Check averages went up, tips went up. And it gave us the ability to move forward with a serious coffee program.

Like many of our initiatives, this idea came from our ongoing dialogue with Danny. We said, "Why can't we serve world-class coffee here?" And at the time, Danny couldn't stop raving about Blue Bottle Coffee in the Ferry Building in San Francisco. So I went to the West Coast,

where I met and tasted with three top roasters. Blue Bottle was head and shoulders above the others; James Freeman, its principled owner, is fanatic about his coffee and exacting about how it is roasted, ground, and served. Of course, making that commitment to excellence meant a great deal more than just the expense of a top-of-the-line espresso machine, but we were willing to invest in a coffee program in order to offer Blue Bottle's organic coffee, becoming the first big restaurant to serve artisanal, coffee-bar-type coffee in New York.

When we added the position of glass polisher, the impact was tremendous. For years, we'd begun each dinner service with a full set of polished glassware on every table, but as tables turned and wine flowed, we'd quickly go through the initial round of polished glasses. A table of eight might drink two white Burgundies, two red Burgundies, and finish with a Bordeaux. We're talking forty glasses that you have to get to that table in the middle of a busy Friday night. Immediately. And if you don't have the glasses, you have to find them, and if they're hot from the dishwasher, you have to ice them down, and then polish them. That means it could be a *very* long time to get that wine to the table. Then imagine that the last of a bottle is drained midway through the entrée course: you have a tiny window to get the glassware down, to get the next bottle up, present it, and pour it before the last bites are taken. If we can't manage it, guests end up disappointed. Next time, they might not ask for another bottle.

So we introduced the idea of a glass polisher. We didn't invent that position. We were at Jean Georges and saw they had a *whole room* for a dedicated glass polisher. We were sick with envy; in the middle of a busy service, servers there could just stop by that room and pick up fresh glasses. So we hired a glass polisher. Part of our staff's job at the end of the night had been to polish all of the glassware, so not only did the new position eliminate the stress of emergency polishing during service, it also lessened the staff's late-night side work. The glass-polishing position became a win-win for everybody!

—*Kevin Mahan*

Even though she's polishing glasses, Ana Flores is not a glass polisher. She's a captain in the dining room, carrying on the family tradition; her two older brothers, Manny and Gabe, were captains, too.

SEAFOOD CHOWDER WITH SQUASH

SERVES 6

In every good restaurant kitchen, there's a combination of thrift and innovation. We always have a dish like this chowder on the menu because when we portion fish for main courses, there are inevitably some pieces of our excellent, sushi-quality fish too small to serve on their own. And that is another great reason to buy your fish whole: not only can you save the bones and head for stock, but you'll be generating two meals from one shopping trip.

We call it chowder to give the idea of a hearty, chunky fish soup (sea bass, shrimp, mussels) with a lot of texture from the vegetables. Our version shows off kabocha squash and ají dulce peppers. These are specific varieties of squash and pepper that I search for at the Greenmarket for their deep flavor and beautiful aroma. If you can't find these, use another variety of squash and a mild pepper.

CHOWDER BASE

1 tablespoon olive oil

1/2 small white onion, minced

1/2 leek (white and pale green parts), halved lengthwise and thinly sliced

1 shallot, minced

1 garlic clove, minced

1 tablespoon peeled and minced ginger

2 cups peeled, seeded, and cubed winter squash, such as kabocha

1 carrot, sliced

1/2 teaspoon mild curry powder

Salt

1 lemongrass stalk, bruised with the side of a chef's knife and halved

1 bay leaf

3/4 cup unsweetened coconut milk

3 1/2 cups Vegetable Broth (page 118) or water

MUSSELS

1 tablespoon olive oil

1 shallot, minced

1 garlic clove, minced

1/2 cup white wine

1 pound mussels, cleaned

1 cup diced winter squash, such as kabocha

1 cup diced potatoes

8 baby turnips, peeled and quartered

8 baby radishes, halved

1/2 pound medium shrimp, peeled, deveined, and halved

1/2 pound skinless black sea bass fillet, cut into small chunks

1 ají dulce or other small red pepper, cored, seeded, halved crosswise, and julienned

Salt and pepper

Extra-virgin olive oil

2 tablespoons minced red onion

1 tablespoon finely chopped chives

Aleppo pepper

Make the chowder base. In a medium pot, heat the olive oil over medium-low heat. Add the onion and cook until softened, about 6 minutes. Add the leek, shallot, garlic, and ginger and cook, stirring occasionally, until the leek is softened, about 6 minutes. Add the squash, carrot, and curry powder, season with salt, and cook, stirring, for a few minutes.

Raise the heat to medium-high, add the lemongrass, bay leaf, coconut milk, and broth, and bring to a simmer. Cook the chowder base until the squash and carrots are very tender, about 30 minutes.

Meanwhile, make the mussels. In a medium pot, heat the olive oil over medium-low heat. Add the shallot and garlic and cook, stirring often, until softened, about 3 minutes. Increase the heat to high, add the wine, and bring to a boil. Add the mussels, cover the pot, and steam them until they just open wide, 3 to 4 minutes.

Using a slotted spoon, transfer the mussels to a medium bowl. Remove the mussels from the shells; discard the shells and any mussels that haven't opened. Strain the broth into a small bowl.

Once the squash is tender, discard the lemongrass and bay leaf. Process the chowder base in a blender until very smooth and creamy, then pass through a fine-mesh strainer into a large pot.

Bring the chowder base to a simmer, then add the raw diced squash, potatoes, and turnips and cook until tender, about 10 minutes. Add the radishes, shrimp, and sea bass and simmer for about 3 minutes. Stir in the mussels and red pepper. The soup's consistency should be thinner than a traditional chowder—add a splash of the reserved mussel liquid, if needed. Season with a touch of salt and pepper. Serve the chowder in bowls, topped with a drizzle of extra-virgin olive oil, the red onion, chives, and Aleppo pepper.

BRAISED LAMB SHOULDER
WITH BROCCOLI PUREE

SERVES 4

We have developed a close relationship with Keith Martin at Elysian Fields Farm in western Pennsylvania; every week, he supplies us with wonderful pasture-raised lamb. While the shoulder cut requires an investment of time to cook, it delivers the most incredible flavor. I've trained our butchers to remove the bones (which are roasted for stock) and marinate the meat in garlic confit and herbs. The large pieces of shoulder meat are first caramelized on the stovetop in heavy pans until evenly browned, then braised slowly in the oven in our aromatic lamb stock until meltingly tender and glistening. In order to achieve a stunning presentation, once the shoulders are cooked, we press them with weights to create even layers of meat that can later be cut into individual portions.

At home, you can re-create these aromas and flavors without restaurant-style precision and portioning, or the extra hours of work that we put in at the restaurant to get the lamb's deep, dark glazed color. The meat is so tender when it comes out of the oven that you could just pull the whole shoulder apart and serve it as is. Or begin the whole process with smaller, more manageable pieces (ask the butcher to cut boneless lamb shoulder into large cubes, about 4 ounces each). At home, the sauce will be lighter in color but still aromatic and delicious. The tender braised meat goes perfectly with vibrant vegetables like this broccoli puree. But throughout the year, I reach for all kinds of colorful seasonal vegetables to serve with the succulent lamb.

BRAISED LAMB

1 tablespoon olive oil

One 2-pound boneless lamb shoulder, tied (or cut into large cubes)

Salt and pepper

1 onion, chopped

6 garlic cloves, minced

2 shallots, minced

1 carrot, chopped

1 celery stalk, chopped

½ tablespoon tomato paste

½ cup red wine

3 sprigs thyme

1 sprig rosemary

1 bay leaf

About 5 cups Chicken Broth (page 59) or water

½ cup White Beans (page 129)

1½ cups Broccoli Puree (page 251)

20 bite-sized broccoli florets

4 baby turnips, peeled and quartered

Salt and pepper

Extra-virgin olive oil

2 tablespoons finely chopped chives

Preheat the oven to 325°F.

Make the braised lamb. In a heavy ovenproof pot with a lid, large enough to hold the meat snugly, heat the olive oil over medium-high heat. Season the lamb with salt and pepper, add to the pot, and brown well on all sides, about 15 minutes. Transfer the lamb to a platter.

Reduce the heat to medium and add the onion, garlic, shallots, carrots, and celery to the pot. Cook the vegetables, stirring occasionally, until softened, about 6 minutes. Stir in the tomato paste and cook for a minute. Add the wine and stir, scraping the bottom of the pot to loosen the browned bits, then simmer until the wine is almost gone. Patience! This is the magic moment for flavor.

Return the lamb to the pot, along with its accumulated juices, and add the thyme, rosemary, bay leaf, and enough broth to almost cover the meat. Bring to a simmer over high heat, cover the pot, and transfer to the oven. Cook, turning once about halfway through, until the lamb is very tender, 2 to 2½ hours.

RECIPE CONTINUES

Transfer the meat to a cutting board. Pass the liquid through a fine-mesh strainer into a wide saucepan, pushing down on the solids with a spoon to extract every last bit of juice. Bring the liquid to a simmer and reduce until it has thickened (you should have about a cup of sauce; this can take about 30 minutes). Season with salt and pepper.

Just before serving, finish the broccoli puree. In a medium saucepan, gently warm the white beans in the broccoli puree, making sure not to boil the puree. Meanwhile, blanch the broccoli florets and turnips in boiling salted water until crisp, about 2 minutes. Drain and then add to the broccoli puree. Season with salt and pepper and keep warm.

Serve the lamb shoulder whole or in pieces with the broccoli puree. Coat the meat with some of the reduced sauce, then sprinkle with extra-virgin olive oil and the chives.

BROCCOLI PUREE

MAKES ABOUT 2 CUPS

I use vegetable purees every day in the kitchen to bring a loose and satiny-smooth texture to a dish. A powerful Vitamix blender helps us achieve this lovely consistency. For me, a puree acts like a backdrop that helps show off the other ingredients and add moisture, without having to use cream or butter. Color, too, plays an important role. The brightness of the broccoli puree contrasts perfectly with the glazed braised lamb. I actually remember the moment when I first saw how bright colors were used playfully on the plate. I was working in the kitchen at Daniel. It was the first American kitchen I'd worked in after cooking abroad, and I was delighted that the dishes looked like *fun*! They were intricate and beautiful. Frequently I'll look at an array of dishes in the GT kitchen ready to go out to the dining room and I'll marvel at how much color and vibrancy there is on the plate. Even in winter.

You can make this puree with many green vegetables, such as spinach, kale, or nettles. Consider purees of other colors, too, like carrots, fennel, parsnips, beets, corn, or sunchokes. It's as simple as making soup—you're just aiming for a bit more body.

½ cup spinach leaves

2 cups broccoli trimmings (stems peeled and cut into small pieces; florets separated)

1 tablespoon olive oil

¼ cup minced shallots

1 small garlic clove, minced

4 basil leaves

1 tablespoon extra-virgin olive oil

About 1½ cups Vegetable Broth (page 118) or water

Salt and pepper

Blanch the spinach in boiling salted water for 15 seconds. Remove the spinach with a slotted spoon, shock in ice water, and remove with a slotted spoon. Blanch the broccoli until quite tender, about 3 minutes. Drain, shock in the ice water, and drain again. Squeeze out excess water from the vegetables.

In a very small skillet, heat the olive oil over medium-low heat. Add the shallots and garlic and cook until the shallots are soft, about 5 minutes.

In a blender, combine the spinach and broccoli, shallot mixture, basil, extra-virgin olive oil, and enough broth to make a thin puree and process until smooth. Season with salt and pepper, then pass through a fine-mesh strainer. The broccoli puree will keep, covered, in the refrigerator overnight.

APPLE PIE

MAKES ONE 9-INCH DOUBLE-CRUST PIE

If you've tasted a better apple pie, please tell me where, because I'd put Nancy's apple pie up against any in the nation! She has such a special touch in the way she handles ingredients. When you taste the crust, you just imagine her hands working the dough. While you can certainly make this pie with just one kind of apple, we suggest a combination of flavors and textures, such as Winesap, Mutsu, and Honeycrisp; Fuji and Granny Smith are also great. Nancy piles the apples amazingly high when building this dessert. They cook down into the most wonderful, intensely flavored pie. We serve it with Sweet Cream Ice Cream (page 173).

3/4 cup sugar, plus more for sprinkling

3 tablespoons cornstarch

1 teaspoon ground cinnamon, plus more for sprinkling

1/2 teaspoon salt

Flaky Pie Dough (page 170)

All-purpose flour for rolling

8 medium apples (about 3 1/2 pounds), peeled, cored, and cut into 1/4-inch slices

Preheat the oven to 400°F, with a rack in the bottom position.

In a large bowl, whisk together the sugar, cornstarch, cinnamon, and salt.

On a lightly floured surface, roll one disk of dough into a 13-inch circle, then fit it into a 9-inch pie dish. Roll the other disk into a 13-inch circle.

Add the apples to the sugar mixture and toss thoroughly. (We combine the apples with the sugar at the last minute so the mixture stays drier and doesn't weight down the dough.) Pour the apple mixture into the dish. We call for just the right amount of apples. Don't be afraid if you see them piled high. Cover with the remaining dough circle, then trim the excess dough, and crimp the edges.

Cut about a dozen slits all over the pie. Sprinkle liberally with sugar and cinnamon and place on a baking sheet lined with aluminum foil. (This way you needn't worry about any juices that may bubble over.) Bake until the crust is golden and the filling is bubbly, 65 to 75 minutes. Transfer the pie to a rack and serve warm or at room temperature.

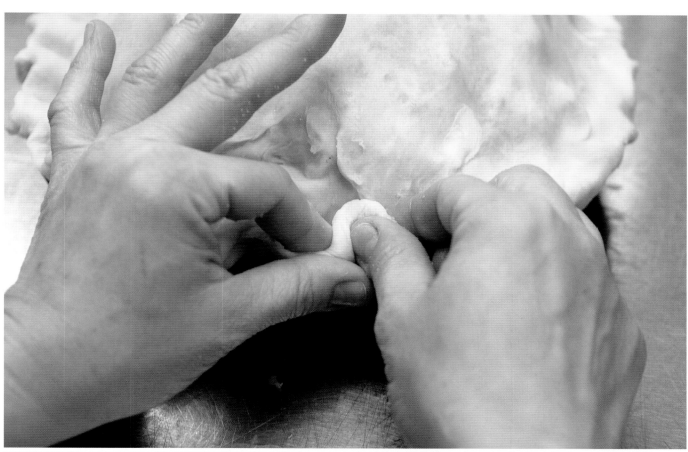

CARROT CAKE

MAKES ONE 9-BY-13-INCH CAKE

This is a surprisingly light version of carrot cake, not weighed down with nuts. It's topped with a stunning carrot-colored glaze made with carrot juice. If you would like to include nuts, add 1½ cups toasted chopped pecans or walnuts to the batter.

4 tablespoons (½ stick) unsalted butter, melted and cooled, plus butter for the pan

1½ cups all-purpose flour, plus more for the pan

3 large eggs

1¼ cups granulated sugar

1½ teaspoons baking powder

½ teaspoon baking soda

½ teaspoon salt

½ teaspoon ground cinnamon

¼ cup vegetable oil

1 teaspoon vanilla extract

2 cups lightly packed peeled and shredded carrots

FROSTING

8 ounces cream cheese, at room temperature

1 cup confectioners' sugar

8 tablespoons (1 stick) unsalted butter, at room temperature

Carrot Glaze (opposite; optional)

Preheat the oven to 350°F, with a rack in the middle position. Butter and flour a 9-by-13-inch baking pan.

In the bowl of a stand mixer, combine the eggs and sugar and mix on medium-high speed until light and fluffy, 8 to 10 minutes.

Meanwhile, in a small bowl, whisk together the flour, baking powder, baking soda, salt, and cinnamon. In another small bowl, whisk together the oil, melted butter, and vanilla.

When the eggs are ready, slowly drizzle the oil mixture down the side of the mixer bowl and continue mixing on medium-high speed until the mixture is emulsified and looks like a light, fluffy mayonnaise. Fold the dry ingredients into the egg mixture until just barely combined, then stir in the carrots.

Pour the batter into the prepared pan. Bake until the cake springs back when touched, 25 to 30 minutes. Let cool completely in the pan on a wire rack.

Meanwhile, make the frosting. In the bowl of the mixer fitted with the paddle attachment, beat the cream cheese and confectioners' sugar until light and fluffy, about 2 minutes. Add the butter and mix until completely incorporated and creamy, about 2 minutes more.

Invert the cake onto a serving platter. Using a serrated knife, cut the cake horizontally in half; lift off the top layer. Frost the top of the bottom layer, then top with the other layer and spread the remaining frosting over the top (we don't frost the sides). If you're not using the carrot glaze, the cake can be served immediately.

If you are using the carrot glaze, smooth the frosting on the top of the cake as evenly as possible. Pour the glaze over the middle of the cake and then gently and evenly spread it out to the edges. Refrigerate the cake until the glaze sets and serve.

CARROT GLAZE

MAKES ABOUT ½ CUP

½ teaspoon unflavored gelatin

1 tablespoon sugar

½ cup carrot juice

Pour 1 tablespoon water into a very small bowl. Sprinkle the gelatin over the top and let it sit for 3 to 5 minutes to soften.

In a very small saucepan, combine 1 tablespoon water and the sugar and bring just to a boil over medium-high heat, then remove from the heat and add the gelatin. Stir gently until the gelatin is completely dissolved. Gradually stir in the carrot juice, then strain the glaze through a piece of cheesecloth into a small bowl. Set the bowl over an ice bath and stir regularly with a spatula, scraping down the sides of the bowl, until it starts to thicken. When the glaze lightly coats the spatula, it is ready to use.

MONKEY BREAD

MAKES ONE 9-BY-13-INCH PAN

We don't serve this sweet bread at the restaurant, but Nancy manages to make her version of the 1950s American classic quite often because it's a staff favorite, whether at family meal, for birthdays, or whenever someone needs a little lift. Make it yourself, and you'll know what I mean.

²/₃ cup plus ½ cup heavy cream

1 cup packed dark brown sugar

2 tablespoons light corn syrup

6 tablespoons (³/₄ stick) unsalted butter

½ teaspoon salt

1 vanilla bean, split lengthwise

2 teaspoons fresh lemon juice

Brioche dough (page 260), refrigerated for at least 8 hours

4 tablespoons (½ stick) unsalted butter, melted

1 cup sugar

1 tablespoon ground cinnamon

In a small saucepan, combine ²/₃ cup of the cream, the brown sugar, corn syrup, the 6 tablespoons butter, and the salt. With the tip of a paring knife, scrape the seeds from the vanilla bean into the pan, then add the bean itself. Bring the mixture to a boil over high heat, stirring until the sugar is dissolved, then reduce the heat and simmer for a few minutes to thicken.

Remove from the heat and stir in the lemon juice and the remaining ½ cup cream. Remove the vanilla bean. Pour the toffee sauce into a 9-by-13-inch baking pan.

Divide the brioche into 20 golf ball–sized pieces and roll. Put the melted butter in a small bowl. In another small bowl, combine the sugar and cinnamon. Dip each ball in the butter, roll in the sugar mixture, and arrange in the baking pan so you end up with 4 rows of 5 balls each.

To proof the dough, loosely cover the pan with plastic wrap and put it in a warm place until the dough is light and has doubled in size, about 1½ hours. (The dough is very forgiving, so don't worry if it rises longer. You can even leave it out overnight.)

Preheat the oven to 350°F, with a rack in the middle position.

Bake the monkey bread until cooked through and golden brown, about 30 minutes. Let cool for about 10 minutes. Serve the bread straight from the pan. It's so much more fun to pull it apart by hand instead of cutting it. The bread will keep, tightly covered, at room temperature for up to 2 days.

BRIOCHE

MAKES ONE 1¼-POUND LOAF

Brioche dough is easy to make if you use a sturdy stand mixer and the dough hook. You can bake it in a regular loaf pan. We use this brioche for the croutons for Chocolate Pudding (page 110) and in the Chocolate Bread Pudding (page 337). Of course, it is also delicious sliced and toasted with Chicken Liver Mousse (page 88) or Rhubarb Jam (page 105).

⅓ cup warm whole milk

2 teaspoons active dry yeast

2 cups all-purpose flour

2 tablespoons sugar

¼ teaspoon salt

2 large eggs

12 tablespoons (1½ sticks) unsalted butter, at room temperature, plus more for the bowl and pan

1 egg, lightly beaten with 1 tablespoon milk, for egg wash

In a very small bowl, combine the milk and yeast. Let sit for several minutes, then stir to dissolve the yeast.

In the bowl of a stand mixer fitted with the dough hook, combine the flour, sugar, and salt and mix briefly. Add the eggs and the milk mixture and mix on low speed, scraping the sides and bottom of the bowl and the hook as needed, until a smooth ball forms, about 4 minutes.

With the mixer on low speed, add the butter a tablespoon at a time, allowing each piece to be incorporated before adding the next; this can take up to 30 minutes or so. The dough will likely creep up the hook during the process; stop the machine occasionally and push it back down.

After all the butter has been added, stop the machine and scrape down the sides of the bowl and the hook. The dough will be very soft and sticky. Increase the speed to medium-low, then to medium, and knead the dough until it is smooth, shiny, and completely homogenous and comes away from the sides of the bowl, 10 to 15 minutes.

Butter a medium bowl. Turn the dough out into the bowl and cover with plastic wrap. Refrigerate for at least 8 hours, or overnight.

Butter a 9-by-5-inch loaf pan. Push the air out of the dough and fit it into the pan, flattening it into an even rectangle. To proof the dough, loosely cover the pan with plastic wrap and put it in a warm place until the dough has tripled in size, 2½ to 3 hours.

Preheat the oven to 375°F, with a rack in the middle position.

Lightly brush the top of the risen dough with the egg wash. Bake until the brioche is golden brown and sounds hollow when you knock on it, about 35 minutes. Turn the loaf out onto a rack and let cool.

PEANUT BUTTER SEMIFREDDO
WITH CHOCOLATE MACARONS

SERVES 14

This dessert comprises a number of recipes, but each of them—the Candied Peanuts, Caramel Sauce, Semifreddo, Chocolate Macarons, and Hot Fudge—can be made and enjoyed separately. We make the luscious, creamy semifreddo in 2-ounce flexible silicone savarin molds, which are easy to unmold; the ring shape is also perfect for holding the caramel sauce. But you can use individual ramekins (no need to unmold them if you aren't doing all the accompaniments; simply bring them straight from the freezer to the table). Or simply pour the mixture into a loaf pan, then unmold it and serve it cut into slices.

SEMIFREDDO

9 large egg yolks

1/2 cup plus 2 tablespoons sugar

3/4 cup smooth peanut butter

3/4 teaspoon vanilla extract

1/4 teaspoon salt

1 1/2 cups heavy cream, whipped to very soft peaks and refrigerated

Hot Fudge (page 109)

Chocolate Macarons (page 264)

Caramel Sauce (page 267)

Sea salt

1 cup heavy cream, lightly whipped

Candied Peanuts (page 267)

Make the semifreddo. In the bowl of a stand mixer, combine the yolks and 2 tablespoons of the sugar and whip on medium-high speed until the mixture is pale yellow and holds a line drawn with a finger down the back of a wooden spoon, about 3 minutes.

Meanwhile, in a small saucepan, combine the remaining 1/2 cup sugar and 1/4 cup water (being careful not to get sugar on the sides of the pan, where it can crystallize) and bring to a boil over medium-high heat, stirring until the sugar is dissolved. Boil the syrup, without stirring, until it reaches the soft ball stage (235° to 240°F on a candy thermometer), about 5 minutes. Immediately remove from the heat.

Reduce the mixer speed to medium and gradually and carefully pour the syrup in a thin stream into the whipped yolks. Increase the speed to medium-high and whip until the bowl feels completely cool, 7 to 10 minutes.

In a large bowl, combine the peanut butter, vanilla, and salt. Using a large rubber spatula, stir in one-third of the whipped egg yolks to lighten the peanut butter mixture, then fold in the remaining whipped yolks. Stir in one-third of the whipped cream, then gently fold in the remaining whipped cream.

Spoon the mixture into fourteen 2-ounce silicone savarin molds or ramekins. Freeze until firm.

To serve, pour some hot fudge on the bottom of each shallow bowl. Put one macaron upside down on the bowl, top with a semifreddo, and then tilt another macaron against the side. Fill the centers of the semifreddo with caramel sauce and sprinkle with sea salt. Dollop whipped cream on each bowl and scatter with the candied peanuts.

CHOCOLATE MACARONS

MAKES ABOUT TWENTY-EIGHT 2¾-INCH MACARONS

Here's how to make the iconic Parisian macaron, which is essentially a flavored meringue with nuts. We serve these large cookies with the semifreddo or on their own. You can also make smaller ones and sandwich a layer of ganache, buttercream, or jam between two cookies. Note that smaller cookies will cook faster, so reduce the cooking time.

2⅓ cups almond flour

2 cups plus 2 tablespoons confectioners' sugar

¼ cup unsweetened cocoa powder

1 cup granulated sugar

5 large egg whites, at room temperature

Preheat the oven to 350°F, with racks in the lower and upper-middle positions. Line two baking sheets with parchment paper. Fit a pastry bag with a ½-inch (#6) plain tip.

In a food processor, pulse the flour, confectioners' sugar, and cocoa powder until combined. Sift by scraping the mixture through a fine-mesh strainer with a rubber spatula into a large bowl. (These steps may seem unnecessary, but sometimes there are larger bits of almonds in the flour or lumps in the cocoa, which can make the tops bumpy.)

In a very small saucepan, combine the granulated sugar and ⅓ cup water (being careful not to get sugar on the sides of the pan, where it can crystallize) and bring to a boil over medium-high heat, stirring until the sugar is dissolved. Boil the syrup, without stirring, until it reaches the soft ball stage (235° to 240°F on a candy thermometer), about 5 minutes. Immediately remove from the heat.

Meanwhile, in the bowl of a stand mixer, whip 2 of the egg whites on medium-low speed until foamy, about 2 minutes. If the syrup isn't ready by the time the whites are foamy, turn off the mixer while you wait for it to heat. When the syrup is ready, increase the mixer speed to medium and gradually pour the syrup in a thin stream into the whites. Increase the speed to medium-high and whip the

meringue until soft peaks form and the bowl feels completely cool, 7 to 10 minutes.

Meanwhile, mix the remaining 3 egg whites into the dry ingredients, using a sturdy spatula. (This takes some time and a little arm strength, so be patient.)

Stir half of the cooled meringue into the almond flour mixture, using the spatula to scrape the bottom and sides of the bowl. Gently fold in the remaining meringue; the mixture will resemble a thick cake batter. Stir the mixture several times to thin it. It takes practice to know exactly how much to stir—too much, and your macarons will spread; not enough, and they will be lumpy. But they'll taste great either way.

Transfer the batter to the pastry bag and pipe about twenty-eight 2-inch circles about 2 inches apart on each prepared baking sheet. Let the macarons sit until a skin forms on top, about 10 minutes.

Bake, rotating the sheets halfway through, until the cookies puff up and the tops are hard but still jiggle around when you touch them, 8 to 10 minutes. Let cool completely on the baking sheets. The macarons will keep in a covered container for up to 5 days.

CANDIED PEANUTS MAKES 1½ CUPS

These sweet and salty nuts are also great on top of ice cream sundaes or as a cocktail snack.

1 tablespoon unsalted butter

½ cup sugar

1½ cups unsalted roasted peanuts

⅛ teaspoon salt

Lightly coat a baking sheet with ½ tablespoon of the butter.

In a small saucepan, combine the sugar and 2 tablespoons water (being careful not to get sugar on the sides of the pan, where it can crystallize) and bring to a boil over medium-high heat, stirring until the sugar is dissolved. Boil the syrup until it reaches the thread stage (220° to 235°F on a candy thermometer), about 2 minutes.

Remove from the heat, add the peanuts, and stir with a wooden spoon or heatproof spatula until the sugar turns white and crystallizes on the nuts. Cook the peanuts over medium-low heat, stirring constantly, until the sugar turns an amber color, about 5 minutes. (It will take a while for the sugar to melt again, so be patient and keep stirring.) Immediately remove the pan from the heat and stir in the remaining ½ tablespoon butter and the salt.

Turn the nuts out onto the buttered baking sheet. Quickly and carefully separate the peanuts with your fingers. This can be tricky—the peanuts are really hot! Or do it after the nuts cool; you won't get perfect pieces, but they'll be just as delicious. Let the nuts cool completely. The candied peanuts will keep in a covered container for up to 2 weeks.

CARAMEL SAUCE MAKES ABOUT 2⅓ CUPS

Of course you can buy caramel sauce, but it's incredibly easy to make and keep. There's another caramel sauce in this book: the salted caramel sauce that accompanies the Chocolate Pudding (page 110). This version is richer and has a candylike quality that pairs well with the semifreddo's peanuts and hot fudge.

1½ cups sugar

One 14-ounce can sweetened condensed milk

2 teaspoons vanilla extract

⅛ teaspoon salt

In a small saucepan, combine the sugar and ½ cup water (being careful not to get sugar on the sides of the pan, where it can crystallize) and bring to a boil over medium-high heat, stirring until the sugar dissolves. Boil the syrup, without stirring, until it becomes an amber color (about 340°F on a candy thermometer), about 10 minutes. Immediately remove from the heat.

Very slowly and carefully pour ⅓ cup water down the side of the pan into the caramel, making sure your hand and arm are not over the saucepan. Carefully add the condensed milk, vanilla, and salt and stir to combine, making sure to get into the edges of the saucepan. If the sauce is lumpy, stir it over medium heat until the lumps dissolve. Transfer to a container and let cool to room temperature. The caramel sauce will keep, covered, in the refrigerator for up to a month.

WINTER

BAKED CLAMS

MAKES 20 CLAMS

My wife, Mindy, grew up eating classic baked clams on the East End of Long Island. I wanted to tap into her nostalgic feelings for summertime and the beach and amplify them by cooking the clams over our open wood-burning fire in the Tavern. It took a number of tries to get it right. I chop the clams first and then add scallops for their sweetness and irresistible flavor. In fact, the dish has become so popular that, along with Roasted Oysters (page 274), it's often the first thing that our staff and regulars order when they come to the Tavern. Baked clams are great for parties: you can assemble them up to a day ahead, refrigerate, and then cook them when you're ready—in a baking pan in the oven or directly on the grates of a hot grill.

1 cup white wine

1 shallot, sliced, plus ¾ cup minced shallots

3 garlic cloves, smashed, plus 2 tablespoons minced garlic

⅓ cup finely chopped flat-leaf parsley, plus a few flat-leaf parsley stems

20 large cherrystone clams, cleaned

¼ cup olive oil

4 tablespoons (½ stick) unsalted butter

1¼ cups minced onions

1¼ cups minced leeks (white parts)

1½ tablespoons peeled and minced ginger

2 teaspoons thyme leaves

Salt and pepper

1¾ cups panko or dried bread crumbs

7 ounces sea scallops, cut into small pieces

1 tablespoon fresh lemon juice

5 cups rock salt

1 lemon, cut into 8 wedges

In a large pot, bring the wine, 1 cup water, the sliced shallot, 2 of the smashed garlic cloves, and the parsley stems to a boil over high heat. Add the clams, cover the pot, and steam until they open, 6 to 8 minutes. Using a slotted spoon, transfer the clams to a large bowl and discard the sediment.

Remove the clams from the shells and save half the shells. Cut the clams into quarters and transfer to a small bowl; cover and refrigerate. Separate the 10 reserved shells and rinse them. Strain the broth into a small container.

Make the filling. In a large skillet, heat 2 tablespoons of the oil and 2 tablespoons of the butter over medium-low heat. Add the onions, leeks, minced shallots, minced garlic, ginger, and 1 teaspoon of the thyme and cook until the onions are softened, 12 minutes. Reduce the heat, pour in the reserved clam broth, and simmer until the pan is almost dry. Season with salt and pepper. Transfer the onion mixture to a large bowl and set aside to cool.

In a large skillet, heat the remaining 2 tablespoons oil and remaining 2 tablespoons butter over medium heat. Add the panko, the remaining teaspoon of thyme, and the remaining smashed garlic clove and toast, stirring constantly, until golden brown, about 4 minutes. Season with salt, discard the garlic, and transfer the panko to a medium bowl.

To finish the filling, add the clams, scallops, chopped parsley, and lemon juice to the onion mixture, season with salt and pepper, and mix well.

Preheat the oven to 375°F. To keep the clams from tipping, spread the rock salt in a large baking pan.

Gently pack the filling into the reserved shells. Cover the packed clam shells evenly with the browned panko, lightly patting to help them stick. Nestle the clams in the salt. Bake just until hot, 15 to 20 minutes. Serve with the lemon wedges.

Cooking the clams over an open fire gives them an amazing smokiness. We prepare them in advance and you can, too. Just before we're ready to serve, we flash them in a hot oven or over our wood-burning grill. The salt is simply used to balance the shells; seaweed also works well.

ROASTED OYSTERS

MAKES 20 OYSTERS

"You could hear people eating in the roast oyster place from five blocks away. There is something about a roast oyster, a clean, stinging taste of the blue sea, hotter than boiling oil, neatly packaged in its own bone-dry kiln, that makes even the most refined diners snort, sniffle, and hum as they eat." I love this passage from Mark Helprin's *Winter's Tale*, which evokes the legendary oyster houses that defined lower Manhattan in the nineteenth century. It inspired me to think of how oysters—and taverns—are connected to old New York.

Starting a meal at Gramercy Tavern with a platter of raw oysters and following that with roasted oysters right from the smoky fire shows off the most elemental way we know to cook an ingredient that is completely representative of the East Coast. The heat of the wood-fired grill is transferred gently through the oyster shells, slowly cooking the oysters. I serve oysters that come from nearby because they embody the distinctive qualities of our region. I'm particularly fond of Island Creek Oysters and Fisher Island oysters, from Long Island Sound. Buy the best local oysters you can find.

1½ tablespoons olive oil

¼ cup minced leek (white part)

1 shallot, minced

1 garlic clove, minced

Salt and pepper

6 tablespoons (¾ stick) unsalted butter, cubed

20 oysters on the half shell (detached from the bottom shells)

5 cups rock salt

¼ cup Pickled Radishes, Carrots, and Celery Root (opposite)

2 tablespoons minced chives

In a medium skillet, heat the oil over medium-low heat. Add the leek, shallot, and garlic and cook until soft, about 7 minutes. Season with salt and pepper and set aside to cool.

Meanwhile, make the brown butter. In a small skillet, cook the butter over medium heat, swirling the pan, until the butter melts and the milk solids turn golden brown, about 3 minutes. Set aside to cool.

Preheat the oven to 450°F, or prepare an outdoor grill and let the coals burn until they turn white.

To keep the oysters from tipping, spread the rock salt in a large baking pan and nestle the oysters in the salt, being careful not to spill the juices. With a spoon, gently lift each oyster from the shell, slip about ¼ teaspoon of the cooked leek mixture into the shell, and set the oyster on top. Drizzle with a little brown butter.

Bake in the oven or cook on the grill until the oysters are just heated through, about 5 minutes. Top each oyster with a few pieces of pickled vegetables and the chives.

PICKLED RADISHES, CARROTS, AND CELERY ROOT

MAKES ABOUT 2 PINTS

These are my favorite pickles to top roasted oysters, but I also like to serve them with Chicken Liver Mousse (page 88), or just sprinkle them like confetti over a salad. Follow the Basic Pickling Recipe (page 86), substituting these ingredients. Because they're cut so small, these pickles are ready after about an hour in the refrigerator.

½ cup minced radishes

½ cup minced carrot

½ cup minced celery root

¾ cup rice vinegar

¼ cup water

¼ cup sugar

1 tablespoon kosher salt

SCOTT REINHARDT

ASSISTANT GENERAL MANAGER •
SINCE 1997

I grew up on Long Island, where my family has always been sort of in the restaurant business. My dad decided that he wanted to open a bar and serve food. It was a family affair. My mom was the daytime bartender and I was the bartender at night and managed the place. It was called Reinhardt's and it was successful for a while. I ended up opening my own restaurant in 1989, when I was twenty-four. I didn't know much, but we did very well. Then our landlord quadrupled the rent. I sold the restaurant and moved into the city. My life changed.

I met my partner, Paul (a cop at the time but now the office manager of Gramercy Tavern). And I got a job as a waiter at Bobby Flay's Mesa Grill. A bartender took me under his wing, and the first thing he told me was to get rid of that Long Island accent. I asked him to repeat what I'd said; I had no idea I talked like that! It was a good run there, but in 1997, I decided that I wanted to work for the best. That meant Gramercy Tavern. Gramercy hired me as a waiter. I was happy, but I worried that it would be too much for me, that I was underskilled. They promised to train me and they did.

I'll never forget the day my mom came in and Danny walked over to her table and said, "You must be so proud." I was like, "Oh, my God!" It was just a comment, but it made me feel so good about working here. This was sixteen years ago and it has stuck with me. I became the daytime maître d'. I still enjoy plotting the room: seating people is like a jigsaw puzzle—putting industry-related diners together so they'll see each other when they're coming and going. That's what Danny talks about: making the dining room feel lively. We've discovered over the years that you never seat the closest room first; you seat the farthest room first, so you're not walking by tables full of people to get to an empty room.

Looking around this buzzing dining room now, it's hard to believe that GT wasn't all that busy for lunch when I started. We used to call over to Union Square Cafe and ask them to send their overflow. I can't even imagine doing that now.

I became a floor manager (I still supervise host reservations), and eventually the AGM. This means that I'm here all day Monday to Friday. The hardest lesson for me has probably been how to be nice to staff all the time. Between running the floor for lunch and maintaining the physical plant of the restaurant, there's a lot to juggle. If I'm cranky, it is usually not about the person in my path, it's the exploding toilet or the broken air conditioner. Gradually I learned that it's much easier to be nice, to be on the staff's side, and to let them know that I'm on their side. The goal is to keep morale high.

I've come to love everything about being a manager, including being the first person the staff sees in the morning. Guests ask me, "How do you manage to hire such nice people?" The thing is, that's exactly what we do: we look at who the person is, not how much he or she knows in the interview. Once here, I think they're happy and nice to our guests because they like everyone they're working with and are having a good time! The staff has to feel good for our guests to feel good. If you really want to describe what we do in one sentence, that's it.

We do push our staff with, to use a Danny phrase, "constant, gentle pressure." But they do feel that they can make a difference—empowered. Our employees are great. One challenge is when restaurant work is not someone's chosen career; that person may need an extra push. But really the staff is a delight to work with and they appreciate our guidance. The best compliment is when someone leaves GT for another job and then reports back, "I channel you guys almost every day: What would Scott do? What would Kevin do? What would Juliette do?" We must be doing something right!

BACON CHEDDAR BISCUITS

MAKES ABOUT 50 SMALL BISCUITS

We make these mini-biscuits as a snack in the Tavern, but I'll make them anywhere, anytime. Try them for breakfast, split in half and topped with a spoonful of scrambled eggs and melted Cabot Clothbound Cheddar; it's a favorite, made by Jasper Hill in Vermont. Since the biscuit dough balls can be frozen and then baked straight from the freezer, it's easy to keep some on hand. (You can make bigger biscuits if you like; just increase the baking time.) If you have the time, freeze the mixed dry ingredients overnight. When the dough is really cold it is more difficult for gluten to form. Less gluten means softer biscuits.

½ cup diced slab bacon (about 3 ounces)

2¼ cups all-purpose flour

3¾ teaspoons baking powder

1 teaspoon salt

⅛ teaspoon cayenne pepper

3 tablespoons unsalted butter, cubed and chilled

¾ cup shredded sharp Cheddar cheese (about 4 ounces)

1½ cups heavy cream

2 tablespoons unsalted butter, melted

Preheat the oven to 425°F.

In a medium skillet, cook the bacon over medium-low heat until the fat is rendered and the bacon is browned but not crunchy, about 6 minutes. Drain the bacon on a paper towel–lined plate and allow to cool completely.

In a large bowl, mix the flour, baking powder, salt, and cayenne with a rubber spatula. Add the cubed butter and toss to coat with the flour mixture, then flatten the pieces of butter between your fingertips. Flattening the bits of butter to mix them with the flour helps produce a really tender biscuit. Stir in the bacon and cheese. Add the cream and mix with the spatula until just combined.

Divide the dough into about 50 tablespoon-sized pieces and shape into balls, handling the dough as little as possible. Put the balls about 1 inch apart on a baking sheet. (The dough balls can be frozen at this point; once hard, transfer them to a freezer container for up to 2 weeks.)

Bake until golden and cooked through, 8 to 10 minutes (add a few minutes if frozen). Brush with the melted butter and serve hot or at room temperature.

RUBY RED SHRIMP WITH WHITE BEANS AND KALE SALSA VERDE

SERVES 4

Ruby Reds are wild American shrimp that come from the warm waters of the Atlantic and the Gulf of Mexico. Unlike shrimp imported from Southeast Asia (which are frequently farmed unsustainably), these wild American beauties have a soft, meaty texture and rich flavor. For the beans, I like to use different varieties of organic ones like yellow-eye, orca, turtle, and navy beans from Cayuga Pure Organics in the Finger Lakes. Although they're simple to cook, they are every bit as important as the shrimp in adding complex flavor.

2 cups cooked White Beans (page 129)

1 cup Vegetable Broth (page 118), or bean liquid plus water

2 tablespoons extra-virgin olive oil

Salt and pepper

2 teaspoons minced garlic, plus 2 garlic cloves, smashed

¼ cup chopped mixed herbs, such as parsley, cilantro, chives, and/or tarragon

3 tablespoons olive oil

20 medium shrimp, peeled and deveined

Large leaves from 4 Brussels sprouts

Kale Salsa Verde

Combine 1 cup of the beans with ½ cup of the broth and the extra-virgin olive oil, season with salt and pepper, and process in a blender until smooth. Transfer the bean puree to a medium saucepan and heat over medium heat. Add the remaining cup of beans and heat through. Stir in the minced garlic, the herbs, and the remaining ½ cup broth. The bean mixture should be quite loose and creamy. Keep warm.

In a large skillet, heat 2 tablespoons of the olive oil over medium-high heat. Add the smashed garlic and the shrimp, season the shrimp with salt and pepper, and cook, turning once, until they just become opaque, about 3 minutes.

Meanwhile, in a small skillet, heat the remaining 1 tablespoon olive oil over medium-high heat, then add the Brussels sprout leaves and toss for a minute. Add a splash of water, cook a minute more. Drain.

Divide the bean mixture among bowls, add the shrimp and Brussels sprout leaves, and drizzle the salsa verde over the top.

KALE SALSA VERDE

MAKES ABOUT 1 CUP

I make this elemental green sauce with kale, but you can pack a mortar with any combination of fresh herbs and greens you like, such as Swiss chard or spinach. Do try making this by hand; it's really satisfying to observe the leaves transform into a condiment.

2 cups kale leaves (center ribs discarded)

2 teaspoons pine nuts

2 tablespoons roughly chopped flat-leaf parsley

2 tablespoons roughly chopped cilantro

¼ cup roughly chopped chives

⅔ cup extra-virgin olive oil, or more if needed

Salt and pepper

Bring a medium pot of salted water to a boil. Add the kale and cook until tender, about 5 minutes. Drain the kale and shock it in ice water. Drain again and squeeze it between your hands to remove excess water.

Transfer the kale to a mortar or food processor, add the nuts, and pound with the pestle or pulse until coarsely chopped. Add the parsley, cilantro, chives, and olive oil, season with salt and pepper, and pound or process, adding more olive oil if needed, until the mixture thickens.

SQUASH AND ENDIVE SALAD WITH MAPLE VINAIGRETTE

SERVES 4

I love salads, but mixed greens alone are usually not hearty enough to completely satisfy my craving, even as an appetizer. So I choose to include a wide variety of ingredients and make composed salads with more interesting textures and body. Here I channel wintertime with squash, endive, and a spicy vinaigrette. Pay attention to those endives! They're worth cooking and serving on their own.

1 teaspoon coriander seeds

1 teaspoon black peppercorns

2 cloves

1 star anise

2 sprigs thyme

1 bay leaf

1 lemongrass stalk, bruised with the side of a chef's knife and quartered

One 1/2-inch piece of ginger, bruised

2 cups orange juice

1 teaspoon olive oil

2 cups peeled, seeded, and cubed (1-inch) winter squash, such as kabocha

Salt

1/3 cup verjus

1 tablespoon fresh lemon juice

2 tablespoons sugar

2 tablespoons dried sweet cherries or raisins

3 endives, 2 halved lengthwise, 1 julienned

Pepper

Maple Vinaigrette

2 handfuls baby mustard greens

1 1/2 tablespoons roasted, salted sunflower seeds

1 1/2 tablespoons roasted, salted pumpkin seeds

Tie up the coriander, peppercorns, cloves, star anise, 1 thyme sprig, the bay leaf, lemongrass, and ginger in a piece of cheesecloth to make a sachet. In a small saucepan, combine 1 cup of the orange juice, 1 cup water, and the olive oil, add the squash, season with salt, and add the sachet. Bring to a simmer and cook until the squash is just tender but still holds its shape, 8 to 10 minutes.

Transfer the braised squash to a medium bowl and refrigerate until cold. Discard the sachet and cooking liquid.

Meanwhile, in a medium saucepan, combine the remaining 1 cup orange juice, 1 cup water, 1/3 cup of the verjus, the lemon juice, sugar, and the remaining thyme sprig, add the dried cherries and halved endives, and season with salt and pepper. Bring to a simmer and cook until the endives are tender but still hold their shape, 7 to 9 minutes. Transfer the braised endives and cherries to a plate and refrigerate until cold. Discard the thyme sprig and cooking liquid.

In a medium bowl, toss the braised squash, endives, and cherries together with a little of the maple vinaigrette. Put on plates.

Toss the mustard greens, julienned endive, and sunflower and pumpkin seeds with a little vinaigrette, scatter over the braised squash mixture, and drizzle with a little more vinaigrette.

MAPLE VINAIGRETTE

MAKES ABOUT 1/3 CUP

1 tablespoon maple syrup

2 teaspoons Dijon mustard

2 teaspoons fresh lemon juice

1 teaspoon sherry vinegar

Pinch of Aleppo pepper

Salt and pepper

3 tablespoons extra-virgin olive oil

In a small bowl, whisk together the maple syrup, mustard, lemon juice, vinegar, and Aleppo pepper; season with salt and pepper. Slowly add the oil, whisking constantly until the dressing is emulsified.

HOWARD KALACHNIKOFF

EXECUTIVE SOUS CHEF •
SINCE 2006

I grew up two blocks from Gramercy. My mom was a caterer and we had a commercial kitchen in a big loft on 22nd Street. The rest of my family lives in Spain, Portugal, and Switzerland, and we'd often vacation in Europe. I went to college in Boston and did a joint program at Northeastern and the Museum School of Fine Arts, in sculpture. I was always interested in food and music, but sculpting gave me a way to work with my hands. And even though my summer jobs were food jobs, and cooking was built into the family dynamic, I didn't think cooking school was an option.

So, I moved to Paris, where my grandmother had a tiny apartment. I thought I'd give it six months, but I fell in love with a girl and stayed for three years. I ended up working at a French-Italian bistro before I returned to New York in 1996. But I wasn't doing serious cooking, and becoming a chef was not in my head—I knew how difficult it is, and it scared me a little. When I came back to the city, I had friends working in music studios and I took a job with a small record company for seven or eight years. I became a partner and we produced underground house music. Our success was thrilling to a young guy. But one day Napster struck. This could not last.

Then my friend Charles Masson, from La Grenouille, gave me a chance to spend some time in his kitchen. After six months, I realized that I was slow and unaware of the skills and language that swirled around me. It dawned on me that if I wanted to get into serious cooking, I needed to either go into another kitchen and begin picking parsley or go to school and gain some confidence. I was twenty-eight; it took me that long to figure out that cooking isn't something you just fall into.

I checked out the French Culinary Institute (now the International Culinary Center). I got a loan, started a one-year program, and immersed myself in school. Jacques Pépin, Alain Sailhac, André Soltner—all the greats were there. When I had a question, I'd go ask *André Soltner*—how cool was that! I took full advantage of it and I kicked ass. After graduation, a friend suggested I meet Peter Hoffman at Savoy. By then I knew that my food sensibilities were natural—the way my grandmother grew up eating—seasonal and market-driven.

I didn't come out of school with a hot-shot attitude. The work of a chef has always been very humbling to me. When Peter offered me a job as *the* (only) prep cook of the restaurant, I eagerly accepted. A few weeks into it, though, I couldn't sleep because I was panicked that I couldn't get it all done. How did my predecessor, this Mexican genius, complete the work so quickly that he had time for a nap, and here I was struggling? But I spent three years at Savoy, two as sous chef.

I realized then that I needed to get into other kitchens I respected and learn not just about food but also about how they managed to sustain a consistently high level of cooking. The first person I approached was Mike Anthony. I hadn't been that interested in Gramercy until Mike became chef, but now the restaurant had a freshness that made me realize fine food could be timely and seasonal, too. It turned out that Mike's trust in me was the best thing that ever happened to me. I know now that owning a restaurant isn't just some shop with a few cooks and a cash register. It's a way of life, and where I will spend most of my time. I know, too, to be as generous as Mike is with me. That's what makes a truly successful restaurant. Yes, you need discipline. But what you really have to do is open your arms super wide and guide people and teach them. And hopefully that generosity will spark the interest of a younger generation.

PUFFED POTATOES

MAKES ABOUT 40 PUFFS

I vividly remember the first time I saw a cook in France make these potatoes. We were late preparing the staff meal and there wasn't much to serve. He told me to boil and rice some potatoes, and I thought, "Oh no, not boiled potatoes again." But unbeknownst to me, he had made a batch of pâte à choux (a wet dough of flour, eggs, and butter) and heated a pot of oil. With a swift gesture, he folded the riced potatoes into the dough and started plopping spoonfuls of the mixture into the hot oil. What happens when you do that? Crispy, fluffy, mouthwatering little teardrops of potato joy! Serve them as a snack or an appetizer, or with a main dish.

1 pound Yukon Gold potatoes, peeled and cut into chunks

Salt

3 tablespoons unsalted butter

½ cup all-purpose flour

2 large eggs

Pepper

Canola oil for frying

In a medium saucepan, combine the potatoes, a large pinch of salt, and enough water to cover the potatoes by an inch or so. Bring to a boil over high heat, reduce the heat, and simmer until the potatoes are just tender, 10 to 15 minutes.

Drain the potatoes, then return to the pan, and toss over medium heat until dry, about a minute. Push the potatoes through a ricer or food mill back into the pan. Season with salt and keep warm.

In a small saucepan, bring the butter and ½ cup water to a boil over high heat. Off the heat, add the flour and stir until combined. Reduce the heat to medium and cook the dough, stirring constantly, until it comes together and pulls away from the sides of the saucepan, about 3 minutes.

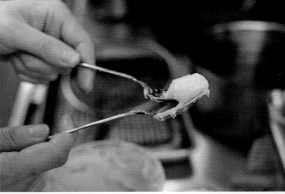

Transfer the dough to a stand mixer fitted with the paddle attachment. With the mixer on medium speed, add the eggs one at a time, mixing until well incorporated and the dough comes together again, scraping the sides of the bowl as needed. Add the riced potatoes and mix until smooth. Season with salt and pepper.

In a medium deep saucepan, heat about 1½ inches of oil to 325°F. Working in batches, carefully drop rounded teaspoons of dough into the pan and fry, turning once, until golden brown and cooked through, about 3 minutes. With a skimmer transfer the puffed potatoes to paper towels to drain. Lightly salt and serve immediately.

SNAPPER WITH TOASTED GREEN WHEAT AND SQUASH SAUCE

SERVES 4

Cooking seasonally in the winter need not be a dull, dreary proposition. Kabocha and red kuri squash are as bright as the sun and we use them to add vibrancy and life to our food. Green wheat, frik or freekeh, is harvested literally green and then roasted to create a wonderful smoky flavor. The lore is that a fire broke out in a wheat field while the grain was still young, and frik was born. Frik is high in protein and so easy to prepare: no soaking, just cover it with water or broth and boil it, season with a splash of olive oil and a pinch of salt, and the wheat's delicious and complex flavor will do the rest. For this recipe I cook it in vegetable broth with kale, but it's just as delicious cooked in water, or as part of Toasted Green Wheat and Warm Beets (page 228).

3 tablespoons olive oil

7 shallots, 3 minced, 4 thinly sliced

3 garlic cloves, 2 minced, 1 smashed

1 cup toasted green wheat (frik or freekeh)

3⅓ cups Vegetable Broth (page 118) or water, or more if needed

Salt and pepper

½ onion, thinly sliced

1 cup white wine

1½ cups peeled, seeded, and cubed winter squash

½ lemongrass stalk, bruised with the side of a chef's knife

2 tablespoons extra-virgin olive oil

Fresh lemon juice

2 cups sliced kale (center ribs discarded)

1 tablespoon Garlic Puree (page 231)

3 tablespoons unsalted butter

Four 6-ounce skinless snapper fillets

1 sprig thyme

2 tablespoons trout roe (optional)

In a small saucepan, heat 1 tablespoon of the olive oil over medium-low heat. Add the minced shallots and half of the minced garlic and cook until softened, 2 to 3 minutes. Add the wheat, stir for a minute, and then add 2 cups of the broth; season with salt and pepper. Cover, bring to a simmer, and cook until the wheat is tender, about 35 minutes.

Meanwhile, make the squash sauce. In a small saucepan, heat 1 tablespoon of the olive oil over medium-low heat. Add the sliced shallots, onion, and remaining minced garlic and cook, stirring often, for 5 minutes. Add the wine and simmer to reduce until the pan is almost dry. Add the squash, lemongrass, and 1 cup of the broth, bring to a simmer, cover, and cook gently until the squash is very tender, about 20 minutes.

Discard the lemongrass stalk and transfer the squash mixture to a blender. Add the extra-virgin olive oil and process until smooth. Pass the squash sauce through a fine-mesh strainer into a small saucepan. Season with salt, pepper, and lemon juice; keep warm.

In a large pot of boiling salted water, blanch the kale for 2 minutes; drain well. When the green wheat is tender, add the kale, along with the garlic puree and 2 tablespoons of the butter and season with salt, pepper, and lemon juice. Stir over low heat. The mixture should be moist; add a bit more broth if needed. Cover and keep warm.

In a large skillet, heat the remaining 1 tablespoon olive oil over medium-high heat. Season the snapper with salt and pepper. Lay the fillets in the pan and cook until light brown on the bottom, about 3 minutes. Carefully flip the fillets and cook until almost cooked through, about 2 minutes more. Add the remaining 1 tablespoon butter, the smashed garlic, thyme, the remaining ⅓ cup broth, and a splash of lemon juice. Baste the fillets (see page 216) with the pan juices and continue to cook, basting, until just cooked through, 1 to 2 minutes more.

Mound some of the wheat in the middle of each plate and top with a snapper fillet. Generously smother the fillets with the squash sauce and top with the roe, if you like.

COUNTRY TERRINE

MAKES 1 TERRINE

Charcuterie is a complex subject, but here is an easy way for you to discover at home the pleasure of transforming seasoned ground meats into wonderful-tasting terrines. Traditionally, terrines were simply a way to use and preserve every cut of the animal. They are uncommonly tasty. If you have a grinder attachment for your mixer, use it to grind the meat (chill the attachment first), or ask your butcher to grind it for you. If pork livers prove hard to find, chicken livers can be used instead. Plan to make this terrine in advance; it needs a night of chilling to develop the flavors.

1¼ pounds lean pork, finely ground

1 pound plus 2 ounces fatback, finely ground

1 pound pork liver (or chicken livers), trimmed of veins and finely ground

1 tablespoon olive oil

½ cup minced onion

2 large eggs

2 garlic cloves, minced

2 tablespoons Armagnac

3 tablespoons plus 1 scant teaspoon salt

½ tablespoon finely ground pepper

Preheat the oven to 250°F. Line a 1½-quart lidded terrine with plastic wrap, leaving enough of an overhang to cover the pâté later.

Keeping the equipment and ingredients cold helps to make a smooth-textured terrine, so put the ground pork, fatback, and liver in the mixer bowl, along with the paddle, and stick them in the freezer for about 15 minutes.

Meanwhile, in a medium skillet, heat the oil over medium-low heat. Add the onion and cook, stirring often, until soft, about 10 minutes. Transfer to a small bowl and chill in the refrigerator.

Remove the chilled bowl and paddle from the freezer and attach to the mixer. Add the onion, eggs, garlic, Armagnac, salt, and pepper to the meat mixture. Mix on medium-low speed just until the ingredients come together, about a minute.

Firmly pack the mixture into the terrine. Cover the mixture tightly with the plastic and then the lid. Put the terrine into a larger pan (such as a roasting pan) and fill the pan with enough hot water to reach halfway up the sides of the terrine. Bake until the internal temperature reaches 165°F, about an hour and a quarter.

Transfer the terrine to another baking pan. Remove the lid and weight down the terrine with heavy cans. Refrigerate overnight. (The terrine will keep, tightly covered, in the refrigerator for up to a week.)

To serve, unmold by inverting the terrine onto a platter.

Sous chef Paul Wetzel *(above left)* is meticulous about every aspect of our charcuterie program. We make small batches of carefully seasoned terrines *(top)*. They are cooled in an ice bath, temperatures are recorded, then they're pressed with a wooden board *(above right)*.

THE ART OF CURING MEAT

The urge to understand the basics of natural preservation methods and the desire to build great authentic flavor has led a whole new generation of American cooks to study charcuterie—preserving meat. I got hooked when I was in cooking school in Paris and became friendly with the butcher at one of the last great butcher shops, La Boucherie Bajon in the 15th arrondissement. That shop looks just like you'd picture it, with sawdust on the floor and a deeply worn butcher's block next to the showcase of wonderful meats. The shop was near my school, and I bought meat and other delicious charcuterie there for the family I cooked for to pay my tuition. Jean-Pierre Bajon was generous enough to take an interest in teaching me some basics. Some days, I would walk into the shop and he'd have several cuts of meat waiting for me. In order to buy the meat, he'd tell me, I'd first have to learn how to butcher it and bone it out. It surprised my chef/instructor at school in my final exam that I was able to prepare a lamb shoulder so quickly.

Over the years, I've stayed in touch with Monsieur Bajon. He is the one who got me started making sausages for Gramercy. Almost every time I'm in Paris, I'll stop by his shop to say hello and tell him how indebted I am to him. Monsieur Bajon is one of the last of the real butchers. There's a thin thread that connects us to authentic practices like his. But it's exciting that enthusiasm for this craft is resurfacing all across this country.

After I arrived at GT, we made the commitment to purchase special equipment for butchering, smoking, curing, grinding, and stuffing. In fact, preserving meat has become so important that we created a full-time position for a line cook who makes our sausages, terrines, and cured meats from the whole animals we butcher: entire sides of Piedmontese beef, Berkshire hogs, whole lambs, ducks, and chickens from local family farms. Besides the goal of creating satisfying dishes for our guests, other motivations come into play: the communal responsibility to purchase healthy and sustainably raised meat and the financial responsibility to the restaurant to use every last bit of that meat. In the kitchen, there is a heightened sense of respect for the producers and the animals themselves, which leads to uncommon creativity.

I'm not saying I think you should go out and buy an entire side of beef; most of us don't have the space to work with whole animals and don't cook for hundreds of people a night! Happily, great sources for smaller quantities of excellent meat are increasingly accessible. Searching them out makes all the difference.

In the last few years, there has been a welcome and renewed interest in developing distinctive regional recipes for cured and fresh meats. At Gramercy, in addition to Pastrami (page 294), we make our own smoked hams, bacon, smoked pork shoulder, smoked kielbasa, cured coppa, Country Terrine (page 286), Chicken Liver Mousse (page 88), mortadella, merguez (lamb sausage), blood sausages, Meatballs (page 296), and hamburgers from a special mixture we grind daily.

As a way to utilize every scrap of pasture-raised Elysian Fields lamb, we regularly make merguez, a spicy lamb sausage, to serve on other lamb dishes, in soups, or simply grilled as an appetizer.

SPAETZLE WITH SMOKED KIELBASA

SERVES 4

What I love about making spaetzle is that you're doing the essential work of a cook: making a satisfying meal from very little. While you begin with a dough as for other pastas, there is no rolling and cutting; you just pass the soft dough through a colander into boiling water, creating rough noodles or mini-dumplings. For me, the best part is once the spaetzle is cooked, I like to brown it by tossing it in a skillet with a little olive oil, which adds complexity of flavor. Browning is where all the deliciousness happens.

We make our own smoked kielbasa, but we don't expect you to, unless of course, you're up for that culinary adventure. (There's more about our charcuterie program at GT on page 288.) Just track down the best sausage you can find from a good artisanal producer.

1½ cups all-purpose flour

2 tablespoons mustard powder

½ teaspoon salt, plus more for seasoning

2 large eggs

½ cup sour cream

3 tablespoons Dijon mustard

3 tablespoons whole-grain mustard

2 tablespoons olive oil

2 tablespoons unsalted butter

Pepper

2 pounds smoked kielbasa

Bring a large pot of water to a boil. Have ready a bowl of ice water.

Meanwhile, in a large bowl, combine the flour, mustard powder, and ½ teaspoon salt. In a medium bowl, whisk together the eggs, sour cream, Dijon mustard, whole-grain mustard, and ¼ cup water. Using a rubber spatula, fold the egg mixture into the flour mixture until the dough is homogenous.

Salt the boiling water. Making the noodles is simple, but do be careful: you'll be balancing the colander over steaming water. Put about a cup of the dough into a colander and press it through with a wooden spoon. When the spaetzle floats to the surface, use a skimmer to transfer it to the ice water. Repeat with the remaining dough. Drain the spaetzle, then pat dry and toss with 1 tablespoon of the oil to keep it from sticking together.

In a large skillet, heat the remaining 1 tablespoon oil and the butter over medium-high heat. Add the spaetzle and let sit undisturbed for about a minute to take on some color, then stir and cook until browned and crispy, about 5 minutes. Season with salt and pepper.

Grill the kielbasa or cook in a large skillet until browned and warm. Slice and serve with the spaetzle.

GRAMERCY AND CRAFT BEER

Gramercy Tavern was the first fine-dining restaurant in New York City to feature craft beer front and center, without any particular fanfare, right next to their stellar wine list. They began with a nice selection of American craft beers on draft and a wide array of European bottled beers, some fairly obscure. The message was clear: "These beers belong here with our food and this experience." When they launched a vintage beer list in 2006, it was a concept most people had never even heard of. And then they actually asked us to brew beer in their kitchen so that the entire staff could learn about the brewing process. They had me come and teach the staff about beer service in a fine-dining environment, asking questions that no one had ever asked before. Many restaurants make good food, but a truly great restaurant actually leads. Gramercy Tavern leads. They are the gold standard for the role of craft beer as a part of a great restaurant experience.

—Garrett Oliver,
Brewmaster, Brooklyn Brewery;
Editor-in-Chief, *The Oxford Companion to Beer*

The idea of introducing people to new experiences is part of the DNA of Gramercy Tavern and is what our guests expect of us. When I arrived at Gramercy in 1999, Paul Grieco's energies were devoted to wine, so he handed the beer program to me in my first year. I'm still doing it, and I love it. We have always featured only North American microbreweries on tap, but in the beginning it was difficult to keep a commitment to small brewers. Sometimes it was hard even to get the beer to New York City. Carol Stoudt, still one of the most respected brewers in the country, used to drive her Stoudt's Pils beer to Gramercy from Pennsylvania in the back of her car! We served it in 1999 and still do. Our commitment to microbreweries back then helped put many of them on the map.

Today craft beer has come into its own as a serious drink and shares the stage with great cocktails, wine, and liquor; we almost take it for granted. More microbreweries now open every year than existed in the United States in 1999. And we remain steadfast in our support of the best: our relationship with a craft brewer who's in a week-to-week struggle to establish his or her business is just like our commitment to the small farmers who pour their love and guts into the soil.

Whether guests choose the Tavern tasting menu with listed beer pairings or just want to eat à la carte with appropriate beers, our bartenders and servers can offer intelligent suggestions. When a guest says, "I'll have a Heineken" (which is not on our list), they are prepared with alternatives by the bottle or on draft. In that way, our craft beer list is just another way we bring about an interesting dialogue with our guests.

—*Kevin Mahan*

Here are some of the American craft breweries we've built relationships with over the years and are proud to feature at Gramercy:

Alchemist Brewery, Waterbury, VT
Allagash, Portland, ME
Anchor Brewing, San Francisco, CA
Ballast Point, San Diego, CA
Bear Republic, Healdsburg, CA
Brooklyn Brewery, Brooklyn, NY
The Bruery, Orange County, CA
Captain Lawrence, Elmsford, NY
Cigar City, Tampa, FL
Dogfish Head, Milton, DE
Firestone Walker, Paso Robles, CA
Founders, Grand Rapids, MI
Goose Island, Chicago, IL
Great Divide, Denver, CO
Hill Farmstead, Greensboro, VT
Jolly Pumpkin, Ann Arbor, MI
Maine Beer Company, Portland, ME
Nectar Ales, Paso Robles, CA
Ommegang, Cooperstown, NY
Oskar Blues, Longmont, CO
Rogue, Ashland, OR
Sierra Nevada, Chico, CA
Sixpoint Brewery, Red Hook, NY
Smuttynose, Portsmouth, NH
Southampton, Southhampton, NY
Southern Tier Brewery, Lakewood, NY
Stillwater, Baltimore, MD
Stone Brewing Co., Escondido, CA
Stoudt's, Adamstown, PA
Victory Brewery, Downingtown, PA

PASTRAMI

MAKES ABOUT 4 POUNDS

Curing pastrami is a celebration of great craftsmanship. This pastrami begins with a great cut of beef—a 5-pound piece of brisket from the fatty end, which is called the point—and is transformed by salt, smoke, and time into something magical. Not only is the experience of preparing pastrami a worthwhile exercise, the meat that results is free of commercial artificial preservatives, and its wonderfully salty and spicy flavor is reminiscent of what this cured meat is *supposed* to taste like. The process is not complicated, but it does take some planning. We use our restaurant smoker. You could certainly try it in a backyard smoker, but in this recipe, the pastrami is cooked in the oven. We add shiro dashi to give it a bit of smoky flavor. A tiny bit of pink salt (sodium nitrite) is necessary to preserve the meat and protect it from dangerous bacteria.

3½ tablespoons black peppercorns

3½ tablespoons coriander seeds

2 tablespoons mustard seeds

½ teaspoon red pepper flakes

½ teaspoon allspice berries

½ teaspoon whole cloves

¼ teaspoon ground mace

¼ teaspoon ground ginger

1 bay leaf, crumbled

¼ cinnamon stick, crushed

1¼ cups kosher salt

2⅔ tablespoons pink salt (sodium nitrite)

1 cup granulated sugar

½ cup packed dark brown sugar

¼ cup honey

5 garlic cloves, minced

One 5-pound beef brisket from the fatty end (point), untrimmed

1½ tablespoons fennel seeds

½ cup shiro dashi

In a small skillet, lightly toast ½ teaspoon of the peppercorns, ½ teaspoon of the coriander, and ½ teaspoon of the mustard seeds over medium heat until fragrant, about 3 minutes. Grind in a spice mill.

Put the ground spices in a large pot and add the pepper flakes, allspice, cloves, mace, ginger, bay leaf, cinnamon stick, kosher salt, pink salt, granulated sugar, brown sugar, honey, garlic, and 4 quarts water. Bring the brine to a simmer, stirring until the salt and sugar are dissolved. Remove from the heat and let cool to room temperature.

Transfer the brine to a vessel large enough to hold it and the meat—which will be added later— and refrigerate until chilled.

Put the brisket in the brine and weight it down (with a plate and tomato cans, for example) to keep it completely submerged. Cover and refrigerate for 5 days.

Remove the brisket from the brine, rinse it, dry it, and put it on a large platter. Discard the brine. In a spice mill, process the remaining peppercorns, coriander seeds, mustard seeds, and the fennel seeds. Transfer the spices to a small bowl and mix well. Coat the brisket with the spice mixture and sprinkle the shiro dashi over it. Cover the platter and refrigerate for about 12 hours.

Preheat the oven to 250°F.

Put the brisket on a rack in a roasting pan. Add a cup of water to the pan and tightly cover the pan with aluminum foil. Cook the brisket until it reaches 165°F on a meat thermometer, 3 to 4 hours. (If you don't have a thermometer, the brisket is ready when it is very tender.) Let the meat rest for at least 2 hours at room temperature, or cover and refrigerate overnight. To serve, transfer the pastrami to a cutting board and cut against the grain into thin slices. The pastrami will keep, tightly covered, in the refrigerator for up to a week.

MEATBALLS WITH BRAISED ONIONS AND MASHED POTATOES

SERVES 4

Since I was the first grandchild in my Italian-American family, I was the only one who was allowed to eat meatballs in my grandmother's kitchen before they went into the sauce. My love of eating them straight out of the pan sparked the idea that with a little care and with some good-quality beef, a meatball could be a satisfying experience, even at a restaurant like Gramercy Tavern. We use this recipe as one of many ways to show off the sustainably raised local beef we buy. I can picture Nick Anderer's hands carefully crafting this humble mixture with all the care in the world. Nick, now the executive chef at Maialino, has a particular way of handling food and has passed on that attention to detail to countless cooks over the years.

4 tablespoons (½ stick) unsalted butter

1 cup minced onion

½ tablespoon very finely chopped rosemary

1 tablespoon dried oregano

1 teaspoon pimentón

½ teaspoon Aleppo pepper

¼ teaspoon cayenne pepper

2 tablespoons salt

1 teaspoon finely ground pepper

1½ pounds freshly ground beef (ask your butcher for meat with a 25% fat content)

1 cup freshly grated Parmigiano cheese

⅔ cup panko or dried bread crumbs

¼ cup finely chopped flat-leaf parsley

2 large eggs

3 tablespoons Garlic Puree (page 231)

8 thin slices Fontina cheese

Braised Onions (opposite)

Mashed Potatoes (opposite)

1 tablespoon finely chopped chives

Preheat the oven to 325°F.

In a medium skillet, melt the butter over medium-low heat. Add the onion and rosemary and stir for about 30 seconds, then add the oregano, pimentón, Aleppo pepper, and cayenne. Stir for 30 seconds more, then add the salt and pepper and cook, stirring often, until the onions are soft, about 10 minutes. Transfer the onion mixture to a large bowl and refrigerate until cold.

Add the beef, Parmigiano, panko, parsley, eggs, and garlic puree to the chilled onions and mix well by hand. Divide the meat into four 1-cup portions (you're making *big* meatballs!). Moisten your hands with cold water and gently shape the meat into smooth balls, rewetting your hands as needed. Put the meatballs in a small baking dish. Bake until cooked through, about 40 minutes.

Preheat the broiler.

Transfer the meatballs to a cutting board, cut them in half, and top each half with a slice of Fontina cheese. Spoon off and discard excess fat from the baking dish, then return the meatballs to the dish and melt the cheese under the broiler. Serve with the braised onions and mashed potatoes, and top with the chives.

BRAISED ONIONS SERVES 4

Cooked onions are naturally sweet and make an irresistible flavor combination when braised with garlic in olive oil and seasoned with a drop of vinegar. These onions are so simple you'll want to serve them with countless dishes.

2 tablespoons olive oil

2 large onions, halved and thinly sliced

1 teaspoon minced garlic

Salt and pepper

2 tablespoons red wine vinegar, plus a drop for serving

2 cups red wine

1 tablespoon extra-virgin olive oil

In a large skillet, heat the olive oil over medium heat. Add the onions, garlic, and a pinch each of salt and pepper and cook, stirring often, until the onions are softened, about 9 minutes. Add the vinegar and cook until it's almost gone. Pour in the wine and 1 cup water, bring to a simmer, and cook, stirring occasionally, until the liquid is almost gone, about 20 minutes.

Remove from the heat and season the onions with salt, pepper, another drop of vinegar, and the extra-virgin olive oil.

MASHED POTATOES SERVES 4

I like mashed potatoes that are satiny-smooth and very loose, so they contrast beautifully with the texture of the meatballs. One key to making great mashed potatoes is never to let them cool, from start to finish.

2 pounds Yukon Gold potatoes, peeled and cut into large chunks

1 garlic clove

1 bay leaf

Salt

3/4 cup whole milk

8 tablespoons (1 stick) unsalted butter

Pepper

In a medium saucepan, combine the potatoes, garlic, bay leaf, and a large pinch of salt. Add enough water to cover the potatoes by an inch or so, bring to a simmer, and cook until the potatoes are just tender, about 15 minutes.

Drain the potatoes, discard the garlic and bay leaf, and toss the potatoes in the pan for about a minute to dry them out. Remove from the heat.

In a small saucepan, combine the milk and butter and heat over medium heat until the butter is melted.

Meanwhile, transfer the potatoes to a ricer or food mill and process them back into the warm saucepan. Gently stir in the hot milk mixture, mix well, and season with salt and pepper.

THE NIGHT BEFORE CHRISTMAS

No sooner has the last guest left Gramercy at 2 a.m. on the Friday after Thanksgiving than Roberta Bendavid and her team of elves work through the night to bring on Christmas. It's au revoir pumpkins, hello pomegranates. A hundred voluptuous handmade balls of fruits and flowers, carefully stored for a year, are hung from the rafters with care and lush garlands are woven into chandeliers. And on the Tavern table *(following pages)* sit branches of radiant red ilex berries, amaryllis, and blowsy red velvet roses; rosemary topiaries; crabapples; and fragrant cinnamon sticks.

GRAMERCY

TAVERN

RESTAURANT

CHRISTMAS CAROL
BY
CHARLES DICKENS
Illustrations by
I.M. GAUGENGIGL & T.V. CHOMINSKI

H.M. CALDWELL CO.
BOSTON

GUINEA HEN TWO WAYS

SERVES 4

Here's a chance to broaden your poultry repertoire. Guinea hens are just a bit more wild in nature than chickens, and that's how they taste. Since the breasts are thin and the legs are lean, the meat requires two cooking methods—the birds don't lend themselves to roasting whole the way chickens do. But the steps in this recipe are easy and the flavor is its own reward. Remove the breasts and legs yourself or ask the butcher to do it. Save the bones for stock; they'll work perfectly in the recipe for Chicken Broth.

Breasts and legs from one 3- to 4-pound guinea hen

Salt and pepper

¼ cup plus 1 teaspoon olive oil

½ onion, chopped

1 carrot, chopped

1 celery stalk, chopped

1 garlic clove, chopped

½ cup white wine

2⅓ cups Chicken Broth (page 59)

⅓ cup diced pancetta

1 tablespoon green peppercorns in brine, rinsed

2 teaspoons red wine vinegar

2 tablespoons unsalted butter

5 cups sliced mushrooms (such as hen of the woods, oyster, shiitake, or cremini)

2 teaspoons thyme leaves

Celery Root Puree (page 304)

Preheat the oven to 350°F.

Season the guinea hen legs with salt and pepper. In a heavy ovenproof pot just large enough to hold the legs snugly, and with a tight-fitting lid, heat 1 tablespoon of the oil over medium-high heat. Add the legs skin side down and brown well on both sides, about 5 minutes per side. Transfer to a platter.

Reduce the heat to medium, add the onion, carrot, celery, and garlic, and cook, stirring occasionally, until softened, about 7 minutes. Add the wine, stir, and simmer until it's almost gone. Another magic flavor moment.

Return the legs to the pot, along with any accumulated juices, and add 2 cups of the broth. Bring the liquid to a boil, cover the pot, and transfer to the oven. Braise until the meat is cooked through, about 30 minutes. (Leave the oven on.)

Transfer the legs to a plate. Pour the liquid through a fine-mesh strainer into a small saucepan. Bring the liquid to a gentle simmer and reduce it to about ⅔ cup, then set the sauce aside. When the leg meat is cool enough to handle, pull the meat into big pieces, discard the skin, and reserve the bones for stock.

In a small saucepan, heat 1 teaspoon of the oil over medium-low heat. Add the pancetta and cook until it is lightly browned and the fat is rendered, about 4 minutes. Drain the fat, then add the pancetta to the sauce, along with the peppercorns and vinegar. Season the sauce with salt and pepper and keep warm.

In a medium ovenproof skillet, heat 1 tablespoon of the oil over medium-high heat. Season the guinea hen breasts with salt and pepper. Add the meat skin side down to the pan and cook until the skin is golden brown, 4 to 6 minutes. Transfer the skillet to the oven and bake the breasts until just cooked through, about 8 minutes. Flip the breasts in the pan, then remove immediately to a cutting board and let rest for 5 minutes.

Meanwhile, cook the mushrooms. In a large skillet, heat the remaining 2 tablespoons oil and the butter over high heat. Add the mushrooms, season with salt and pepper, and cook, stirring often, until soft and browned, about 3 minutes. Stir in the reserved leg meat, the thyme, and the remaining ⅓ cup broth and heat gently. Season with salt and pepper.

Slice the guinea hen breasts in half lengthwise. Serve the breasts on a bed of the mushroom mixture and the celery root puree, smothered with the sauce.

CELERY ROOT PUREE

SERVES 4 TO 6

Every time I make this puree, it amazes me that such a gnarly root can be transformed into something so satiny-smooth and elegant. I distinctly remember when I first saw a chef in France work his hocus-pocus on this humble vegetable; I was astounded then and I'm still astounded every time I cook it.

Here are two pointers for working with celery root: first, peel it well, and then cut it into large chunks. Peeling isn't easy—the root is so big, hard, and round that if you go at it with a large knife, you'll take too much of the flesh away. I've learned to take my time and slowly peel the root with a thin sharp knife, or just with a good peeler. Large chunks matter, because they allow the flesh to cook slowly and not to absorb too much liquid. Since you're cooking the celery root in a combination of milk and water, the milk will throw off some odd-looking solids that only strengthen your belief that there's no way this concoction will puree smoothly. Rest assured, these milk solids will help silken the puree. After you brown the butter and add it to the celery root in the blender, along with a drop of lemon juice and the cooking liquid, you'll watch this elemental transformation take place.

Besides serving as a cushion for the guinea hen, celery root puree can replace mashed potatoes with the Meatballs (page 296), is delicious with Braised Lamb Shoulder (page 249), and works wonderfully with fish.

4 tablespoons (½ stick) unsalted butter

1 shallot, minced

1 garlic clove, minced

1½ pounds celery root, peeled and cut into large chunks

2 cups whole milk

Salt and pepper

Fresh lemon juice

In a medium saucepan, melt 1 tablespoon of the butter over medium-low heat. Add the shallot and garlic and cook, stirring, until softened, about 3 minutes. Add the celery root, milk, and 2 cups water, or as needed (the liquid should cover the celery root by an inch or so). Bring to a simmer and cook until the celery root is completely tender, 15 to 20 minutes. Remove from the heat.

Transfer the solids to a blender, reserving the cooking liquid. Add 1 cup of the cooking liquid and process.

Make the brown butter. In a small saucepan, melt the remaining 3 tablespoons butter over medium heat. In a couple of minutes, it will start crackling. Listen carefully: when it stops making noise, it will begin browning. Wait for a minute more, then remove from the heat. You'll see lots of speckled brown particles in the butter—that is the good stuff!

Immediately pour the butter into the blender and process for a few minutes to thoroughly mix. Season with salt, pepper, and lemon juice. Add a little more cooking liquid if needed to make the puree satiny-smooth.

DUCK CONFIT

MAKES 4 DUCK LEGS

The whole notion of confit may sound mysterious and difficult, but it is a useful, basic technique that is not complicated. Confit is a fine way to cook duck legs at home and preserve them for several dishes. First the legs are seasoned with citrus peel, herbs, spices, sugar, and salt and chilled for at least 6 hours, or overnight. Then the legs are cooked slowly in the oven, submerged in liquid duck fat. At the restaurant, we spend hours rendering duck fat from whole birds, and while it's easy enough to do, it's time-consuming. Instead, buy rendered duck fat from a good source like D'Artagnan. You can serve the whole legs just warmed, with a green salad or White Beans (page 129). Or shred the meat for a ragout, as in the Spinach Fettuccine with Tomato and Duck Ragout (page 204), or Duck Breast and Confit with Quinces (page 309).

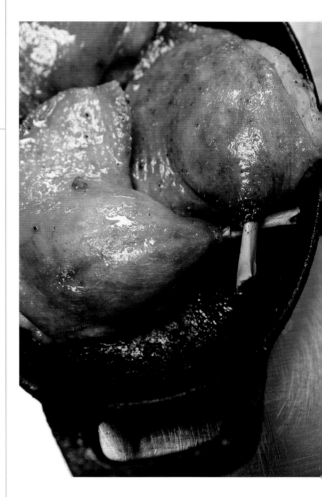

4 duck legs (about 8 ounces each)

1 teaspoon ground cinnamon

1 teaspoon ground nutmeg

1 cup kosher salt

¼ cup sugar

4 garlic cloves, smashed

Several sprigs of thyme and rosemary

Several strips of lemon and orange zest

1 bay leaf

Duck fat to cover (about 3½ cups), melted

Sprinkle the duck legs with the cinnamon and nutmeg and transfer to a baking pan. Toss together the salt, sugar, garlic, thyme, rosemary, citrus peels, and bay leaf, and combine with the duck legs. Cover with plastic wrap and refrigerate for at least 6 hours, or overnight.

Preheat the oven to 225°F.

Rinse the duck legs, pat dry, and put in a wide ovenproof saucepan (with a lid) just large enough to hold them snugly in a single layer. Add enough duck fat to cover the legs. Cook over medium heat until the first bubbles appear in the fat, then cover the pot, put it in the oven, and cook the meat at a very slow simmer until it is tender and can be easily pulled from the bone, 2½ to 3 hours.

Remove from the oven and let the legs cool in the fat, then transfer both to a covered container. Or, if using the legs immediately, remove them from the fat when cool enough to handle. The duck legs will keep, submerged in the fat and covered, in the refrigerator for several weeks.

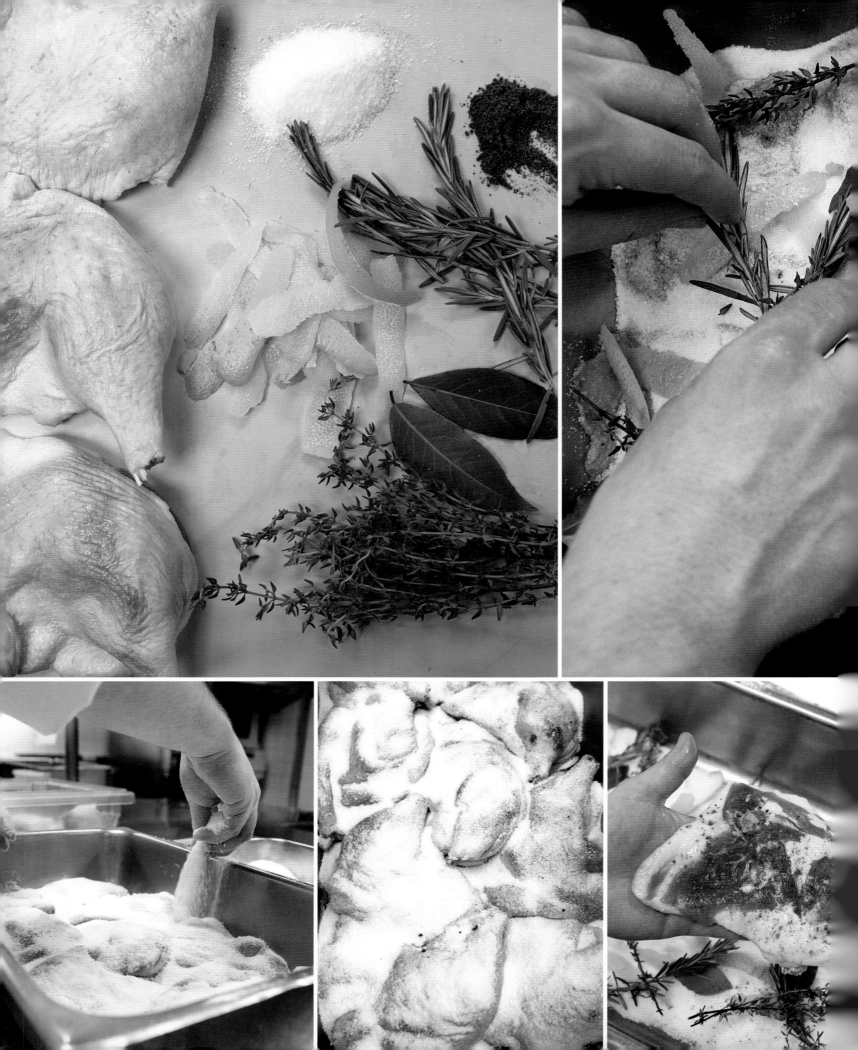

MAKING DUCK CONFIT

Buy the whole duck and use everything but the quack. The legs are the easiest and most satisfying parts to cook. Above we show the progression of this classic preserving technique. We use salt, sugar, citrus zest, thyme, rosemary, and bay leaves to perfume the duck legs. I like to keep the duck in the salt cure for at least 6 hours, or better yet, overnight. Then the legs are rinsed, patted dry, and put in a single layer in a pan. Melted duck fat is ladled over the legs slowly, heated, and then transferred to the oven for $2\frac{1}{2}$ to 3 hours.

DUCK BREAST AND CONFIT WITH QUINCES

SERVES 4

Duck is hardly a new ingredient in the kitchen, but it is so versatile and flavorful, it is recapturing the attention of cooks everywhere. Duck is the new pork! You can make so many things from one bird, from crispy cracklings and succulent confit to sausage and even duck prosciutto. Here I combine two ways of cooking duck and pair it with sweet, aromatic quinces in a memorable dish. The quinces are also cooked two ways: poached and pureed. Since we buy whole birds for the restaurant, we include both breasts and legs in this recipe, though you can certainly make the dish with one or the other. Because the Duck Confit takes some time, it's also fine to buy it.

3 tablespoons olive oil

1 leek, thinly sliced (white part)

4 cups peeled, cored, and cubed quinces

3 cups Vegetable Broth (page 118) or water

1/2 cup sweet Riesling

1/2 cup sugar

Salt and pepper

Four 7-ounce duck breast halves, skin scored

1 cup Brown Duck Sauce (page 310)

1 1/2 cups sliced mushrooms (hen of the woods, oyster, shiitake, or cremini)

1/2 pound sunchokes, peeled and sliced

Large leaves from 8 Brussels sprouts

1 cup shredded Duck Confit meat (page 305; from about 2 legs)

1/3 cup peeled, cored, and finely diced sweet firm apple, such as Honeycrisp

Poached Quinces (page 310)

2 tablespoons roasted, salted sunflower seeds

Fresh lemon juice

Make the quince puree. In a medium saucepan, heat 1 tablespoon of the oil over medium-low heat. Add the leek and cook until softened, about 6 minutes. Add the quinces, broth, wine, and sugar, bring to a simmer, and cook until the quinces are completely tender, about 50 minutes. Transfer the solids to a blender and process, adding just enough of the liquid to create a creamy puree. Pass the quince puree through a fine-mesh strainer into a small saucepan, season with salt and pepper, and keep warm.

Heat a large skillet over medium heat. Season the duck breasts on both sides with salt and pepper, put in the skillet skin side down, and cook until most of the fat is rendered and the skin is deep golden brown, 12 to 15 minutes. Pour off excess fat every few minutes (reserve it in a jar and refrigerate). Flip the breasts over and cook until medium-rare, about 2 minutes more. Transfer the breasts to a cutting board, tent with foil, and let rest for about 5 minutes.

Meanwhile, in a small saucepan, bring the duck sauce to a simmer and reduce by half. Season with salt and pepper. While the sauce is reducing, in a large skillet, sauté the mushrooms in 1 tablespoon of the oil over medium-high heat until soft and brown, about 5 minutes. Season with salt and pepper and transfer to a plate. Wipe out the pan and cook the sunchokes in the remaining tablespoon of oil over medium heat until tender, about 10 minutes. Add the Brussels sprout leaves, season with salt and pepper, and toss for a minute. Add the mushrooms, duck confit, apple, poached quinces, and sunflower seeds. Heat through for a minute or two, then season with lemon juice, salt, and pepper.

Slice the duck breasts on an angle. Spoon the quince puree onto the plates, layer on the mushroom mixture and duck confit, followed by the sliced duck breast. Spoon the sauce over the duck.

POACHED QUINCES MAKES ABOUT 1 CUP

Poached quinces can make a mouthwatering condiment that works with such varied dishes as Red Kuri Squash Soup (page 184), Chicken Liver Mousse (page 88), and Squash and Endive Salad (page 281). In winter, we stack crates of whole quinces just inside the front door at Gramercy, where their lovely fragrance becomes yet another welcome to the restaurant.

1 cup peeled, cored, and finely diced quinces

1/2 cup sugar

In a small saucepan, combine the quinces, sugar, and about 1 cup water; the water should cover the quinces. Bring to a simmer and cook until the quinces are just tender, about 30 minutes.

If not using the quinces immediately, let cool in the liquid, cover, and refrigerate. The quinces can be refrigerated for up to several weeks; drain before using.

BROWN DUCK SAUCE MAKES ABOUT 2 1/2 CUPS

This brown sauce is useful in many dishes—to season the Duck Breast, (page 309) and Spinach Fettuccine (page 204). I like to use a few drops in grain or bean dishes to add flavor and character.

1 duck carcass, cut up

3/4 cup red wine

1/4 cup sherry vinegar

7 cups Chicken Broth (page 59)

2 tablespoons olive oil

1 cup thinly sliced shallots

1 cup sliced mushrooms

2 garlic cloves, smashed

1 heaping tablespoon tomato paste

A strip of orange zest

2 sprigs thyme

Salt and pepper

Preheat the oven to 425°F.

Put the duck bones in a roasting pan and roast until well browned, 35 to 45 minutes. Pour off the excess fat (reserve it in a jar and refrigerate). Set the pan over medium heat, and deglaze with the wine and sherry vinegar. Reduce until the liquids are syrupy, add 1 cup of the broth, and set aside.

In a large pot, heat the oil over medium heat. Add the shallots, mushrooms, and garlic and cook, stirring often, until the shallots are softened and the mushrooms are golden brown, about 5 minutes. Stir in the tomato paste, then add the roasted bones and pan juices, the remaining 6 cups of broth, the zest, and thyme.

Bring to a simmer, skimming occasionally, and cook until the liquid is reduced to about 2 1/2 cups, about 2 hours.

Pass the sauce through a fine-mesh strainer into a container and season with salt and pepper. If not using immediately, let cool to room temperature, then cover and refrigerate. The sauce can be refrigerated for up to 3 days or frozen for up to 3 months.

SLOW-ROASTED PORK SHOULDER WITH BACON BROTH AND CORN BREAD

SERVES 8

This is a recipe that allows time and low heat to work their magic. I like to rub the roast with the seasoning and let it cure for a day before cooking. At Gramercy, as a way to use the whole hog, we slow-roast bone-in pork shoulders. At home, it's just as easy to generate that intense flavor with a smaller roast. Make sure to ask your butcher for high-quality, locally raised pork.

One 5-pound bone-in pork roast

6 garlic cloves, smashed

1 tablespoon thyme leaves

Salt and pepper

¼ cup olive oil

6 cups chopped savoy cabbage

6 cups chopped red cabbage

3 tablespoons red wine vinegar

1 teaspoon Aleppo pepper

Bacon Broth (page 314)

Corn Bread (page 315)

In a large bowl, combine the pork, 4 of the garlic cloves, and the thyme, season with salt and pepper, and rub the mixture all over the pork. Cover the meat tightly with plastic wrap and refrigerate for at least an hour or up to a day.

Preheat the oven to 250°F.

Unwrap the pork and discard the garlic. Put the meat in a roasting pan and cook in the oven until the meat's internal temperature reaches about 190°F, about 5 hours. Let the meat cool a little, then pull it into large pieces.

Meanwhile, about 30 minutes before the pork is ready, make the sautéed cabbage. In a large pot, heat the oil over high heat. Add the savoy and red cabbages and the remaining 2 garlic cloves, season with salt and pepper, and cook, stirring often, until the edges of the cabbage are browned, about 5 minutes.

Add about a cup of water and continue to cook until the cabbage is crisp-tender, about 5 minutes more. Stir in the vinegar and Aleppo pepper. The cabbage should have a slight vinegary bite and a little heat; add more vinegar and/or Aleppo pepper if needed. Serve the pork in bowls with the cabbage, bacon broth, and corn bread.

BACON BROTH MAKES ABOUT 4 CUPS

This bacon broth is perfect with the slow-roasted pork, but it can make just about any vegetable taste better; it's light and aromatic, not at all fatty. Whether you use it as a stock for cooking or as the base of a soup studded with your favorite fresh vegetables, it can be handy almost every day. We make the broth from our own smoked bacon. Ask your butcher for high-quality bacon or order it online from heritagefoodsusa.com.

1 tablespoon olive oil

½ pound slab bacon, diced

1 onion, chopped

2 shallots, sliced

5 garlic cloves, smashed

¼ head cabbage, cored and sliced

1 carrot, chopped

1 sweet firm apple, such as Honeycrisp, peeled, cored, and quartered

1 sprig thyme

8 cups Chicken Broth (page 59)

Salt and pepper

In a large pot, heat the oil over medium heat. Add the bacon, onion, shallots, and garlic and cook, stirring often, until the onions are softened, about 10 minutes. Increase the heat to medium-high, add the cabbage and carrot, and cook until the vegetables are wilted, about 3 minutes more.

Drain any excess fat, then add the apple, thyme, and broth. Bring to a gentle simmer and cook for 45 minutes.

Pass the broth through a fine-mesh strainer into a container and season with salt and pepper. Once cooled, the broth will keep, covered, in the refrigerator for about 5 days; it can be frozen for up to 3 months.

CORN BREAD MAKES 20 MINI MUFFINS

This recipe makes wonderfully moist corn bread if you bake it for about 12 minutes, but ever since our former sous chef Kyle Knall, from Birmingham, Alabama, inspired us to use the corn bread as a crunchy crouton with our slow-roasted pork, we bake it longer so you can sop up the broth without it falling apart. We bake the corn bread in wide flat molds, but a mini-muffin pan works, too.

2 tablespoons unsalted butter, at room temperature, plus more for the pan

3/4 cup all-purpose flour

1/2 cup medium-ground cornmeal

1 1/2 teaspoons baking powder

1/2 teaspoon salt

1/4 cup sugar

1 tablespoon honey

1 tablespoon maple syrup

1 large egg

1/2 cup whole milk

Preheat the oven to 350°F, with a rack in the middle position. Butter a mini-muffin pan (20 "holes").

In a small bowl, whisk together the flour, cornmeal, baking powder, and salt. In a medium bowl, work the butter and sugar together with the back of a wooden spoon until smooth. Work in the honey and maple syrup, then stir in the egg until completely combined. Gently stir in the dry ingredients and milk, alternating the two, with 3 additions of the dry ingredients and 2 of the milk. Don't overmix the batter; lumps are okay.

Spoon the batter into the prepared pan. Bake until the corn bread is deep golden brown and slightly hard, about 20 minutes. Unmold onto a wire rack and let cool slightly. Once cool, the corn bread will keep, tightly covered, for up to 4 days.

GERMAN CHOCOLATE CA[KE]
(PAGE 322)

APPLE PIE
(PAGE 254)

CHOCOLATE-COVERED TOFFEE WITH
PUMPKIN SEEDS AND SEA SALT
(PAGE 318)

LEMON MERINGUE PIE
(PAGE 321)

BIG COOKIES
(PAGE 325)

CHOCOLATE-COVERED TOFFEE WITH PUMPKIN SEEDS AND SEA SALT

MAKES ABOUT 1¼ POUNDS

This toffee is the perfect after-dinner chocolate. Or make it for holiday gifts. I like to give away little packages for Halloween. You can use the easy tempering method described below with good bittersweet chocolate to achieve a smooth texture and a good snap. To me, the crunch and savory quality of the pumpkin seeds makes all the difference.

12 tablespoons (1½ sticks) unsalted butter, cubed

1 cup sugar

½ teaspoon salt

1 teaspoon vanilla extract

8 ounces bittersweet chocolate, chopped

¾ cup toasted pumpkin seeds, toasted

Sea salt

Line a large baking pan with parchment paper. Put the pan on a flat surface and protect the surface—because toffee is sugar cooked at a high temperature—with a trivet or a towel underneath. In a small saucepan, combine the butter, sugar, and 2 tablespoons water (being careful not to get sugar on the sides of the pan, where it can crystallize) and bring to a boil over medium-high heat, stirring until the sugar dissolves. Boil the mixture, stirring constantly, until it turns a beautiful caramel color (about 295°F on a candy thermometer), about 7 minutes. Immediately remove from the heat.

Add the salt and stir to combine, then add the vanilla and stir to combine. Be careful: the mixture is very hot and will sputter. Immediately pour the toffee onto the parchment paper–lined pan and, with a heatproof spatula, quickly spread it in an even layer almost to the edges. (This is very hot, so resist the temptation to stick a finger in it.) Let cool completely.

Temper the chocolate. Bring 2 inches of water to a bare simmer in a medium pot. Set a medium metal bowl over it, add two-thirds of the chocolate, and gently melt it. Remove the bowl from the heat and stir in the remaining chocolate until melted and smooth.

Pat the surface of the cooled toffee dry to make sure the chocolate will adhere properly. With the heatproof spatula, spread the melted chocolate in an even layer over the toffee, then quickly scatter the pumpkin seeds on top and sprinkle with sea salt. Let stand until the chocolate hardens.

Break the toffee into large pieces. The toffee will keep, covered, for up to 2 weeks.

LEMON MERINGUE PIE

MAKES ONE 9-INCH PIE

This recipe was developed by Alexandra Ray (now the pastry chef at one of our sister restaurants, North End Grill) when she was Nancy's sous chef at Gramercy. Her inspiration was, not surprisingly, the lemon meringue pie her grandmother used to make. She played with the proportions until she arrived at the perfect ratio of light, fluffy, sweet meringue to thick, soft, tangy curd.

Pastry Dough (page 103)

All-purpose flour for rolling

LEMON CURD

10 large egg yolks (save the whites for the meringue)

⅓ cup cornstarch

1 cup plus 2 tablespoons sugar

Grated zest of 4 lemons

⅔ cup fresh lemon juice

12 tablespoons (1½ sticks) unsalted butter

¼ teaspoon salt

MERINGUE

½ cup plus 2 tablespoons sugar

1 teaspoon cornstarch

10 large egg whites

On a lightly floured surface, roll out the pastry dough. Fit it into a 9-inch pie dish and crimp the edges. Refrigerate for at least 30 minutes.

Preheat the oven to 375°F, with a rack in the middle position.

Line the pie shell with parchment paper and fill with pie weights.

Bake the pie shell for 20 minutes. Remove the paper and weights and continue to bake until the shell is evenly golden brown and cooked all the way through, 10 to 15 minutes more. Let cool. Lower the oven temperature to 350°F.

Make the lemon curd. In a medium bowl, combine the yolks and cornstarch and whisk until smooth, then set aside. In a medium saucepan, combine the sugar, lemon zest and juice, butter, and salt and bring to a boil, stirring until the sugar dissolves.

Slowly whisk about a cup of the hot liquid into the yolk mixture in a steady stream to temper it. Then pour the contents of the bowl into the saucepan and cook over medium heat, whisking constantly and getting into the edges of the pan to keep the curd from sticking or burning, until the first bubbles form. (Lower the heat a little if you see more than a few bubbles.) Immediately remove from the heat and spread the curd into the cooled pie shell.

Immediately make the meringue (the meringue will adhere better to the curd if the curd is still warm). In a small bowl, combine the sugar and cornstarch. In the bowl of a stand mixer, whip the egg whites on medium-low speed until foamy, about 4 minutes. Increase the mixer speed to medium and gradually pour the sugar mixture into the whites. Once the sugar is incorporated, increase the speed to medium-high and whip the meringue until medium-stiff peaks form (a peak of meringue should stand up, then slowly curl over), about 7 minutes.

Spread the meringue over the lemon curd with a small spatula, making sure to seal the meringue to the edges of the crust all the way around the pie. Form peaks on top by lifting up the spatula. Bake the pie until the meringue is golden, about 15 minutes. Let cool, then refrigerate until cold. The pie will keep, covered, in the refrigerator for up to 2 days.

GERMAN CHOCOLATE CAKE

MAKES ONE 9-INCH 3-LAYER CAKE

The is *the* cake for chocolate lovers: rich and soul-satisfying. We use cocoa powder instead of flour for dusting the baking pans because its color blends right into the dark cake. At the restaurant we make six-layer cakes. At home we make three layers.

FROSTING

4 large egg yolks

1 cup sugar

1 cup unsweetened coconut milk

8 tablespoons (1 stick) unsalted butter, cubed

1³/₄ cups sweetened shredded coconut, toasted to light golden brown

1¹/₂ cups chopped pecans, toasted

CAKE

2 tablespoons unsalted butter, melted, plus butter for the pans

7 tablespoons unsweetened cocoa powder, sifted if lumpy, plus more for the pans

1 cup plus 1 tablespoon sugar

³/₄ cup plus 2 tablespoons all-purpose flour

³/₄ teaspoon baking powder

³/₄ teaspoon baking soda

³/₄ teaspoon salt

1 large egg

¹/₂ cup whole milk

2 tablespoons vegetable oil

1¹/₂ teaspoons vanilla extract

7 tablespoons boiling water

Preheat the oven to 350°F, with a rack in the middle position.

Make the frosting. In a medium bowl, whisk the egg yolks until smooth. In a medium saucepan, bring the sugar and coconut milk to a boil over medium-high heat, stirring until the sugar dissolves.

Slowly whisk about a cup of the hot milk mixture into the yolks to temper them, then pour the contents of the bowl back into the saucepan and cook over medium-low heat, stirring constantly with a wooden spoon, until the mixture thickens enough to hold a line drawn with a finger down the back of the spoon, about 10 minutes. (Be careful not to let the mixture boil.)

Stir in the butter, toasted coconut, and pecans, then pour the frosting into a shallow baking pan. Cover the surface with plastic wrap and let the frosting cool until it's spreadable.

Meanwhile, make the cake. Butter three 9-inch round cake pans and dust with cocoa powder.

In a large bowl, whisk together the cocoa powder, sugar, flour, baking powder, baking soda, and salt. In a medium bowl, whisk together the egg, milk, oil, vanilla, and melted butter. Add the wet ingredients to the dry ingredients and whisk until well combined and smooth. Whisk in the boiling water.

Pour the batter (which will be quite thin) into the prepared pans. Bake until the layers spring back when lightly touched, about 12 minutes. Let cool completely in the pans.

Unmold the cake layers. Put one layer on a serving plate and spread one-third of the frosting over the top. Cover with another layer, spread with another one-third of the frosting, and then repeat the process one more time. The cake will keep for up to 3 days.

BIG COOKIES:
CHOCOLATE CHIP–WALNUT AND
WHITE CHOCOLATE CHIP–MACADAMIA NUT

MAKES FOURTEEN 3-INCH COOKIES

This cookie was the result of a friendly baking competition. When Gregory Marchand, now owner of the restaurant Frenchie in Paris, was a line cook in our kitchen, he challenged Nancy to a cookie-off. Nancy won, and you may think I'm exaggerating when I say that this is the best version of the iconic chocolate chip cookie, but truly I have never had a better one! Everyone has a preference: some like them soft; some like them crispy. This one is the best of both, a bit of crunch outside and just the right soft interior. Chocolate chip cookies and a glass of milk are still, for me, an inexplicably soothing and nostalgic combination.

1³/₄ cups plus 1 tablespoon all-purpose flour

³/₄ teaspoon salt

¹/₂ teaspoon baking powder

¹/₈ teaspoon baking soda

10 tablespoons (1¹/₄ sticks) unsalted butter, cubed, at room temperature

1 cup plus 2 tablespoons packed light brown sugar

1 large egg

1 large egg yolk

1¹/₂ teaspoons vanilla extract

1¹/₃ cups semisweet chocolate chips or white chocolate chunks

1 cup walnuts or macadamia nuts, coarsely chopped

In a medium bowl, whisk together the flour, salt, baking powder, and baking soda.

In the bowl of a stand mixer fitted with the paddle attachment, beat the butter and brown sugar on medium speed just until thoroughly combined. Beat in the egg, then the yolk, and finally the vanilla. Reduce the speed to low and add the dry ingredients, mixing just until almost combined. Remove the bowl from the mixer, add the chocolate chips and nuts, and stir until just combined. Cover the bowl and refrigerate for at least 6 hours or overnight for the best results.

Preheat the oven to 375°F, with racks in the lower and upper-middle positions.

Divide the dough into 14 balls (about ¹/₃ cup). Arrange the balls about 3 inches apart on two large ungreased cookie sheets. Bake, switching the pans halfway through, until the cookies are golden brown but a little underbaked, 16 to 18 minutes. Let the cookies cool completely on the sheets. The cookies will keep in a covered container, for up to 5 days (but they'll never last that long!).

NANCY'S COOKIE TIPS

• When combining the butter and sugar, don't overmix, or you'll beat in too much air. Air may be desirable in cake batters, but it makes cookies spread too much when baked.

• When mixing the dough, make sure to scrape the bottom of the bowl to scoop up any unmixed ingredients. It's mostly butter and sugar at the bottom of the bowl, and if you don't mix them in, you'll get cookies that spread unevenly in the oven.

• While it's not necessary, refrigerating the dough for at least 6 hours, or overnight, helps create more uniform cookies that spread less, because the flour has time to absorb the liquid in the dough.

• At Gramercy Tavern, we mix large batches of cookie dough, then scoop it onto cookie sheets and freeze it. Then we store the dough balls in sealed bags in the freezer so we can bake fresh cookies whenever we like. Frozen cookies require a little bit more time in the oven, but they'll spread less and have a more beautiful domed appearance. So do try freezing the dough.

• I like to bake cookies that seem slightly underbaked when removed from the oven. They'll continue to bake from the residual heat of the baking pan.

CHOCOLATE–PEANUT BUTTER COOKIES

MAKES ABOUT 30 COOKIES

These peanut butter cookies are topped with Guittard milk chocolate wafers, but Hershey's chocolate kisses work really well, too. Lining the baking sheets with parchment paper is a good idea to keep cookies from sticking, but not mandatory.

8 tablespoons (1 stick) unsalted butter, at room temperature

½ cup sugar

½ cup creamy peanut butter

1¼ cups all-purpose flour

About 60 Guittard 38% cacao milk chocolate wafers or 30 Hershey's chocolate kisses

Preheat the oven to 350°F, with racks in the lower and upper-middle positions.

In the bowl of a stand mixer fitted with the paddle attachment, beat the butter and sugar until light and fluffy, about 5 minutes. Add the peanut butter and beat until combined, about a minute. Add the flour and mix, scraping down the sides of the bowl as needed, until just combined.

Divide the dough into about thirty 1-inch balls and put them about 2 inches apart on two ungreased cookie sheets. Bake until the cookies are almost two-thirds cooked and still soft enough to yield to the wafers, about 10 minutes.

Remove the cookie sheets from the oven and gently push 2 stacked chocolate wafers (or 1 chocolate kiss) into the center of each cookie, slightly flattening it; the cookies will crack in various places. Work quickly, because they'll start to harden. Return to the oven and bake until the wafers melt slightly, about 2 minutes more. Let the cookies cool completely on the sheets. (They are very fragile until they cool.) The cookies will keep in a covered container for up to 5 days.

CRANBERRY-PISTACHIO BISCOTTI

MAKES ABOUT THIRTY-SIX 3-INCH COOKIES

At Gramercy, we make our biscotti small and elegant. We use this basic recipe for many different combinations, such as hazelnut–cacao nib, apricot-almond, and candied lemon–pine nut (right).

1 cup all-purpose flour, plus more for rolling

⅓ cup sugar

½ teaspoon baking powder

Pinch of salt

Grated zest of ½ orange

4 tablespoons (½ stick) unsalted butter, cubed and chilled

1 large egg

½ cup chopped or sliced pistachios

⅓ cup chopped dried cranberries

Preheat the oven to 350°F, with a rack in the middle position.

In the bowl of a stand mixer fitted with the paddle attachment, combine the flour, sugar, baking powder, salt, and zest. Add the butter and mix until the mixture is sandy, then add the egg, pistachios, and cranberries and mix on medium speed just until a dough forms, about a minute.

Shape the dough into a ball and cut it in half. Roll each half into a 12-inch-long log, flouring the dough as needed.

Transfer the logs to a baking sheet and bake until pale golden, about 20 minutes. Remove from the oven and let the logs stand on the baking sheet until they are cool enough to handle but still warm. Reduce the oven temperature to 275°F.

Using a serrated knife, cut each log on an angle into ⅓-inch-thick slices. Arrange the slices on the baking sheet cut side up and bake until dry and crisp, about 10 minutes. Let cool completely. The biscotti will keep in a covered container for up to 2 weeks.

MAKING CHRISTMAS COOKIES

Every year, the entire pastry team participates in this long-standing Gramercy Tavern tradition. Savory cooks, too, can help, and even my executive assistant, Catherine Hines (second from right in the photograph at bottom), who spent three years in our pastry kitchen, joins in on the fun. They make dozens and dozens of cookies to decorate the tree on the Tavern bar.

THE LIGHTING OF THE TREE

At 7:00 a.m., after Roberta Bendavid and her team have decorated all night, Ben Fischer *(above)*, the grower and horticulturist who is as crucial to Roberta as farmers are to the kitchen, arrives with the Christmas tree, measuring to make sure it will fit. Installation (on the Tavern bar) is exciting. Assistant General Manager Scott Reinhardt's nephews, Quinn and Oliver *(far left)*, arrive to decorate, as Roberta makes the final touches.

CHRISTMAS COOKIES

MAKES SIXTEEN 3½-INCH ROUND COOKIES

Gramercy has long had a wonderful tradition of baking cookies as ornaments for the Tavern Christmas tree. The pastry team makes about two hundred of these cookies every year, and everyone on our staff can pitch in. We use this recipe for cookies that will be eaten. To use the cookies only as ornaments, omit the lemon zest, vanilla seeds, and baking powder (no need to flavor cookies made for show, and baking powder makes them puff up more and lose their shape).

2 cups all-purpose flour, plus more for rolling

¼ teaspoon salt

½ teaspoon baking powder

8 tablespoons (1 stick) unsalted butter, cubed, at room temperature

1 cup sugar

Grated zest of ½ lemon

Seeds from ½ vanilla bean

1 large egg

2 tablespoons heavy cream

½ teaspoon vanilla extract

Royal Icing (opposite)

Assorted decorations, such as dragées, sprinkles, peppermint candies, licorice, and Red Hots

In a medium bowl, whisk together the flour, salt, and baking powder.

In the bowl of a stand mixer fitted with the paddle attachment, beat the butter, sugar, lemon zest, and vanilla seeds at medium speed just until thoroughly combined. Beat in the egg, then reduce the speed to low and add the dry ingredients. Add the cream and vanilla, mixing just until a dough forms, about a minute.

Wrap the dough in plastic and refrigerate for at least an hour, or preferably overnight. (Letting the dough rest overnight gives it time to absorb the egg and cream.)

Preheat the oven to 350°F, with racks in the lower and upper-middle positions.

On a lightly floured surface, roll out the dough to about ¼ inch thick. Use cookie cutters to cut into shapes. (If you're using the cookies as ornaments, with a toothpick, make a small hole about ⅓ inch from the top of each cookie for

hanging them.) Transfer the cookies to two ungreased cookie sheets, leaving about an inch between them. Press the dough scraps together, reroll, and cut out more cookies.

Bake, rotating the sheets about halfway through, until the edges are golden, about 15 minutes. Transfer the cookies to racks to cool completely.

To ice the cookies, spoon the contents of each bowl of icing into a Ziploc bag, seal, pressing out the excess air, and snip off a corner of the bag. The size of the cut depends on how thin you want to pipe the icing. Pipe the icing onto the cookies and have fun decorating them. Let the icing dry completely (from an hour to overnight) before moving/hanging/eating/storing the cookies. The cookies will keep in a covered container for up to a week, or as decorations for about a month.

ROYAL ICING

MAKES ABOUT 3 CUPS

This recipe yields enough icing to make both thinner and thicker consistencies and a variety of colors; you can scale it down if you won't need as much. Let the first coating of icing dry completely if you'd like to pipe detailed designs over it.

1 pound confectioners' sugar
5 tablespoons egg white powder
Food coloring

In a medium bowl, whisk together the sugar and egg white powder. Whisk in 6 to 10 tablespoons of water, depending on the consistency you want; use more water if you're covering the cookies, less if you want to pipe edges and borders. Or, to do both, divide the sugar mixture and add water accordingly. Whisk until the mixture is smooth. Divide the icing among small bowls and color each as you like. (If you're not using the icing immediately, tightly cover the bowls with plastic wrap and refrigerate for up to a day.)

CHOCOLATE BREAD PUDDING

MAKES ONE 9-BY-13-INCH PAN

Bread pudding is a way for an inexperienced cook to feel triumphant and an experienced cook to feel deeply satisfied by making something wonderful from leftovers. Brioche works best, but you can use challah or croissants. Bread pudding reheats really well, and it's even good cold for breakfast. I like it with homemade ice cream or whipped cream.

Unsalted butter for the pan

3 cups heavy cream

2 cups whole milk

1½ cups sugar

1 vanilla bean, split lengthwise

4 large eggs

2 large egg yolks

4 ounces bittersweet chocolate, melted in a small bowl

2 ounces bittersweet chocolate pieces (about ⅓ cup)

¾ teaspoon vanilla extract

1 pound Brioche (page 260), crusts removed and cut into ¾-inch cubes

2 ounces milk chocolate pieces (about ⅓ cup)

1 cup heavy cream, lightly whipped (optional)

Preheat the oven to 325°F, with a rack in the middle position. Butter a 9-by-13-inch baking pan.

In a large pot, combine the cream, 1 cup of the milk, and the sugar. Scrape the seeds from the vanilla bean into the pot, then toss in the bean. Bring the mixture to a boil over medium heat, whisking until the sugar dissolves.

Meanwhile, in a medium bowl, combine the remaining 1 cup milk, the eggs, and yolks and whisk until smooth.

When the cream mixture boils, remove it from the heat and steadily whisk about a cup of the liquid into the egg mixture to temper it. Pour the egg mixture back into the pot, whisking constantly. Gradually whisk about a cup of the egg mixture into the bowl of melted chocolate, then pour the chocolate mixture back into the pot, whisking constantly. Whisk in the vanilla extract. Add the brioche to the pot and stir the chocolate mixture well to break up the bread. Let the mixture stand for about 30 minutes so the brioche can absorb the liquid.

Pour the brioche mixture into the buttered pan. Sprinkle the bittersweet and milk chocolate pieces on top. Bake the bread pudding until it's just set, 45 to 55 minutes; when it is ready, the pudding will puff up. Let the pudding cool for about 15 minutes before serving. Serve with the whipped cream, if you like.

WHERE WE SHOP

We could not cook the way we do at Gramercy Tavern without the collaboration of so many extraordinary regional producers.

Some of our closest sources—amazing producers such as Pierless Fish, Early Morning Seafood, Nantucket Specialty Seafood, Four Story Hill Farm, Wholesale Greenmarket, and our forager for wild foods, Evan Strusinski—only sell wholesale.

The others listed below are my favorites in the New York area and have retail and/or direct mail businesses. If you are cooking in another part of the country, I am confident that you can surely find producers of great quality local food. I encourage you to search them out, support them, and treat yourself to those fresh ingredients.

GREENMARKET SOURCES

All these vendors are found at our beloved Union Square Greenmarket and at other locations.

UNION SQUARE GREENMARKET
Union Square Park, Park Avenue at 17th Street
Monday, Wednesday, Friday, and Saturday
8:00 a.m.–6:00 p.m.

BERRIED TREASURES FARM
248 Beaver Kill Mountain Road
Cooks Falls, NY 12776
(646) 391-3162

Franca Tantillo's 36-acre farm is in the western Catskills. Strawberries are the farm's main claim to fame, but she grows about seventeen varieties of potatoes, sunchokes, and a variety of beans.

BODHITREE FARM
2116 Jacksonville Road
Jobstown, NJ 08022
(201) 401-5865
bodhitreefarm.com

Nevia No, a Korean-American grower and former concert pianist, produces some of the most beautiful Korean cucumbers, avocado squash, okra, and chameh melons.

CARADONNA FARMS
1394 US Route 9 W
Marlboro, NY 12542
(845) 236-1344

We buy peaches and plums here, plus Honeycrisp and Winesap apples, and apple cider for the bar.

CAYUGA ORGANICS
18 Banks Road
Brooktondale, NY 14817
(607) 793-0085
cporganics.com

When Cayuga Organics began selling at the Greenmarket, they changed the landscape of healthy and local eating. We buy their black turtle, red merlot, and pinto beans, and well as grains like farro, freekeh, and spelt.

CHERRY LANE FARM
802 Roadstown Road
Bridgeton, NJ 08302
(856) 455-7043

Originally Suzy Dare's farm focused on asparagus. Now we count on them for corn, zucchini, eggplant, Brussels sprouts, cauliflower, and more.

ECKERTON HILL FARM
117 Lobachsville Road
Fleetwood, PA 19522
eckertonhillfarm.com

Tim Stark is one of our primary sources for heirloom tomatoes and peppers. Check out his book, *Heirloom: Notes from an Accidental Tomato Farmer.*

HAWTHORNE VALLEY
327 Route 21C
Ghent, NY 12075
hawthornevalleyfarm.org

This 400-acre biodynamic farm has operated since 1972. We like their history and philosophy and we buy their yogurt and beautiful greens.

KERNAN FARMS
196 Macanippuk Road
Bridgeton, NJ 08302

Fresh produce from warmer southern New Jersey farms like this one extends our season.

LANI'S FARM
924 Jacksonville Mount Holly Road
Bordentown, NJ 08505
lanisfarm.blogspot.com

Steve Yoo, a Korean-American farmer, never stops experimenting with Asian varietals grown with limited or no herbicides or insecticides. I prize new discoveries such as Fairy Tale eggplant, padrón peppers, husk cherries, and purslane. We buy those tiny edible flowers and greens like tatsoi here.

MAX CREEK HATCHERY
484 Monkey Run Road
East Meredith, NY 13757

Dave Harris is famous for his rainbow and brook trout raised in man-made ponds. He grows arugula, sunchokes, and potatoes. On Wednesdays, he brings watercress harvested from his spring.

MIGLIORELLI FARM
46 Freeborn Lane
Tivoli, NY 12583
migliorelli.com

We buy sugar snap peas, broccoli raab, Japanese turnips, summer squash, pears, and nectarines from Kenneth Migliorelli's sustainable 600-acre Duchess County farm. Don't miss their cider, baked goods, and preserves.

MOUNTAIN SWEET BERRY FARM
Box 667
Roscoe, NY 12776

Rick Bishop is a leader in the organization of our local foodshed who's fostered a return of small-scale alternative agriculture. Rick champions the production of distinctive ingredients like La Ratte potato, sucrine lettuce, day-neutral Tristar strawberries, wild ramps, and green garlic.

MUDDY RIVER FARM
123 Celery Avenue
New Hampton, NY 10958
muddyriverny.com

Located in the Black Dirt region of Orange County, John Schmid produces amazing artichokes, cabbages, carrots, kohlrabi, salsify, parsnips, garlic, and leeks.

NORWICH MEADOWS FARM
105 Old Stone Road
Norwich, NY 13815
norwichmeadowsfarm.com

Taste their vegetables and you'll know why Zaid and Haifa Kurdieh are one of our favorite growers. They share invaluable information and build strong community. They've grown many varieties based on our requests: Canestrino tomatoes, Kyoto carrots, Whippoorwill cowpeas. You must experience their beans!

PAFFENROTH GARDENS
95 Little York Road
Warwick, NY 10990
(845) 258-4746

Alex and Linda Paffenroth took over his father's farm in Orange County, New York, and transformed it from an onion farm to one of the region's most diversified, excelling at growing distinctive carrots, sunchokes, potatoes, parsnips, onions, and corn.

PHILLIPS FARMS
290 Church Road
Milford, NJ 08848
phillipsfarms.com

This family farm provides a wide variety of excellent fruits, berries, and vegetables in every season.

RED JACKET ORCHARDS
957 New York 5
Geneva, NY 14456
(315) 781-2749
redjacketorchards.com

The Nichols family grows the difficult but wonderful-tasting apricot variety "Red Jacket" in the Finger Lakes region. They bring amazing fruits to the market and they have become justly famous for their juices: Fuji Apple and Tart Cherry Stomp are my favorites.

W. ROGOWSKI FARM
327-329 Glenwood Road
Pine Island, NY 10969
rogowskifarm.com

Cheryl Rogowski is a forward-thinking farmer who fully utilizes her resources, championing Community Supportive Agriculture (CSA's), the Field to Fork Supper Club, and Breakfast at the Farm.

TREMBLAY APIARIES
154 Warner Road
Van Etten, NY 14889
tremblayapiaries.com

Their honey is pure, sustainable, and delicious.

VAN HOUTEN FARM
68 Sickletown Rd
Orangeburg, NY 10963
(845) 735-4689
vanhoutenfarmsny.com

Each season we depend on this family farm to bring a variety of vegetables, fruits, perennials, and annuals. We love their Cherry Berry tomatoes, eggplant, and peppers.

WILD HIVE FARM
2411 Salt Point Turnpike
Clinton Corners, NY 12514
(845) 266-0660
wildhivefarm.com

In our taste test of grits against all the great Southern producers, Wild Hive won hands down. Their stone-ground organic corn from their micro-mill produces polenta that bursts with fresh corn flavor.

OTHER PURVEYORS

BATTENKILL VALLEY CREAMERY
691 County Road 30
Salem, NY 12865
(518) 854-9400
battenkillcreamery.com

As dairy farms disappear from our region, we are proud to support Seth McEachron's Battenkill Creamery. We are a loyal customer, buying his high-quality, New York State farm-fresh milk and cream.

GARDEN STATE URBAN FARMS
406 Tompkins Street
Orange, NJ 07050
gardenstateurbanfarms.com

When Tony Gibbons is not working in Garden State's greenhouse or field, he greets our guests at the front door of Gramercy Tavern as maître d'. The company he co-owns with his mother produces many of the microgreens and small lettuces we serve at the restaurant.

GOTHAM GREENS
818 Humboldt Street
Brooklyn, NY 11222
(347) 799-1099
gothamgreens.com

Viraj Puri, Eric Haley, and Jennifer Nelkin launched this sophisticated hydroponic farm in a greenhouse rooftop in Greenpoint in 2011. We buy their butterhead lettuce that is harvested before breakfast and serve it at lunch! Besides lettuce, they produce Swiss chard, arugula, and basil year-round and are experimenting with new varieties for our restaurant.

LIBERTY GARDENS
232 E. Wall Street
Bethlehem, PA 18018
libertyorganic.com

The high quality of vegetables grown by Jeffrey Frank and Kristin Illick in eastern Pennsylvania is based on constantly improving soil fertility, identifying superior plant varieties, and building a greater trust between farms and chefs.

SPICES, OILS, AND VINEGARS

KALUSTYAN'S
123 Lexington Avenue
New York, NY 10016
(800) 352-3451
kalustyans.com

I have felt a special connection to this amazing store for over fifteen years. We buy mild curry powder, Aleppo pepper, dried Ancho chiles, pimentón, and papadum crackers, among other ingredients. In the small deli upstairs they make my favorite sandwich: Mujadarra made with soft, braised lentils, crispy shallots, garam masala spice, and pickles. They have a robust mail-order business.

SEAFOOD

ISLAND CREEK OYSTERS
PO Box 348
Duxbury, MA 02331
islandcreekoysters.com

A perfect example of great oysters grown by great people.

AMERICAN CAVIAR
(212) 226-5252
americancaviarco.com

In an effort to provide a sustainable alternative to imported caviars, Robert Gardner sources domestic fish from the Mississippi and Missouri rivers for paddlefish roe, and farm-raised trout for great-textured trout roe.

MEAT AND POULTRY

D'ARTAGNAN
280 Wilson Avenue
Newark, NJ 07105
(800) 327-8246
dartagnan.com

Ariane Daguin has built a brand of gourmet meat, poultry, and mushrooms that is synonymous with excellence.

ECOFRIENDLY FOODS
3397 Stony Fork Road
Moneta, VA 24121
(540) 297-9582
ecofriendly.com

I buy entire sides of Piedmontese beef and whole heritage breed pigs from Bev Eggleston. With his network of farmers and our dedicated staff, we demonstrate how a regional livestock program can really work.

ELYSIAN FIELDS FARM
Waynesburg, PA
purebredlamb.com

Keith and Mary Martin have been a role model for holistic livestock operations through their close observation of their animals and insistence on staying in rhythm with the natural world. The quality of the meat they produce has consistently been among the very best tasting in the world.

FLYING PIGS FARM
246 Sutherland Road
Shushan, NY 12873
(518) 854-3844
flyingpigsfarm.com

Mike Yezzi and Jennifer Small raise rare heritage breeds of pig such as Large Blacks, Gloucestershire Old Spots, and Tamworths. We buy them whole and serve every part with pleasure in order to preserve a market for these rare breeds.

HERITAGE FOODS
heritagefoodsusa.com

I support Patrick Martins's vision for sourcing meat with integrity on a national level. We buy sustainably raised pork to augment our whole animal program. I appreciate his encouragement to try less familiar meat like whole goats, which we've come to love. We offer our staff the chance to buy Thanksgiving turkeys from the country's last producer of heritage breed poultry.

RAVEN & BOAR
111 County Route 34
East Chatham, NY 12060
(518) 794-0125
ravenandboar.com

We've fallen in love with the American whey-fed pigs Ruby and Sather Duke produce on their farm in Columbia County, New York. Their company, Hivemind Design, manufactures furniture and designs interiors.

CHEESE

FORMAGGIO ESSEX MARKET
120 Essex St
New York, NY 10002
(212) 982-8200
formaggioessex.com

We buy many European cheeses here; the shop, in the colorful Essex Street Market, is a good source of specialty oils and vinegars.

MURRAY'S CHEESE
254 Bleecker Street
New York, NY 10014
(212) 234-3289
murrayscheese.com

This iconic New York resource (with a branch in Grand Central Station) has an outstanding selection of the world's greatest cheeses and an aging cellar that allows us to serve those cheeses at the peak of their maturation.

SAXELBY CHEESEMONGERS
120 Essex Street
New York, NY 10002
(212) 228-8204
saxelbycheese.com

One of the great sources of new American farmstead cheese, with an experienced and enthusiastic cheese guru, Anne Saxelby, at the helm. Her tiny shop in the Essex Street Market sells yogurt, milk, and cream, too.

JAPANESE INGREDIENTS

KATAGIRI JAPANESE GROCERY STORE
224 E. 59th Street
New York, NY 10022
(212) 755-3566
katagiri.com

This store has made typical Japanese ingredients like shiro dashi, kombu, white miso paste, and bonito flakes readily available; I use them discreetly in my dishes at home and at work.

ACKNOWLEDGMENTS

Roots run deep here at Gramercy Tavern. . . . I would like to thank the people who have nurtured this restaurant with wisdom and love, who celebrated its evolution and shared their tireless support and encouragement for this book.

Danny Meyer, for his wonderful vision of an adored restaurant where people and food matter. Endless thanks for putting his trust in me to steward this dream. And for writing his compelling history of GT for this book.

Kevin Mahan, general manager and partner of Gramercy Tavern, who has been the protector of the spirit of GT for all of these years as the business manager, service director, beer master, coach, friend, brother, father, therapist, and head custodian of this huge family.

Paul Bolles-Beaven, the wisest and most nurturing man I know; his constant encouragement and mentoring helped me and this book happen.

Jeff Flug, the president of USHG, who supports our passion and has given structure and longevity to our business.

David Black, our literary agent and friend, who always offers invaluable counsel, insight, and encouragement.

Nancy Olson, pastry chef, for her beautiful creations and inspired attention to detail.

The incredibly dedicated, courageous, thoughtful, and talented team at Gramercy Tavern: Howard Kalachnikoff, executive sous chef; and Modesto Batista, chief steward. To sous chefs Saman Javid, Duncan Grant, Suzanne Cupps, John Patterson, Paul Wetzel, Jessica Perkiss, and Joanne Courounis. Special thanks for the hard work and expertise of former sous chefs Geoff Lazlo, Kyle Knall, and Alexandra Ray.

FOH managers: Kim DiPalo, Dave Goodwin, Isabella Fitzgerald, Aimee Rials, and Elizabeth Carr Eubanks. Scott Reinhardt, assistant general manager, and Juliette Pope, beverage director.

With awe and admiration for the creative work of floral designer Roberta Bendavid. And artist Robert Kushner, for opening his notebooks for us to use as endpapers.

Peter Bentel, for articulating his timeless vision of GT.

The many food-loving souls who have been employed at Gramercy Tavern and who have shared their hard work, warmth, and expertise, adding their own imprint on our story.

Thanks to the masterfully creative Dorothy Kalins—writer, project manager, and fairy godmother. Without your experience, vision, love, and understanding of Gramercy Tavern, as well as your sense of humor and insatiable passion for food and people, we could not have even considered beginning this story. Thanks for taking us on such a fun journey filled with so many valuable lessons.

Rica Allannic, our editor at Clarkson Potter, both your family at Random House and your family at home for believing in the evolution of GT and for your enthusiastic support. And to creative director Marysarah Quinn, who lovingly designed each page.

Kathy Brennan, diligent recipe editor and new keeper of all GT gossip, and her family. Thanks for having the patience to put up with us and for fighting to make our recipes accessible to cooks everywhere.

Photographer Maura McEvoy, you charmed us all with your sharp eye and ability to reveal both the obvious beauty as well as the hidden character of GT. It was such a pleasure to work together.

Big gratitude to Catherine Hines, my executive assistant, who kept us all on time, on target, and sane.

Jim and Jan Anthony, my parents, taught me the value of a strong work ethic and a respect for people. They have supported me through every decision I've ever made.

Thank you to my loving, supportive family: my wife, Mindy Dubin, and our three beautiful daughters, Gabrielle, Colette, and Adeline.

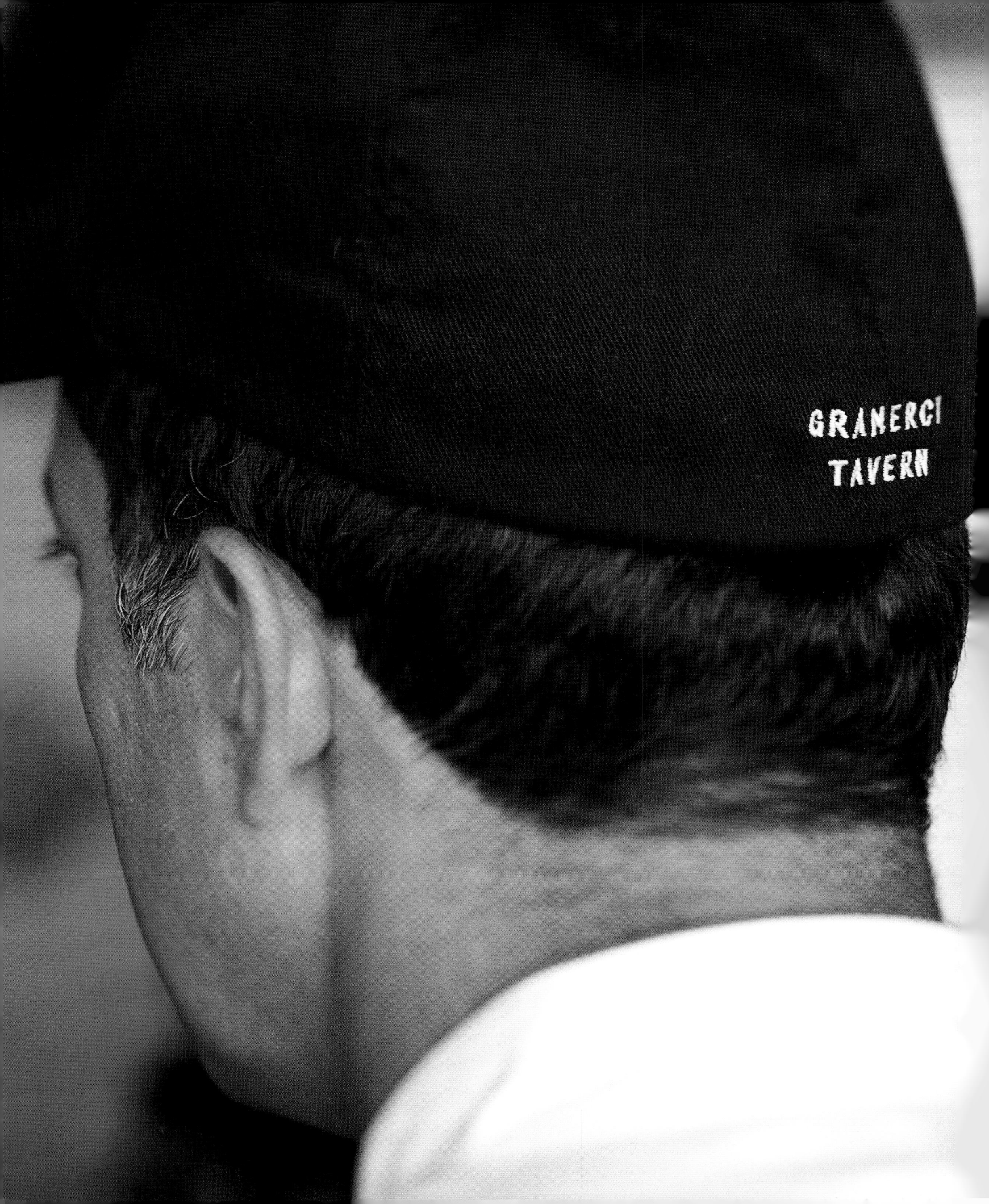
GRAMERCY
TAVERN

INDEX

GRAMERCY

TAVERN

RESTAURANT

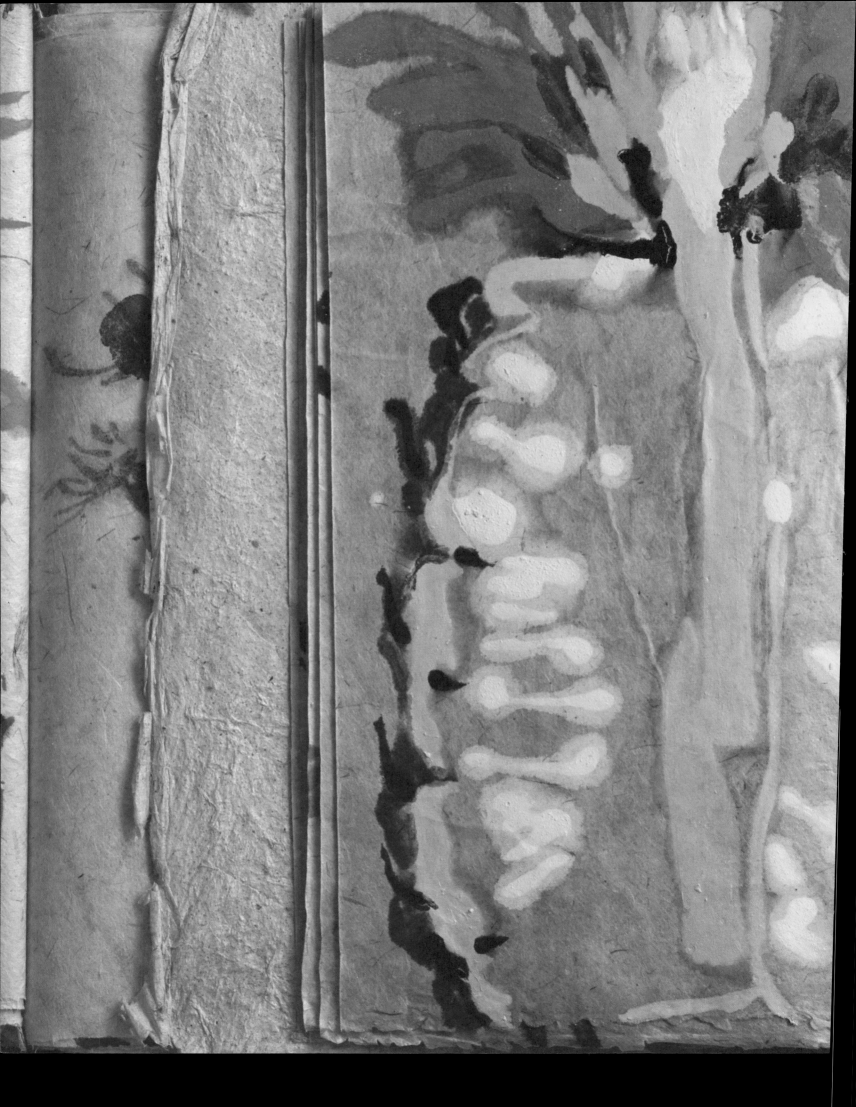